The Life and Rituals of the Nanai People

This work was supported by the National Research Foundation of Korea Grant funded by the Korean Government. (NRF-2010-32A-A00075)

THE LIFE AND RITUALS OF THE NANAI PEOPLE

KIM Juwon

KO Dongho

Antonina KILE

CHOI Moonjeong

Seoul National University Press

KIM Juwon	Department of Linguistics, Seoul National University, Korea
KO Dongho	Department of Korean Language and Literature, Chonbuk National University, Korea
Antonina KILE	Department of Art and Crafts, Far Eastern State University of Humanities, Russia
CHOI Moonjeong	Department of Russian Language and Literature, Kyung Hee University, Korea

Altaic Languages Series 8

The Life and Rituals of the Nanai People

Printed in Seoul, Korea

Seoul National University Press
1 Gwanak-ro, Gwanak-gu, Seoul 08826, Korea

E-mail: snubook@snu.ac.kr
Homepage: http://www.snupress.com

First Printing: April 30, 2015

ISBN 978-89-521-1743-4 93700

Contents

Figures

Figure 1. The Late Professor A. Kile narrating on the life and rituals of the Nanai People in February, 2013

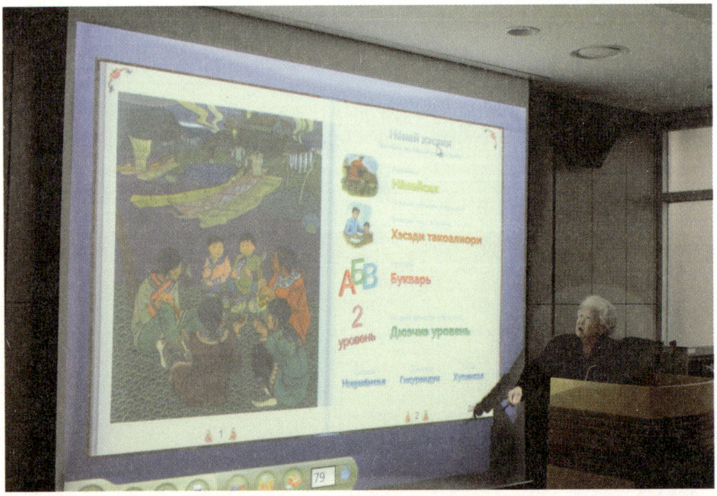

Figure 2. Professor A. Kile introducing the Electronic Textbook of Nanai (2011) to the audience at lecture at Seoul National University in February, 2013

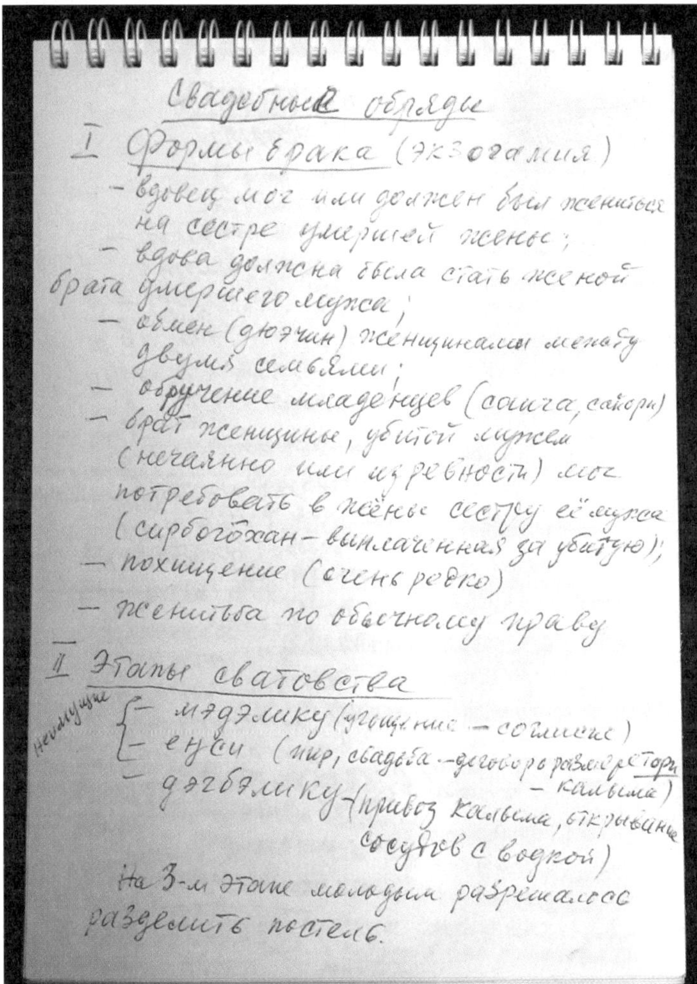
Свадебные обряды
I Формы брака (экзогамия)
– вдовец мог или должен был жениться на сестре умершей жены;
– вдова должна была стать женой брата умершего мужа;
– обмен (дюэчин) женщинами между двумя семьями;
– обручение младенцев (саига, сайори)
– брат женщины, убитой мужем (нечаянно или из ревности) мог потребовать в жёны сестру её мужа (сирбогохан – выплаченная за убитую);
– похищение (очень редко)
– женитьба по обычному праву
II Этапы сватовства
– мэдэлику (угощение – согласие)
– енсу (пир, свадьба – договор о
– калыма)
– дэгбэлику – (привоз калыма, открывание сосудов с водкой)
На 3-м этапе молодым разрешалось разделить постель.

Figure 3. Professor A. Kile's note written in preparation for her spontaneous narratives

Figure 4. The cover of *The Art of Nanai* by Professor A. Kile featuring with the "clan tree"

Figure 5. Nanai Textbooks written by Professor A. Kile

Figure 6. The First Far Eastern International Festival of Indigenous Art Forms and Crafts (Khabarovsk, Russia, 2008) with the theme of "Indigenous Art: Connecting the Past and the Present"

Figure 7. Nanai drum dancing

Figure 8. A bridal robe

Figure 9. A cradle

Figure 10. Birch bark containers

Figure 11. *Saoris*, *Sewens*, and a shaman's belt with bells

Figure 12. Dolls in traditional costumes

Acknowledgements

We received the help of the following people during the development of this book. KO Seongyeon (CUNY) reviewed the overall contents of this book, including its structure and expressions, brought any flaws to our attention and contributed recommendations for improvements. CHOI Woonho (Mokpo University) laid the groundwork for Chapter 4 of this book. PARK Sangchul, LEE Hyoungmee, DO Jeong-up, JIN Hui, and CHOE Gyeyeong (PhD candidates at Seoul National University) worked on the initial stages of the grammatical analysis and compilation of the Nanai speech materials. KIM Byung (CUNY) provided the English translation and revisions. The relatives of Professor A. Kile, who live in Naikhin, assisted with deciphering difficult sentences, and Professor A. Kile's daughter, Mrs. Valentina Shabelnikova, contacted these relatives in our stead. We would like to express our sincere gratitude here. Any mistakes found in this book remain ours.

Abbreviations

1	first person
2	second person
3	third person
ABL	ablative
ACC	accusative
ADD	additive
AGT	agentive
ANT	anterior
CAUS	causative
CNTR	contrastive
COHOR	cohortative
COMPR	comparative
CON	consecutive
CONC	concessive
COND	conditional
DAT	dative
DES	desiderative
DIM	diminutive
DIR	directive
DISTR	distributive
DSG	designative
DUR	durative
EMP	emphatic
EXCL	exclusive
EXTR	extreme degree
FR	frequentative
FUT	future
HAB	habitual
IMP	imperative
IMPS	impersonal
INCH	inchoative

INF	infinitive
INS	instrumental
INT	intentional-directional
ITER	iterative
LIM	limitative
LOC	locative
MIR	mirative
NEG	negative
NMLZ	nominalizer
OBLG	obligative
OCM	oblique case marker
P	participle
PASS	passive
PL	plural
PROP	proprietive
PRS	present
PST	past
PURP	purposive
Q	question
RECP	reciprocal
REFL	reflexive
REP	repetitive
REPO	reportative
REV	reversive
SEL	selective
SG	singular
SIM	simultaneous
SML	similative
SUFF	sufficient degree
TOP	topic
TR	transitivizer
VBZ	verbalizer

Transliterations

а	б	в	г	д	е	ё	и	й	к	л	м	н
a	b	w	g	d	jə	jo	ɪ/i	ɪ/i	k	l	m	n
ӈ	о	п	р	с	т	у	х	ч	э	ю	я	
ŋ	o	p	r	s	t	u	x	č	ə	ju	ja	
ā	ō	ӣ	ӯ	э̄								
aa	oo	ɪɪ/ii	uu	əə								
де	дё	дю	дя	ди								
ǰə	ǰo	ǰu	ǰa	ǰɪ/ǰi/dɪ/di								

1

Introduction

1.1. Outline of the study

1.1.1. Research purpose and significance

In this study, we transcribed data that was dictated by a Nanai person in the Nanai language about the traditional way of life of the Nanai people, and we interpreted and added grammatical and lexical annotations for every sentence spoken in Nanai. The goals of this study are twofold. The first is to elicit and analyze sentence-level spontaneous speech in Nanai to reveal its grammatical characteristics. The second is to show the traditional life and culture of the Nanai people such as their child rearing, birth rituals, wedding ceremonies, and funeral rites.

The Nanai language is a seriously endangered and under-documented language. It is difficult to find a fluent speaker even in Nanai villages nowadays. Therefore, both their cultural and linguistic heritages are at the verge of extinction. Under these rather tragic circumstances, we hope that this book will make a significant contribution to the field of Nanai studies by its vivid documentation of the traditional lifestyle as well as the language of the Nanai people.

It is worth noting that until now the lifestyle and culture of the Nanai people have been introduced partially and narrowly through an outsider's lens, that is, through works written in Chinese or Russian. In contrast, this book describes the Nanai culture from the perspective of an insider, a Nanai speaker.

1.1.2. About the Nanai language and the Nanai people

The Nanai people (also known as Hezhe in China) are a minority ethnic group that lives in regions midstream of the Amur River in Russia and near the Heilong River and Songhua River in China. Their language is a member of the Manchu-Tungusic group of the so-called Altaic Languages.

There are 12,460 Nanai people in Russia (as of 2002) and an estimated 4,640 Nanai people living in China (as of 1999). Of those in Russia, 30% or 3,886 people can speak Nanai, while of those in China, there are only about 10 people who use Nanai (Ko & Yurn 2011:6). The language of the Nanai people is not being passed down to the next generations, making it a seriously endangered language.

According to the Ethnologue (accessed on February 15, 2015), the Nanai language is judged to be a Level 7 (on the EGIDS scale). In other words, it is in a state known as "Shifting", which means "the child-bearing generation can use the language among themselves, but it is not being transmitted to children." It is highly likely that their culture is not being transmitted, either.

The following map in page 3 shows the residential areas of the Nanai people, including the Hezhe people in China. See Ko & Yurn 2011 for more detailed information on the Nanai language.

1.1.3. Research methods

We filmed and recorded audio of spontaneous speech data as shown below:

Narrator: KILE Antonina Sergeevna
(КИЛЕ Антонина Сергеевна)

Interviewer: Kim Juwon, Ko Dongho

Interpreter: Choi Moonjeong

Recording: Park Sangchul, Do Jeong-up

Location: Kim Juwon's office (Room 307, Building 3, Seoul National University)

Date and Time of Recording: 10:30–12:30 PM, February 14th, 2013, and 10:30–3:00 PM, 9:00–10:00 PM, February 16th, 2013.

The fieldwork equipment was as follows:

Audio recording:

Digital audio recorder setting: Sound Device 722 16 bit, 44.1 kHz, Stereo (one channel for consultant, the other channel for interpreter)

Microphone: AKG C-420 (professional headset condenser microphone, for consultant) and Audio-Technica ATM 15A (Cardioid condenser microphone, for interpreter)

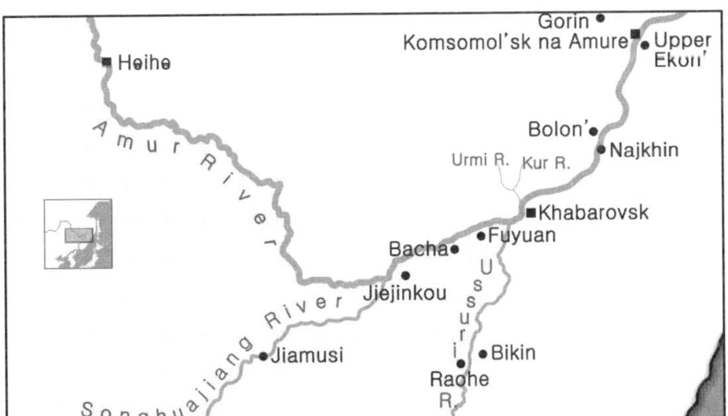

Map. The Nanai people's main residential areas in Russia and China marked with '•' (Ko & Yurn 2011:2)

Video recording:
Camcorder: SONY DSR-PDX10
Microphone: Audio-Technica AT831B (unidirectional cardioid condenser type, for consultant)

Since 2005, Professor Kile has collaborated with us and provided us with many materials about the Nanai language. In 2013, in response to the invitation by the Institute of Altaic Studies at Seoul National University, Professor Kile visited us to give a public lecture on the language education in the Nanai community. During her visit, she was also requested to narrate the life and rituals of the Nanai people in both Nanai and Russian. Professor Kile divided her oral narrative into four sections: childhood education and child rearing rituals, birth rituals, wedding rituals, and funeral rituals. For each section, she first spoke in Nanai and then repeated nearly the same content in Russian. Through this process, we were able to record very natural and vivid Nanai speech. The original Nanai sentences were first transcribed in the Cyrillic alphabet by Kile herself, and later annotated and interpreted by Kim Juwon and Ko Dongho. The corresponding Russian text was translated into Korean by Choi Moonjeong.

1.1.4. Professor KILE Antonina Sergeevna (1929–2014)

Professor Kile[1)] was a scholar who, in spite of her old age, had been passionately working for the revitalization of the Nanai language and the preservation of Nanai tradition. In Ko

1) During the development of this book, co-author Professor A. S. Kile passed away. Despite her advanced age of 85, she provided a very accurate and precise Cyrillic transcription of her own speech materials, which was instrumental in writing this book. We would like once again to express our sincere gratitude for her contribution to this book, and we know her spirit lives on in her many contributions to the field.

& Yurn (2011:5), Professor Kile is introduced as follows.

Name: Kile Antonina Sergeevna
Sex: Female
Year and place of birth: 1929, Naikhin situated in Nanai District, Khabarovsk Krai, where she lived until 15 years old.
Occupation: Associate Professor of Department of Art and Crafts, Far Eastern State University of Humanities, Khabarovsk, Russia. Also taught Nanai language and literature.
Linguistic characteristics: Spoke only Nanai until 7 years old, and learned Russian after that time, but used Nanai with those who spoke the language such as brothers and sisters in Naikhin.

1.1.5. Contents of this book

This book is organized as follows: Following the introduction (Chapter 1), Chapter 2 presents the annotated Nanai text with interlinear glosses. The Nanai text consists of the following four sections:

1. Childhood education and child rearing rituals
2. Birth rituals
3. Wedding rituals
4. Funeral rituals

For each topic, the talk in Nanai and the corresponding Russian portion together was generally about an hour each, and it came to a total of six hours.

The main points of each section are as follows: Section 1 describes how the Nanai people who have no writing system put all their effort and pedagogical methods in transmitting their experiences to young children, the next generation. Section 2 explains how the Nanai people prepare for child birth and describes various rituals performed to protect the newborn children from death. Section 3 delineates the procedures for a blessed wedding in detail and clearly shows the aspects of meticulous exchanges between the two families of the bride and groom. Section 4 depicts the process of funeral rites for the deceased as well as the effort for the bereaved to disconnect themselves from the deceased to ensure the peace and stability of the family.

Chapter 3 presents the English translation of the recitation delivered in Russian. It should be noted that there are quite a few differences in their contents between the Nanai portion in Chapter 2 and the Russian portion in Chapter 3. This is due to the fact that the Russian portion was not a sentence-by-sentence translation of the Nanai speech data. Sometimes the description in Nanai is more elaborate, while at other times that in Russian is more detailed. Therefore, the contents of Chapter 2 and 3 should be viewed as complementary to each other. For those more interested in the lifestyle of the Nanai people than the Nanai language may find Chapter 3 more useful. Chapter 4 provides the lists of all the lexical and grammatical items arranged in alphabetical order.

1.2. Explanatory notes for annotations

The method used in this book for the annotations is as follows:

First, following the Leipzig Glossing Rules (http://www.eva.mpg.de/lingua/resources/glossing-rules.php), all morpheme boundaries are marked with hyphens both in the Nanai texts and in the gloss.

Second, multiple meaning components and/or multiple grammatical properties of a single morpheme are separated by period mark [.] in the gloss.

Third, a particle boundary is marked with [=].

Nouns and verbs in Nanai have different morphological properties as follows:

[1] Nouns

Nouns in the Nanai language are composed of the following elements and in the following order.

stem-(derivational suffix)-case ending-(personal ending)

Derivational suffixes, e.g., diminutive and plural suffixes, and personal endings, are not obligatory. Case endings are often omitted as well.

The most typical example is as shown below:

kusun-ǰi-əri
power-INS-REFL.PL

Accusative case endings, which is normally realized as *-wa*, *-wə*, *-ba*, *-bə* are occasionally omitted. They are often realized as *-a*, *-ə* depending on the phonological environments.

torɪ-a
bridewealth-ACC

The following example shows that *xaǰom*, the spoken form of *xaǰon-ba* 'stuff-ACC', ends with the final consonant [m] and thus is annotated as 'stuff.ACC' with a period intervening between stuff and ACC.

xaǰom
stuff.ACC

There are often cases that allow more than one analysis.

For example, In case of *ənim* that is morphologically ambiguous as illustrated below, the selection of the right annotation is made between the two possibilities based on the context.

ənin-bə 'mother-ACC' > ənim
ənin-bi 'mother-REFL' > ənim

[2] Verbs
Nanai verbs are structured as follows:

stem-(derivational suf.)-finite ending -personal ending
participle ending -(personal ending)
converbal ending -(personal ending)

In principle, if a finite ending is attached to the stem, it should be followed by personal ending. In contrast, a personal ending may or may not be attached after a participle ending. In the case of the converbal endings, some require a personal ending obligatorily and others do not. Personal endings are often omitted in verbal inflection. They may optionally undergo certain formal changes when co-occurring with another morpheme.

Using a few cases as examples, we will show the conventions used for annotation.
Primarily, the functions of each morpheme are annotated below using previously designated abbreviations (see page xiv-xv above). The following are some examples.

piktə-gu-ji
child-DSG-REFL

bi-či-či
be-PST.P-3PL

ta-ɪ-wa-nɪ
do-PRS.P-ACC-3SG

However, there are many instances where various phonological processes may change the original forms of a morpheme attached to a stem, as illustrated below:

un-dii
say-PRS.P.

Note that, in the two examples above, there may be a hidden personal ending after the gerund ending *-dɪɪ*. This will not be marked in the gloss because the conventions adopted in this book does not allow it. Also, recall that a personal ending following the participle ending is optional. Therefore, whether or not the personal ending is present, we annotated *-dɪɪ* as PRS.P.

Like in the example below, if two morphemes (*kin-bi*) are only realized as one (*kim*), the two morpheme categories are connected using a period mark.

olbɪn-kɪm
bring-PST.P.REFL

Also, in Nanai, there are cases in which a stem-final vowel is fully assimilated to the following vowel [ɪ] or [i] resulting in the change of the stem form. This change is illustrated in the following examples. (Note that this rule is optional.)

ǰapa-ɪ 'take-PRS.P' > ǰapɪ-ɪ
čɪxala-ɪ 'allow-PRS.P' > čɪxalɪ-ɪ
ičə-i 'see-PRS.P' > iči-i
urə-i=dəə 'grow-PRS.P=ADD' > uri-i-dəə

In these cases, the Nanai elements simply reflect their surface realizations. In these cases, we transcribed the stem-final vowel in its original form.

ǰapa-ɪ	čɪhxla-ɪ	ičə-i
take-PRS.P	allow-PRS.P	see-PRS.P

Conjunctions in Nanai, although most of them consist of two or more words, are treated as if they were mono-morphemic words.

totam(ɪ), tui tam(ɪ)	therefore
totamaar(ɪ), tui tamaar(ɪ)	therefore
totamɪa	lastly
totap(ɪ)	then
totapaar(ɪ)	then
totapɪa	a bit later
totapaarɪa	a bit later
totaraa, tui taraa	and then

2

Nanai Speech Materials with Linguistic Annotations

2.1. Childhood education and child rearing rituals

Balana	xəǰəni	ǰooŋkanı	əgǰi	piktə-ku	gurun-bə
long.ago	Nanai	family.3SG	many	child-PROP	people-ACC

«kəsi-ku=əm»,	un-dii	bi-či-či.
happiness-PROP=REPO	say-PRS.P	be-PST.P-3PL

Long ago, a Nanai family with many children was said to be blessed.

Əgǰi-ə	baa-rii=daa,	puril-či	bu-dii
many-ACC	get-PRS.P=ADD	children-3PL	die-PRS.P

bi-či-či	goan.
be-PST.P-3PL	certainly

Even if one got many children, one lost their children in part.

Totamı	əgǰi	puril-ku	aso	əgǰi	ǰooŋkan=daa
therefore	many	children-PROP	so.much	many	family=ADD

bi-əči-ni.
be-NEG.PST.P-3SG

Therefore, a family with many children was not a particularly large family.

Əmun	ǰuər.	Ixon-do	əgǰi	puril-ku	gurun
one	two	village-DAT	many	children-PROP	people

čuu	kəsi-ku-ǰi	naɪ	gərbiə-si-i	bi-či-ni.
most	happiness-PROP-INS	person	call-DUR-PRS.P	be-PST.P-3SG

There was only one or two. In a village, a man with many children was being praised as the happiest person.

Xusə	piktə	balǰɪ-waan-ɪ	təŋ	agda-nasɪ-ɪ
male	child	be.born-CAUS-PRS.P	very	be.glad-REP-PRS.P

bi-či-či	goanɪ.
be-PST.P-3PL	certainly

The birth of a son was a most delightful occasion.

Xusə	piktə	amɪn-bɪ	ǰooŋkan-ba-nɪ	daaɪ-laa
male	child	father-REFL	family-ACC-3SG	large-SUFF

osɪ-waan-dɪɪ-nɪ	goan.
become-CAUS-PRS.P-3SG	certainly

The father of the son himself makes the family somewhat large.

Čado=tanɪɪ,	guči	xusə	piktə,	balǰɪ-pɪ,
then=TOP	again	male	child	be.born-COND.IMPS

amɪn-bɪ	ta-xa-nɪ	ǰaka-wa	sɪra-go-ɪ-nɪ.
father-REFL	do-PST.P-3SG	thing-ACC	continue-ITER-PRS.P-3SG

Again then, when the son grew up, he would continue jobs that his father had done.

Əktə	piktə-kəən	balǰɪ-ɪ=daa,	čačɪ=daa
female	child-DIM	be.born-PRS.P-ADD	that.DIR=ADD

agda-nasɪ-ɪ	bi-či-či	goanɪ.
be.glad-REP-PRS.P	be-PST.P-3PL	certainly

The birth of daughter was also a joyous occasion of course.

əktə piktə-wə, əǰi-gu-ji baa-rɪɪ-do-jɪ
female child-ACC husband-DSG-REFL get-PRS.P-DAT-REFL

(əktə piktə xoda-wa-nɪ čaa asɪ-go-jɪ ǰapa-ɪ
female child price-ACC-3SG that.ACC wife-DSG-REFL take-PRS.P

gurun buu-rii-či bi-či-či goanɪ) torɪ-a
people give-PRS.P-3PL be-PST.P-3PL certainly bridewealth-ACC

ǰapa-ɪ bi-či-či goanɪ təi əktə piktə
take-PRS.P be-PST.P-3PL certainly that female daughter

xoda-wa-nɪ.
price-ACC-3SG

When a daughter got married, people paid a bridewealth. (When a man took a girl as a wife, his parents paid a bridewealth in exchange.)

Təi torɪ=tanɪɪ ambaan daaɪ bi-či-ni.
that bridewealth=TOP fairly large be-PST.P-3SG

That *tori* (bridewealth) was fairly large.

Piktə ənini, amɪnɪ — naɪ kidu-i-ni
child mother.3SG father.3SG person respect-PRS.P-3SG

gurun, bajan-laa bi-i gurun osɪnɪ,
people rich-SUFF be-PRS.P people if

torɪ-nɪ=daa, təi piktə-či torɪ-nɪ=daa
bridewealth-3SG=ADD that child-3PL bridewealth-3SG=ADD

daaɪ-laa bi-či-ni.
large-SUFF be-PST.P-3SG

If the groom's parents were honest and somewhat rich people, the bridewealth was somewhat large.

Torɪ-do njəpultə, boso, səurə, goɪ goɪ xaǰon,
bridewealth-DAT fur fabric silk various thing

ənjuə — əgǰi xaǰom buu-rii bi-či-či goanɪ,

pot many stuff.ACC give-PRS.P be-PST.P-3PL certainly

təi xaǰon xoda-nɪ maŋga bi-či-ni.
that stuff price-3SG expensive be-PST.P-3SG

As a bridewealth they gave various things like fur, fabric, silk and kettles. These were expensive.

Bajan gurun=tənii aɪsɪn-ba, məŋgun-bə buu-rii
rich people=TOP gold-ACC silver-ACC give-PRS.P

bi-či-či.
be-PST.P-3PL

Rich people gave gold and silver.

Puril-bə uruuči-məəri, balana mənə kolɪ-warɪ
children-ACC bring.up-SIM.PL long.ago oneself custom-REFL.PL

təǰuuči-i bi-či-či goanɪ.
try-PRS.P be-PST.P-3PL certainly

While raising children, we tried to maintain our own traditional customs.

Amɪn-bɪ, ənin-bi xaɪ-wa ta-ɪ-nɪ osɪnɪ,
father-REFL mother-REFL what-ACC do-PRS.P-3SG if

puril-či=dəə čawa xəm ta-ɪ.
children-3PL=ADD that.ACC all do-PRS.P

If one's father and mother do something, they also do it together.

Naonǰokaan, njaŋgaa daaɪ-laa osɪ-ɪ-ǰɪ gəsə,
boy a.little large-SUFF become-PRS.P-INS together

amɪn-ǰɪ-jɪ, daaɪ-ǰɪm aag-ǰɪ-jɪ gəsə
father-INS-REFL big-SEL elder.brother-INS-REFL together,

boatoačɪ-orɪ xaǰon-ba xəm saa-rɪɪ bi-či-ni;
hunt-PRS.IMPS.P stuff-ACC all know-PRS.P be-PST.P-3SG

As soon as a boy grew up somewhat, working with his father and brothers, he gained knowledge about hunting equipment.

amın-bı,	aag-sal-bı	čawa	ta-ı-wa-nı,
father-REFL	elder.brother-PL-REFL	that.ACC	do-PRS.P-ACC-3SG

xəm	bələči-i	bi-či-ni.
all	help-PRS.P	be-PST.P-3SG

His father and elder brothers helped him do that.

Tui	ta-mı=tanıı	čawa	xəm	otolı-ı
so	do-SIM=TOP	that.ACC	all	understand-PRS.P

bi-či-ni.
be-PST.P-3SG

By doing so, he became acquainted with the equipment.

Arčokaan=tanıı	ənim	ta-ı-wa-nı	xəm
girl=TOP	mother.REFL	do-PRS.P-ACC-3SG	all

otolı-ı	bi-či-ni.
understand-PRS.P	be-PST.P-3SG

A girl also learned all of her mother's work.

Ulpi-mi,	ılga	aŋgo-mı,	sıa-orı-a
sew-SIM	embroidery	make-SIM	eat-PRS.IMPS.P-ACC

pujuu-či-mi,	ǰoo	doo-wa-nı	oosı-čı-mı	— əktəni
boil-FR-SIM	house	inside-ACC-3SG	clean-FR-SIM	female

ta-ı-wa-nı	xəm	otolı-ı	bi-či-ni	goanı.
do-PRS.P-ACC-3SG	all	understand-PRS.P	be-PST.P-3SG	certainly

Through sewing, embroidery work, cooking food and cleaning the house, she was acquainted with women's tasks.

Čawa=tanıı	nəə	tui	ičəuči-mi	aloosı-ačı-čı
that.ACC=TOP	certainly	so	show-SIM	teach-NEG.PST.P-3PL

bi-či-ni goanɪ.
be-PST.P-3SG certainly

They did not teach but only showed the tasks.

Naɪ xaɪ-wa ta-ɪ-nɪ osɪnɪ, nuučikəənǰuən=dəə,
person what-ACC do-PRS.P-3SG if children=ADD

čawa amda-maarɪ, xupi-i, čawa amda-maarɪ,
that.ACC imitate-SIM.PL play-PRS.P that.ACC imitate-SIM.PL

ta-ɪ bi-či-či goanɪ.
do-PRS.P be-PST.P-3PL certainly

Whatever parents did, children played and did things by imitating them.

Gəə, bi-uri, čaa xaɪ ta-ɪ osɪnɪ, xəm
well be-PRS.IMPS.P that.ACC what do-PRS.P if all

otolɪ-ɪ bi-či-či goanɪ njaŋgaa urə-məəri.
understand-PRS.P be-PST.P-3PL certainly a.little grow-SIM.PL

Generally, while growing a little, children became well accustomed to all that they did.

Totamaarɪ əkəsəl=dəə xəm paksɪ, ulpi-i,
therefore woman.PL=ADD all skillful sew-PRS.P

ɪlga-la-ɪ.
pattern-VBZ-PRS.P

While doing so, all girls become skillful at sewing and embroidery work.

Naonǰokaan-sal=tanɪɪ boatoŋgo, sogdata waa-rɪɪ
boy-PL=TOP hunter fish catch-PRS.P

gurun osɪ-ɪ bi-či-či goanɪ.
people become-PRS.P be-PST.P-3PL certainly

Boys became hunters and fishermen.

Xaɪ-wa=daa   ta-ɪ=daa,   ǰɪa   ǰɪa-warɪ   tul tul
what-ACC=ADD   do-PRS.P=ADD   friend   friend-REFL.PL   always

bələči-i   bi-či-či   goanɪ.
help-PRS.P   be-PST.P-3PL   certainly

Whatever they did, they always helped one another.

Gəsə   ǰobo-ɪ.
together   work-PRS.P

They work together.

ǰooŋkan-do   xaalɪ=daa   tui   əčiə   bi-ə: əmun   naɪ
family-DAT   when=ADD   so   not   be-INF   one   person

ǰobo-ɪ   — goɪ   naɪ   təə-si-i.
work-PRS.P   other   person   sit-DUR-PRS.P

When there is family work, there is never a case that one person works while another just sits around.

Tui   xaalɪ=daa   əčiə   ta-ra.
so   when=ADD   not   do-INF

They never do such a thing.

Əmuni   ǰobo-ɪ-nɪ   osɪnɪ,   naɪ   xəm   ǰobo-ɪ.
one.person   work-PRS.P-3SG   if   person   all   work-PRS.P

When one works the others also do.

Baɪ   tui   təə-si-i   gurun   xaalɪ=daa   aba   bi-či-ni.
just   so   sit-DUR-PRS.P   people   when=ADD   not   be-PST.P-3SG

There was no one who sits around without working.

Ənusi-i   osɪnɪ,   aja.
be.sick-PRS.P   if   good

If someone is sick, he is exempt.

Gəə,	təi	ənusi-i-ni	mutə-əsi-ni	goanɪ
well	that	illness.VBZ-PRS.P-3SG	be.able.to-NEG.PRS.P-3SG	certainly

ǰobo-mɪ.
work-SIM

The sick cannot work.

Totamɪ	təə-si-i,	ao-rɪɪ,	okčɪ-čɪ-ɪ	ta-ɪ.
therefore	sit-DUR-PRS.P	sleep-PRS.P	cure-FR-PRS.P	do-PRS.P

Therefore he sits (to take a break from working) and sleeps, healing himself.

Bəjə-ji	xətə-əsi	osɪnɪ,	tui	osɪ-ɪ-nɪ
body-REFL	withstand-NEG.PRS.P	if	so	become-PRS-3SG

goanɪ.
certainly

This is because he cannot do things with his own power.

Bəjə-ji	xətə-i	osɪnɪ,	naɪ	xaɪ-wa=daa
body-REFL	withstand-PRS.P	if	person	what-ACC=ADD

ta-ɪ-do-a-nɪ,	nəə	ta-orɪ	gəsə=dəə,
do-PRS.P-DAT-OCM-3SG	certainly	do-PRS.IMPS.P	together=ADD

kaokaa	bi-wəsi.
quietly	be-NEG.PRS.IMPS.P

If someone is able to use his own power, he must work with others, and not stand still.

Daaɪ	osɪ-pɪ,	tui	osɪ-ɪ	bi-či-či
large	become-COND.IMPS	so	become-PRS.P	be-PST.P-3PL

goanɪ	nuučikəənǰuən=dəə,	daaɪ	osɪ-pɪ,
certainly	children=ADD	large	become-COND.IMPS

nəə	ǰobo-orɪ-a	gələ-i.
certainly	work-PRS.IMPS.P-ACC	need-PRS.P

When children grew up, it became that way. When they grow up, they need to work.

Kaokaa	təə-si-mi	ačaasɪ,	mutə-wəsi
quietly	sit-DUR-SIM	not.appropriate	be.able.to-NEG.PRS.IMPS.P

kaokaa	təə-si-mi.
quietly	sit-DUR-SIM

It is not right to sit still and it is impossible to sit still.

Totapɪ,	məən	piktə-gu-ji	baa-rɪɪ=daa,	purig-ni
then	oneself	child-DSG-REFL	get-PRS.P=ADD	children-3SG

xəm	njoanɪ=maa	osɪ-ɪ-nɪ	goanɪ.
all	he=SML	become-PRS.P-3SG	certainly

In this way, after people have children, the children all become like their parents.

Tui=dəə.
so=ADD

That's the way it goes.

Nuučikəənǰuən	uləən	gurun	osɪ-go-a-nɪ,	tui
children	good	people	become-PURP-OCM-3SG	so

ta-ɪ-čɪ	bi-či-ni	goanɪ.
do-PRS.P-3PL	be-PST.P-3SG	certainly

For children to become good people, they had done as follows:

Əmutuu	əsi	naɪ	anjaa-wa	aŋgo-ɪ-nɪ=maa=daa.
as.if	now	person	holiday-ACC	make-PRS.P-3SG=SML=ADD

It is like how people celebrate festivals nowadays.

Nuuči-kuukəən naonǰokaan, umәkəəči-ndə-rəə,
small-EXTR boy fish-INT-ANT

sogdata-wa waa-rɪɪ-nɪ osɪnɪ, ambaan daaɪ
fish-ACC catch-PRS.P-3SG if fairly large

sogdata-wa, təi ini, sogdata-wa təlgəči-rəə, talaa-wa
fish-ACC that day fish-ACC bone-ANT tala-ACC

aŋgo-ɪ, tuə osɪnɪ, pɪarmaa-wa aŋgo-ɪ,
make-PRS.P winter if frozen.raw.fish-ACC make-PRS.P

xolto-a pujuu-rii, goɪ sɪaptaŋgɪ-a aŋgo-ɪ.
fish.soup-ACC boil-PRS.P other food-ACC make-PRS.P

When a little boy goes fishing and catches a rather large fish, people bone the fish before the day is over and make *talaa* (sliced raw fish). In the winter, they make *piarmaa* (frozen raw fish) and *holto* (fish soup) or cook various foods.

Totaraa=tanɪɪ sagǰɪ gurun-bə, mənə kidu-i
and.then=TOP old people-ACC oneself respect-PRS.P

gurun-bə gələ-i-či bi-či-ni goanɪ.
people-ACC invite-PRS.P-3PL be-PST.P-3SG certainly

After doing that, they invited elders and other venerable persons.

Təi ǰi-čin gurun=tənii xəm suglən-ku
that come-PST.P people=TOP all gift-PROP

ǰi-či-či.
come-PST.P-3PL

All the invited people brought gifts.

Təi suglən-bə naonǰokaan-du buu-rii-du-əri,
that gift-ACC boy-DAT give-PRS.P-DAT-REFL.PL

tui xɪsaŋgo-ɪ bi-či-či goanɪ:
so say-PRS.P be-PST.P-3PL certainly

Giving the gifts to the boy, they said as follows:

— Gəə, uləən sii, naonǰokaan. İčə-u, sii təi
well good you boy see-2SG.IMP you that

sogdata waa-xa-sɪ, təŋ amta sogdata.
fish catch-PST.P-2SG very tasty fish

"Oh, what a good boy! Look at this! You caught this fish. It is very delicious.

Buə əi=məə bi-i sogdata-wa xaalɪ=daa balana
we this=SML be-PRS.P fish-ACC when=ADD long.ago

əčiə sɪa-ra-pu.
not eat-INF-1PL

We have never eaten anything more delicious than this fish.

Sii waa-xa-sɪ sogdata čuu amta, čuu amta.
you catch-PST.P-2SG fish most tasty most tasty

The fish you caught is the most delicious."

Gəə, tui makta-maarɪ, tui un-dii bi-či-či goanɪ.
OK so praise-SIM.PL so say-PRS.P be-PST.P-3PL certainly

Like this they said words of praise.

Totamɪ təi naonǰokaan=tanɪɪ, čaa dosɪǰa-mɪ,
therefore that boy=TOP that.ACC listen-SIM

agda-ɪ bi-či-ni goanɪ.
be.glad-PRS.P be-PST.P-3SG certainly

Then the boy felt happy hearing it.

Čɪmana=tanɪɪ guči waa-nda-go-ɪ-nɪ goanɪ təi=məə
tomorrow=TOP again catch-INT-ITER-PRS.P-3SG certainly that=SML

bi-i sogdata-wa, sagǰɪ gurun agda-go-a-nɪ.
be-PRS.P fish-ACC old people be.glad-PURP-OCM-3SG

He will go fishing tomorrow in order to make the adults happy.

Suglən-bə=tənii,	tui	bi-i	sugləm
gift-ACC=TOP	so	be-PRS.P	gift.ACC

buu-rii-či	goanɪ.
give-PRS.P-3PL	certainly

The gifts they give are as follows:

Sogdata-wa	sɪa-rɪɪ	osɪnɪ,	sogdata-wa	waa-orɪ
fish-ACC	eat-PRS.P	if	fish-ACC	catch-PRS.IMPS.P

xaǰon-ba:	uməkən-bə,	boŋnan-ba,	xaɪ-wa,
stuff-ACC	fishing.gear-ACC	fishing.rod-ACC	what-ACC

sogdata	waa-orɪ	xaǰon-sal-ba	suglə-i
fish	catch-PRS.IMPS.P	stuff-PL-ACC	present-PRS.P

bi-či-či	goanɪ.
be-PST.P-3PL	certainly

When they eat fish, they presented him with fishing gear, like fishing rod and stuffs to catch fish with.

Nuuči	naonǰokaan,	boatoačɪ-mɪ,	amɪn-ǰɪ-jɪ	gəsə,
small	boy	hunt-SIM	father-INS-REFL	together

čuu	boŋgo	gormaxon-ba	waa-xa-nɪ	osɪnɪ,
most	first	rabbit-ACC	catch-PST.P-3SG	if

gormaxon-ba=daa	goɪ	bəjun-kəən-bə=dəə	waa-xa-nɪ
rabbit-ACC=ADD	other	animal-DIM-ACC=ADD	catch-PST.P-3SG

osɪnɪ,	čawa=daa	tui	anjaara-ɪ	bi-či-či	goanɪ.
if	that.ACC=ADD	so	celebrate-PRS.P	be-PST.P-3PL	certainly

If a little boy, while hunting with his father, caught a rabbit or other small animal for the first time, then this was also celebrated in the same manner.

Čado=tanɪɪ	suglə-i-du-əri	təi=tənii,
then=TOP	present-PRS.P-DAT-REFL.PL	that=TOP

dəəŋgurə-kəən-bə, *tam* xaɪ-wa, ləkəə-wə,

gun-DIM-ACC	R. there	what-ACC	arrow-ACC

buri-wə,	sokta-wa	suglə-i	bi-či-či	goanı.
bow-ACC	ski-ACC	present-PRS.P	be-PST.P-3PL	certainly

Then equipment related to hunting, like small guns, arrows, bows or skis were presented.

Təi	xaǰon-sal=tanıı	xəm	boatoačı-orı	xaǰon
that	stuff-PL=TOP	all	hunt-PRS.IMPS.P	stuff
bi-či-ni	goanı,	duipə	pulsi-uri	xaǰon.
be-PST.P-3SG	certainly	taiga	walk-PRS.IMPS.P	stuff

These were all for hunting and walking in the taiga.

Čado=daa	naonǰokaan	təŋ	maŋga-ǰı	agda-ı
then=ADD	boy	very	strong-INS	be.glad-PRS.P
bi-či-ni	goanı,	tui	murun-du-ji	nəuči-i
be-PST.P-3SG	certainly	so	mind-DAT-REFL	keep-PRS.P
bi-či-ni:				
be-PST.P-3SG				

At that time the boy was very delighted and kept this into his mind:

«Mii,	daaı	urə-pi=tənii,	amaa=maa	uləən
I	large	grow-COND.IMPS=TOP	father=SML	good
boatoŋgo	osı-ǰaan-bı»=am=daa.			
hunter	become-FUT-1SG=REPO=ADD			

"When I grow up, I will be a hunter like father."

Arčokaan-sal-ba=daa	tui	makta-ı	bi-či-či	goanı.
girl-PL-ACC=ADD	so	praise-PRS.P	be-PST.P-3PL	certainly

Girls were also praised in the same way as follows:

Arčokaan-sal	uləən	ılga	ənin-bi=maa

girl-PL good embroidery mother-REFL=SML

aŋgo-ɪ-nɪ osɪnɪ, uləən ulpi-lu-i-ni osɪnɪ,
make-PRS.P-3SG if good sew-INCH-PRS.P-3SG if

čawa=daa xəm makta-ɪ bi-či-či goanɪ:
that.ACC=ADD all praise-PRS.P be-PST.P-3PL certainly

When girls embroidered something and began to sew well as their mother, everyone praised them.

— Gəə, sii, daaɪ urə-pi, paksɪ əktə
OK you large grow-COND.IMPS skillful female

osɪ-ǰaa-čɪ, uləən ulpi-ǰəə-či, uləən xaǰom
become-FUT-2SG well sew-FUT-2SG good stuff.ACC

aŋgo-ǰaa-čɪ, simbiə naɪ xəm makta-ǰaa-ra.
make-FUT-2SG you.ACC person all praise-FUT-INF

"Well, when you grow up, you will become a skillful woman. You will sew well and make good things. People will praise you."

Gəə, njoandoanɪ=daa tui suglə-i bi-či-či goanɪ:
OK she.DAT=ADD so present-PRS.P be-PST.P-3PL certainly

To the girls, gifts were also presented as follows:

kupən-bə, balana=daa kupən aba-do-a-nɪ,
thread-ACC long.ago=ADD thread not-DAT-OCM-3SG

tompo-wa, sumul-ǰi aŋgo-oxan tompo-wa, sogbo-ǰɪ
thread-ACC sinew-INS make-PST.IMPS.P thread-ACC fish.skin-INS

aŋgo-oxan tompo-wa, xaɪ-ǰɪ gɪrmaksa-ǰɪ
make-PST.IMPS.P thread-ACC what-INS bone-INS

aŋgo-oxan xurmə-wə, sogbo-ǰɪ=daa, nanta-ǰɪ=daa
make-PST.IMPS.P needle-ACC fish.skin-INS=ADD leather-INS=ADD

aŋgo-oxan, (xaɪ-wa) čumčuən-bi (xaɪ-wa)
make-PST.IMPS.P (what-ACC) finger-REFL (what-ACC)

pujəli-əsi osɪ-go-a-nɪ, čawa təi xaǰon-ba
get.hurt-NEG.PRS.P become-PURP-OCM-3SG that.ACC that thing-ACC

(xonjapton-ba) buu-rii bi-či-či goanɪ.
(thimble-ACC) give-PRS.P be-PST.P-3PL certainly

Thread, or thread-like material made with animal sinew or fish-skin, when earlier there was no thread, or needle made of bone, or thimbles made with fish skin or leather, which prevented them from being pricked, were presented.

Ənin-bəri xaɪ-wa ta-ɪ-čɪ osɪnɪ, čaa xəm
mother-REFL.PL what-ACC do-PRS.P-3PL if that.ACC all

amda-ɪ bi-či-či goanɪ.
imitate-PRS.P be-PST.P-3PL certainly

Whatever their mothers did, they imitated their deed.

Uləən osɪ-go-a-čɪ, uləən gurun
good become-PURP-OCM-3PL good people

osɪ-go-a-čɪ=tanɪɪ, nuuči-ləə-či-bəki, amɪn-čɪ,
become-PURP-OCM-3PL=TOP small-NMLZ-3PL-CON father-3PL

ənin-či, daanɪn-čɪ, daamɪn-čɪ nuučikəənǰuən-bə
mother-3PL grandmother-3PL grandfather-3PL children-ACC

aloosɪ-ɪ bi-či-či goanɪ.
teach-PRS.P be-PST.P-3PL certainly

Their father, mother, grandmother and grandfather taught them from childhood so that the young children might become good people.

naɪŋgɪ-a ǰapa-mɪ ačaasɪ.
other's.property-ACC take-SIM not.appropriate

It is prohibited to take what belongs to others.

Čawa xaɪ-wa=daa gələ-i osɪnɪ, naɪ-čɪ
that.ACC what-ACC=ADD request-PRS.P if person-DIR

mədəsi-uri.
ask-PRS.IMPS.P

And when someone needs such a thing, he should ask others for it.

Naɪ	čɪxala-ɪ-nɪ	osɪnɪ,	ǰapa-mɪ	aja.
person	agree-PRS.P-3SG	if	take-SIM	good

If the other person agrees, then one may take it.

Čɪxala-asɪ-nɪ	osɪnɪ,	ačaasɪ.
agree-NEG.PRS.P-3SG	if	not.appropriate

If the other person does not agree, then one should not take it.

Xoonɪ=a	murči-i=dəə,	naɪŋgɪ-a	ǰapa-mɪ
how=MIR	think-PRS.P=ADD	other's.property-ACC	take-SIM

ačaasɪ.
not.appropriate

No matter how much someone wants the other person's things, one must not do so.

Tujəə	bi-i	nuuči-kuukəən	piktə-kəən
so.much	bi-PRS.P	small-EXTR	child-DIM

otolɪ-asɪ-nɪ	goanɪ.
understand-NEG.PRS.P-3SG	certainly

Small children do not understand these situations.

Boa-la	xaɪ-wa=daa	ičə-i	naɪ
outside-LOC	what-ACC=ADD	see-PRS.P	person

tuliə-du-ə-ni	ičə-i	osɪnɪ,	gələ-i-ni	goanɪ.
garden-DAT-OCM-3SG	see-PRS.P	if	request-PRS.P-3SG	certainly

When they see something outside the house in someone else's garden, they ask for it.

Xaɪ,	ǰuə ɪlaan	səə	piktə	xaɪ-wa	otolɪ-ɪ?
indeed	two three	age	child	what-ACC	understand-PRS.P

How can a two or three year old child understand this?

Gəə,	tui	nuuči-kuukəən	naonǰokaan=daa,	arčokaan=daa
OK,	so	small-EXTR	boy=ADD	girl=ADD

soŋgo-mɪ	gələ-i-ni	osɪnɪ,
cry-SIM	request-PRS.P-3SG	if

təi	naɪ	ǰoog-čɪ-a-nɪ	ii-wu-i-ni	goanɪ
that	person	house-DIR-OCM-3SG	enter-TR-PRS.P-3SG	certainly

ənini=dəə,	daanɪnɪ=daa.
mother.3SG=ADD	grandmother.3SG=ADD.

If such a little boy or girl is crying, asking for it, his mother or grandmother takes him into that house.

Totaraa	gələ-i-ni	goanɪ:	— Piktə-kəən	maŋga
and.then	request-PRS.P-3SG	certainly	child-DIM	strong

čaa	gələ-i-ni.
that.ACC	request-PRS.P-3SG

And she asks for a favor, saying, "My child wants that."

Təi	ǰoo	əǰəni	əktə=tənii	un-dii:	— Gəə,
that	house	owner.3SG	female=TOP	say-PRS.P	OK

aja,	ǰapa-oso,	un-dii.	Buu-ruu,	nuuči	piktə
good	take-2PL.IMP-2PL	say-PRS.P	give-2SG.IMP	small	child

soŋgo-ɪ-do-a-nɪ,	buu-ruu.
cry-PRS.P-DAT-OCM-3SG	give-2SG.IMP

Then the owner says, "OK. Tell him to take it. Give it to him. Give it to the little child who is crying."

Čaa	xətuli-rəə,	piktə-du-ji	buu-rii-ni	goanɪ.
that.ACC	cut-ANT	child-DAT-REFL	give-PRS.P-3SG	certainly

Then she picks it to give it to the child.

Piktə-ni, sɪa-mɪ, agda-nasɪ-ɪ-do-a-nɪ=tanɪɪ, təi
child-3SG eat-SIM be.glad-REP-PRS.P-DAT-OCM-3SG=TOP that

ənin-ji=dəə, daaɪn[1]=tanɪɪ
mother-REFL=ADD grandmother-REFL=ADD=TOP

un-dii-ni goanɪ:
say-PRS.P-3SG certainly

When the child is eating it feeling happy, his mother or grandmother says the following:

— Gəə, aja, bundu=dəə bi-i xoaŋgoan. Mii
OK good we.DAT=ADD be-PRS.P cucumber I

sindu buu-gu-ən-bi, ǰoog-čɪ ənu-pi.
you.DAT give-REV-PRS-1SG house-DIR go-COND.IMPS

"OK. Thank you so much. We also have cucumber. When I return home, I will give one back for you."

Əktə=dəə: — Xaɪgojɪ buu-gu-i-si?
woman=ADD for.what give-REV-PRS.P-2SG

Buu-gu-əsi=dəə aja. Xaɪ? Xoaŋgoan aba-nɪ=nuu?
give-REV-NEG.PRS.P=ADD good indeed cucumber not-3SG=Q

The host says, "Why do you give me your cucumber back? You don't need to do so. It's merely a cucumber, isn't it?"

— Aba, buu-gu-ən-bi, — un-dii.
not give-REV-PRS-1SG say-PRS.P

She says again, "No, I'll give you my cucumber back."

— Piktə-ji iča-gu-ə-ni: naɪŋgɪ-a ǰapa-mɪ,
child-REFL see-PURP-OCM-3SG other's.property-ACC take-SIM

1) *daanɪnɪ=daa* is shortened to *daaɪn.*

məənčiji	manjaa	ǰapa-wasɪ.
oneself.DIR	only	take-NEG.PRS.IMPS.P

This is to show her child that one must only take what is one's own, and not what is others'.

Naɪŋgɪ-a	ǰapa-ɪ	osɪnɪ,	naɪ-do=daa
other's.property-ACC	take-PRS.P	if	person-DAT=ADD

buu-wuri;	naɪ-do=daa	buu-wuri.
give-PRS.IMPS.P	person-DAT=ADD	give-PRS.IMPS.P

If one takes what belongs to another, one must return it.

Tui	ta-mɪ	buə	naɪ-do-po-wa	čowoo	gurun
so	do-SIM	we	person-DAT-1PL-OCM	thief	people

aba	bi-či-či	goanɪ.
not	be-PST.P-3PL	certainly

There were no thieves among us.

Čowoo	gurun	aba	bi-či-ni.
thief	people	not	be-PST.P-3SG

There were no thieves.

Naɪŋgɪ-a	xaalɪ=daa	ǰapa-asɪ	bi-či-či
other's.property-ACC	when=ADD	take-NEG.PRS.P	be-PST.P-3PL

goanɪ.
certainly

We never took other's things.

Boa-čɪ	ǰoog-ǰɪaǰɪ	naɪ	xəm	ənu-i=dəə,
place-DIR	house-ABL	person	all	go-PRS.P=ADD

ǰoo	gəun=dəə,	joso	aba	bi-či-ni,	joso	aba
house	empty=ADD	locker	not	be-PST.P-3SG	locker	not

bi-či-ni.

be-PST.P-3SG

Even when all of the family members went out and the house was vacant, we never locked the house. There were no locks.

Baɪ	uikə	dasɪ-raa,	tui	xaŋgɪsɪ	ənə-i
just	door	close-ANT	so	away	go-PRS.P

bi-či-ni.
be-PST.P-3SG

One just closed the door and went away.

Totapɪ	əi	o-čɪ-nɪ	goanɪ:	xaosɪ=daa
then	this	become-PST.P-3SG	certainly	where.to=ADD

ənə-i	osɪnɪ,	moo-kaam	ǰapa-raa,	uikə-ji	tuǰu-i.
go-PRS.P	if	rod-DIM.ACC	take-ANT	door-REFL	lean-PRS.P

Then it became like this: wherever we go out, we lean a little rod on the door.

Tui=dəə.	Tuǰu-rəə,	tui	ənə-i.
so=ADD	lean-ANT	so	go-PRS.P

After leaning we go out.

Guči=tənii	nuučikəənǰuən-bə	aloosɪ-ɪ
again=TOP	children-ACC	teach-PRS.P

bi-či-či	goanɪ:
be-PST.P-3PL	certainly

They also taught the children as follows:

ənuu-ku	gurun-bə,	sagǰɪ	gurun-bə,	xaɪ-wa=daa
disease-PROP	people-ACC	old	people-ACC	what-ACC=ADD

ta-mɪ	mutə-əsi	gurun-bə	bələči-uri,
do-SIM	be.able.to-NEG.PRS.P	people-ACC	help-PRS.IMPS.P

nəə bələči-uri.

certainly help-PRS.IMPS.P

One must help the sick and old persons, who cannot do any work.

Xoon bələči-uri? Gəə, tui=dəə.
how help-PRS.IMPS.P OK so=ADD

How should they help the disabled persons? They do as follows:

Jara-raa, sogdata waa-raa, xaa-go-xa-nɪ
navigate-ANT fish catch-ANT go.ashore-REV-PST.P-3SG

osɪnɪ, təi jara-xa-nɪ gurun xəm, ǰuəni=dəə,
if that navigate-PST.P-3SG people all two.people=ADD

ɪlaanɪ=daa — xəm obolago-ɪ-čɪ goanɪ
three.peoples=ADD all share-PRS.P-3PL certainly

məən waa-xan-bɪ ǰɪa ǰɪa-do-arɪ.
oneself catch-PST.P-REFL friend friend-DAT-REFL.PL

When they went fishing on a boat then returned to shore, they shared the catch according to the number of the involved persons, whether there were two or three people.

ǰuəni osɪnɪ, ǰuəni-du; ɪlaanɪ osɪnɪ,
two.people if two.people-DAT three.peoples if

ɪlaanɪ-du.
three.peoples-DAT

If there were two people, then portions were given to two persons. If there were three, then portions were given to three.

Guči=tənii əm obo-a soloogo-ɪ-čɪ.
again=TOP one share-ACC leave-PRS.P-3PL

In addition, they set aside one more portion.

Təi obo-a=tanɪɪ xagoarɪ soloogo-ɪ-čɪ?

that share-ACC=TOP what.for leave-PRS.P-3PL

Why do they leave one more portion?

Təi naɪ xəm məən obo-warɪ ǰapa-go-xa-nɪ,
that person all oneself share-REFL.PL take-REV-PST.P-3SG
təi obo-a=tanɪɪ təi ənusi-i gurun-du,
that share-ACC=TOP that illness.VBZ-PRS.P people-DAT
sagǰɪ gurun-du soloogo-ɪ-čɪ.
old people-DAT leave-PRS.P-3PL

After taking their own portion, they left one more portion for the sick and the elderly.

Čaa ɪra-go-a-nɪ=tanɪɪ, piktə-ji xəəsi-i.[2)]
that.ACC carry-PURP-OCM-3SG=TOP child-REFL call-PRS.P

To send this extra portion to him, he calls his own son.

Təi ogda, ogda, jarako əǰəni, piktə-ji
that boat boat net owner.3SG child-REFL
xəəsi-rəə, təi piktə ɪra-waan-dɪɪ təi
call-ANT that child carry-CAUS-PRS.P that
sogdata-wa təi ənusi-i, sagǰɪ gurun-či.
fish-ACC that illness.VBZ-PRS.P old people-DIR

The owner of the ship and the net calls his son, and lets him take the fish to the sick and the elderly.

Gəə, boatoŋgo-sal, dujə-ǰiə əu-gu-pəəri,
OK hunter-PL taiga-side descend-REV-COND.PL.IMPS
boatoačɪ-xan-bari boa-ǰɪ-arɪ, uliksə
hunt-PST.P-REFL.PL place-INS-REFL.PL meat
əu-gu-i=dəə, gəə, čado=daa tui obola-ɪ
descend-REV-PRS.P=ADD OK then=ADD so share-PRS.P

2) A colloquial form of *xəərsii*.

bi-či-či goanɪ.
be-PST.P-3PL certainly

When the hunters returned from the taiga, then they also divided the meat like that.

Təi əm obo-wa təi ənusi-i gurun-du, sagǰɪ
that one share-ACC that illness.VBZ-PRS.P people-DAT old

gurun-du nuučikəənǰuəm ɪra-waan-dɪɪ bi-či-či
people-DAT children.ACC carry-CAUS-PRS.P be-PST.P-3PL

goan.
certainly

They made children take one portion to the sick and to the old.

Tui tamaarɪ nuučikəənǰuən=dəə, urə-i=dəə,
therefore children=ADD grow-PRS.P=ADD

saa-rɪɪ bi-či-či goanɪ.
know-PRS.P be-PST.P-3PL certainly

In doing so, children grew up and understood.

Njoančɪ, urə-pəəri, tui sagdan-go-xa-nɪ,
they grow-COND.PL.IMPS so get.old-REV-PST.P-3SG

ənusi-i gurun, məəpəəri uǰi-məəri
illness.VBZ-PRS.P people oneself.ACC.PL raise-SIM.PL

mutə-əsi gurun-bə njoančɪ uǰi-i-wə-či
be.able.to-NEG.PRS.P people-ACC they raise-PRS.P-ACC-3PL

gələ-i.
need-PRS.P

Growing up, they should take care of the elderly and the sick who cannot take care of themselves.

Totamɪ təi gurun-bə xaalɪ=daa oŋbo-wasɪ.
therefore that person-ACC when=ADD forget-NEG.PRS.IMPS.P

Xaal=daa	oŋbo-wasɪ.
when=ADD	forget-NEG.PRS.IMPS.P

Therefore, they never forget those persons. No, never.

«Tui	ta-pɪ,	kəsi-gu-ji	baa-orɪ, —	un-dii-či.
so	do-COND.IMPS	happiness-DSG-REFL	find-PRS.IMPS.P	say-PRS.P-3PL

— Boa	čaa	xəm	ičə-i,	totamɪ	simbiə=dəə
heaven	that.ACC	all	see-PRS.P	therefore	you.ACC=ADD

uləən[3]	bi-wəən-dii,	ajaǰɪɪ	bi-wəən-dii.»
good.INS	be-CAUS-PRS.P	well	live-CAUS-PRS.P

"There is a saying that goes: If one do so, he gains happiness. Heavenly God looks down upon it all and have you live well."

Totamɪ	nuučikəənǰuən	təi	ərin-du=dəə	bi-či-či
therefore	children	that	time-DAT=ADD	be-PST.P-3P

goanɪ	poaktanɪ	baakɪ,	poaktanɪ	ǰobo-orɪ-a
certainly	some	lazy	some	work-PRS.IMPS.P-ACC

uləəsi-i	gurun.
love-PRS.P	person

At that time, some children were idle, and other children liked working.

Totamɪ	əsi=məə	bi-i	gurun	bi-əči-či	goanɪ.
therefore	now=SML	be-PRS.P	people	be-NEG.PST.P-3PL	certainly

But they were different from children nowadays.

Balana	balǰɪ-ɪ	gurun,	balana	urə-i	gurun
long.ago	live-PRS.P	people	long.ago	grow-PRS.P	people

mənə	xaɪ-wa=daa	ta-ɪ	ǰaka-sal-ba	nəə
oneself	what-ACC=ADD	do-PRS.P	affair-PL-ACC	certainly

3) A colloquial form of *uləən-ǰi*.

saa-rɪɪ	bi-či-či	goanɪ.
know-PRS.P	be-PST.P-3PL	certainly

People born and brought up in an old-fashioned way, in whatever they did, knew without a doubt what it is they had to do.

Njoanči	ta-ɪ...	ta-asɪ-nɪ	osɪnɪ,	goɪ	gurun
they	do-PRS.P	do-NEG.PRS.P-3SG	if	other	people

ta-asɪ.
do-NEG.PRS.P

If they don't work, others don't do it for them either.

Təi	njoančɪ	ǰaka-čɪ,	njoančɪ	ta-ɪ-nɪ	ǰaka.
that	they	affair-3PL	they	do-PRS.P-3SG	affair

They do their works for themselves.

Totamaarɪ,	məən	urə-i=dəə,	njoančɪ	saa-rɪɪ
therefore	oneself	grow-PRS.P=ADD	they	know-PRS.P

bi-či-či	goanɪ:
be-PST.P-3PL	certainly

Thus growing up, they came to understand the following:

Sogdata	waa-rɪɪ=daa,	daaɪ	gurun[4]	buu-rii;
fish	catch-PRS.P=ADD	large	people-DAT	give-PRS.P

bəjun-bə	waa-rɪɪ=daa,	daaɪ	gurun-du	buu-rii.
animal-ACC	catch-PRS.P=ADD	large	people-DAT	give-PRS.P

When they catch fish, they should give them to the elderly, and when they catch animals, they should give them to the elderly also.

---

4) A colloquial form of *gurun-du*.

Məən	puril-bər=dəə	tui	uǰi-i	bi-či-či
oneself	children-REFL.PL=ADD	so	raise-PRS.P	be-PST.P-3PL

goanı,	čaa	saa-go-a-čı.
certainly	that.ACC	know-PURP-OCM-3PL

People raised their own children to know that.

Gəə,	nuučikəənǰuən-bə	uǰi-i-du-əri,	daaı	gurun
OK	children-ACC	raise-PRS.P-DAT-REFL.PL	large	people

naonǰokaan-sal-ba=daa,	arčokaan-sal-ba=daa	təŋ
boy-PL-ACC=ADD	girl-PL-ACC=ADD	very

toŋdo	bi-i	gurun-ǰi	uǰi-i	bi-či-či	goanı.
honest	be-PRS.P	people-INS	raise-PRS.P	be-PST.P-3PL	certainly

Well, when adult raised their children, they raised their son or daughter to be very honest.

Naı-a	argala-ası,	xaalı=daa	ǰələči-əsi,	təŋ
person-ACC	deceive-NEG.PRS.P	when=ADD	betray-NEG.PRS.P	very

təǰə-wə	manjaa	un-buri-wə,	gusərə-uri-wə	— gəə,
truth-ACC	only	say-PRS.IMPS.P-ACC	say-PRS.IMPS.P-ACC	OK

čaa	tačıo-čı-xa-čı	goanı.
that.ACC	teach-DUR-PST.P-3PL	certainly

They taught their children not to cheat others, not to be sly, but to speak the truth only.

Naı-a	argası-orı	— čuu	orkın,	čuu	orkın
person-ACC	deceive-PRS.IMPS.P	most	bad	most	bad

ǰaka	— naı-a	argala-orı.
affair	person-ACC	deceive-PRS.IMPS.P

Deceiving others is considered the most evil deed.

Totamaarı	xaalı=daa	argası-ası-čı	bi-či-či
therefore	when=ADD	deceive-NEG.PRS.P-3PL	be-PST.P-3PL

goanɪ.
certainly

Therefore they never deceived others.

— Gəə, məəpi=dəə doolaa doolaa nəuči-uri, —
OK oneself.ACC=ADD quietly keep-PRS.IMPS.P

un-dii bi-či-či goanɪ.
say-PRS.P be-PST.P-3PL certainly

They told themselves they should be modest.[5]

— Naɪ, simbiə ičə-mi, xəm saa-rɪɪ, xoonɪ=daa
person you.ACC see-SIM, all know-PRS.P how=ADD

bi-i-wə-si.
be-PRS.P-ACC-2SG

People know all by themselves what you are like just by observing you.

Totamɪ doolaa doolaa bi-uri, məəp xaalɪ=daa
therefore quietly be-PRS.IMPS.P oneself.ACC when=ADD

makta-wasɪ=am=daa.
praise-NEG.PRS.IMPS.P-REPO-ADD

Therefore you must be humble. One always must not praise oneself.

Orkɪn ǰaka — təi məəp makta-orɪ.
bad thing that oneself.ACC praise-PRS.IMPS.P

Praising oneself is a bad thing.

Məəpi əǰi makta-ra. naɪ simbiə ičə-mi,

5) In translating difficult sentences to understand, Mrs. Lidija Timofeevna Kile, who is a relative of A. Kile, helped us. We appreciate her invaluable assistance.

oneself.ACC not praise-INF people you.ACC see-SIM
mənə saa-rɪɪ xoonɪ=daa bi-i-wə-si.
oneself know-PRS.P how=ADD be-PRS.P-ACC-2SG

Do not praise yourself. People know all by themselves what you are like just by observing you.

Balana, nuučikəənǰuən urə-i-du-ə-či,
long.ago children grow-PRS.P-DAT-OCM-3PL
daanɪn-čɪ, ənin-či, akpan-go-ɪ-čɪ
grandmother-3PL, mother-3PL lie.down-REV-PRS.P-3PL
taon-do-a-nɪ, siksə, nɪŋmaan-dɪɪ bi-či-či=kəə.
every-DAT-OCM-3SG night narrate-PRS.P be-PST.P-3PL=CNTR

In the old days when children were young, their grandmother and mother told them fairy tales when they were lying in bed in the night.

Buə nuuči-du-əri təi nɪŋmaan-sal-ba təŋ
we small-DAT-REFL.PL that fairy.tale-PL-ACC very
uləəsi-i bi-či-pu goanɪ.
love-PRS.P be-PST.P-1PL certainly

When we were young, we were very fond of listening to fairy tales.

Daanja=daa, əniə=dəə nɪŋmaan-dasɪ osɪnɪ,
grandmother=ADD mother=ADD narrate-NEG.PRS.P if
oŋasa-wadaasɪ=a, təi nɪŋmaan-ba xalačɪ-mɪ.
sleep-NEG.PRS.IMPS.P=MIR that fairy.tale-ACC wait-SIM

If grandmother or mother do not tell a story, children do not sleep and wait.

Baɪbɪɪ nɪŋmaan-sal nɪŋmaan-dasɪ bi-či-či goanɪ.
just fairy.tale-PL narrate-NEG.PRS.P be-PST.P-3PL certainly

It was more than just telling a story.

Təi nıŋmaam nıŋmaan-dıı=daa, nuučikəənǰuən,
that fairy.tale.ACC narrate-PRS.P=ADD children

xoonı=daa osı-orı-a, otolı-go-a-čı,
how=ADD become-PRS.IMPS.P-ACC understand-PURP-OCM-3PL

nıŋmaan-dıı bi-či-či goanı. Mərgəən-səl=dəə
narrate-PRS.P be-PST.P-3PL certainly hero-PL=ADD

— buə mərgəən-gu-pu.
we hero-DSG-1PL

The purpose of telling fairy tales is to let children understand how our heroes performed good deeds.

Čuu uləən, sokta-ǰı pulsi-i-ni=dəə čuu turgən;
most good ski-INS walk-PRS.P-3SG=ADD most fast

bəjun-bə waa-rıı-nı=daa nəə waa-rıı,
beast-ACC kill-PRS.P-3SG=ADD certainly kill-PRS.P

əgǰi-wə waa-rıı.
many-ACC kill-PRS.P

They are very good at riding skis and walks the fastest. Even when hunting, they are able to hunt many animals without fail.

Puǰin=dəə čuu gučkuli, ərdən-ku,
heroine=ADD most beautiful method-PROP

ılga-la-mı=daa uləən otolı-ı, kusuni=dəə
embroidery-VBZ-SIM=ADD good.INS understand-PRS.P power.3SG=ADD

əgǰi, əmutuu xusəni=məə bi-i.
much as.if male=SML be-PRS.P

Heroines are also very beautiful, clever, and good at embroidery. Moreover, they are very powerful, like men.

Sokta-ǰı=daa pulsi-mi otolı-ı, ogda-ǰı=daa

ski-INS=ADD go-SIM understand-PRS.P, boat-INS=ADD

pulsi-mi otolɪ-ɪ.
go-SIM understand-PRS.P

She can move by ski or by boat.

Gəə, xagoarɪ tui bi-i mərgəən-səl-bə,
well what.for so be -PRS.P hero-PL-ACC

puǰin-səl-bə nɪŋmaan-do nɪŋmaan-dɪɪ bi-či-či=kəə?
heroine-PL-ACC fairy.tale-DAT narrate-PRS.P be-PST.P-3PL=CNTR

Well then, why did they tell such fairy tales about heroes and heroines?

Gəə, təi nuuči gurun, čaa dosɪǰa-maarɪ,
well, that small people that.ACC listen-SIM.PL

murun-du-əri tui murči-i bi-či-či goanɪ:
mind-DAT-REFL.PL so think-PRS.P be-PST.P-3PL certainly

Well, listening to these fairy tales, these children thought themselves in the following way:

«Buə=dəə, urə-pi, təi=məə osɪ-orɪ=am;
we=ADD grow-COND.IMPS that=SML become-PRS.IMPS.P=REPO

təi mərgəən=məə, təi puǰin=məə osɪ-orɪ.»
that hero=SML that heroine=SML become-PRS.IMPS.P

"When we grow, we will also become like a *Mergeen* or a heroine."

Nɪŋmaan-sal-ba uləəsi-i bi-či-či goanɪ
fairy.tale-PL-ACC love-PRS.P be-PST.P-3PL certainly

nuučikəənǰuən.
children

Children enjoyed listening fairy tales.

Guči=tənii,	nuučikəənǰuəm	uruuči-mi,
again=TOP	children.ACC	bring.up-SIM

nuučikəənǰuən	xaɪ-ǰɪ=daa	xupi-wəči	— čawa
children	what-INS=ADD	play-NEG.PST.IMPS.P	that.ACC

təǰuuči-uri	bi-či-ni	goanɪ.
try-PRS.IMPS.P	be-PST.P-3SG	certainly

In addition, while raising children, people did not make them play with something but make them practice things.

Gəə,	xupi-i=dəə,	baɪ	tui	xupi-əsi-či
well	play-PRS.P=ADD	just	so	play-NEG.PRS.P-3PL

bi-či-či	goanɪ.
be-PST.P-3PL	certainly

Well, playing was not just playing.

Naonǰokaan-sal	xupi-i-du-ə-či,	tui	ləkəə-či-uri-wə,
boy-PL	play-PRS.P-DAT-OCM-3PL	so	arrow-VBZ-PRS.IMPS.P-ACC

dəəŋgurə-wə	toɪga-orɪ-wa,	ogda-ǰɪ	pulsi-uri-wə
slingshot-ACC	hit-PRS.IMPS.P-ACC	boat-INS	go-PRS.IMPS.P-ACC

— čaa,	xəm	xupi-i-du-əri,	amda-ɪ
that.ACC	all	play-PRS.P-DAT-REFL.PL	imitate-PRS.P

bi-či-či	goanɪ.
be-PST.P-3PL	certainly

When playing, boys pretended to shoot bows, slingshots and go on boats. They imitated all of them in playing.

Njəŋnjə=tənii,	təi	ǰukə	xəjə-i-du-ə-ni,
spring=TOP	that	ice	float-PRS.P-DAT-OCM-3SG,

naonǰokaan-sal,	əmutuu	ǰɪa	ǰɪa-ǰɪ-arɪ
boy-PL	as.if	friend	friend-INS-REFL.PL

məlǰə-i=məə	məlǰə-i=məət,	təi
compete-PRS.P=SML	compete-PRS.P=SML	that

ogda-čɪ	oo-raa,	ǰoan	ǰoan duin	səə	naonǰokaan-sal,
boat-DIR	board-ANT	ten	fourteen	age	boy-PL

ambaan	daaɪ	naonǰokaan-sal	goanɪ,	taja-čɪ
fairly	big	boy-PL	certainly	there-DIR

bi-i	naonǰokaan-sal	boatoačɪ-maarɪ=daa	mutə-i,
be-PRS.P	boy-PL	hunt-SIM.PL=ADD	can-PRS.P

sogǰama-sɪ-maarɪ=daa	mutə-i.
fish-DUR-SIM.PL=ADD	can-PRS.P

In the spring, when ice is floating on the river, boys of age ten to fourteen who are big enough to hunt and fish, get on a boat as if they compete with one another.

Təi	ǰukə,	xəjə-i-du,	bojaa-mɪ,	xəjə-i-du-ə-ni,
that	ice,	float-PRS.P-DAT	break-SIM,	float-PRS.P-DAT-OCM-3SG,

təi	ǰukə	aldan-do-a-nɪ	ogda-ǰɪ	pulsi-i
that	ice	gap-DAT-OCM-3SG	boat-INS	go-PRS.P

bi-či-či	goanɪ.
be-PST.P-3PL	certainly

When the floating ice was broken, they rode a boat between ices.

Nuuči	gurun=dəə	ŋəələə-či-ni	goanɪ.
small	people=ADD	fear-FR-3SG	certainly

Little children are afraid of this.

Tooɪ-ǰɪaǰɪ	njoančɪačɪ	ičəǰə-i=dəə,	xoonɪ	ələ
riverside-ABL	they.DIR	look-PRS.P=ADD	how	enough

təi	ǰukə	njoambačɪ	ogda-wa-čɪ	bojalɪ-ɪ=daa,
that	ice	they.ACC	boat-ACC-3PL	destroy-PRS.P=ADD,

saawaasɪ.
maybe

When seen from the riverbank, it seems that the ice might break the boat.

Gəə, čaa ələ saago-ɪ-do-arɪ=tanɪɪ,
OK that.ACC enough make.sure-PRS.P-DAT-REFL.PL=TOP,

nuučikəənǰuən=tənii ogda-ǰɪ-arɪ ǰukə ojaa-čɪ-a-nɪ
children=TOP boat-INS-REFL ice surface-DIR-OCM-3SG

puiku-nəsi-i-či goanɪ.
jump-REP-PRS.P-3PL certainly

The older boys who fully know this jump on the ice from the boat.

Tui puiku-gu-rəə=tənii, ogda-warɪ=tanɪɪ
so jump-REV-ANT=TOP boat-REFL.PL=TOP

əjə taja-ǰɪa-nɪ gara-do-a-nɪ ǰapa-raa=tanɪɪ,
here there-side-3SG oarlock-DAT-OCM-3SG take-ANT=TOP

daaɪ ǰukə pasɪ-čɪ-a-nɪ ogda tata-ɪ.
big ice piece-DIR-OCM-3SG boat-ACC pull-PRS.P

After jumping on the ice, they pull the boat, grasping oarlock on both sides, toward the big piece of an ice.

Tolapɪ, tata-paar=tanɪɪ, təi ǰukə-ǰiə-či kutu-məəri,
then, pull-COND.PL.IMPS=TOP, that ice-side-DIR drag-SIM.PL,

goɪ boa-čɪ, muə ojaa-čɪ-a-nɪ ogda-wa xaɪ-raa,
other place-DIR water surface-DIR-OCM-3SG boat-ACC do.what-ANT

ana-go-raa, gučɪ mənə oo-go-raa, čado=ma, xaɪ,
push-REV-ANT again oneself board-REV-ANT then=PTCL what

ǰukə aldan-dola-nɪ ənə-məəri, tooɪ-čɪ
ice gap-LOC-3SG drive-SIM.PL riverside-DIR

xaa-go-ɪ-čɪ.
go.ashore-REV-PRS.P-3PL

After pulling and dragging the boat to the ice and pushing it onto the water, they board again and drive between ice then land on the shore.

Gəə,	tui	xupi-məəri,	baɪ	tui	xupi-mi,
OK	so	play-SIM.PL	just	so	play-SIM

xupi-wəsi-ni	goanɪ.
play-NEG.PRS.IMPS.P-3SG	certainly

Well, playing like this is not simple playing at all.

Tui	xupi-i-du-əri,	njoančɪ,	əmutuu	daaɪ
so	play-PRS.P-DAT-REFL.PL	they	as.if	big

gurun=məə,	məəpəəri	tui	ŋəələə-či-wəsi,
people=SML	oneself.ACC.PL	so	fear-FR-NEG.PRS.IMPS.P

xaɪ-ǰɪ=daa	ŋəələə-či-wəsi,	tui	ənə-mi
what-INS=ADD	fear-FR-NEG.PRS.IMPS.P	so	go-SIM

otolɪ-orɪ,	kutu-mi	otolɪ-orɪ,	ǰukə-səl
understand-PRS.IMPS.P	drag-SIM	understand-PRS.IMPS.P	ice-PL

pasɪ-la-nɪ	ənə-mi	otolɪ-orɪ.
piece-LOC-3SG	drive-SIM	understand-PRS.IMPS.P

Playing like this they, like the adults, are not afraid at all and are able to ride a boat, drag it and maneuver it between pieces of ice.

Njaŋgaa	bəgǰi	muə-či	ənə-xə=dəə	aja.
a.little	foot	water-DIR	go-PST.P=ADD	well

Even their feet get wet a little bit it is all right.

Bəgǰi-ji	tata-go-raa,	ǰukə	ojaa-čɪ-a-nɪ
foot-REFL	pull-REV-ANT	ice	surface-DIR-OCM-3SG

oo-go-orɪ.
board-REV-PRS.IMPS.P

After pulling the ice with their feet, they jump on the ice.

Gəə,	totapɪ,	daaɪ	urə-pəəri=tənii,	uləən	naɪ-sal
well	then	big	grow-COND.PL.IMPS=TOP	good	person-PL

osɪ-ɪ-čɪ	goanɪ.
become-PRS.P-3PL	certainly

Well then, in this way, they grow up to become capable men.

Xawaŋga,	boatoačɪ-maarɪ=daa	uləən	mutə-i,
quickly	hunt-SIM.PL=ADD	good.INS	can-PRS.P,

kusun-či=dəə	əgǰi,	ǰɪa	ǰɪa-warɪ
power-3PL=ADD	much,	friend	friend-REFL.PL

bələči-məəri=dəə	mutə-i.	Tui	osɪ-ɪ
help-SIM.PL=ADD	can-PRS.P	so	become-PRS.P

bi-či-či	goanɪ.
be-PST.P-3PL	certainly

They are able to hunt quickly and skillfully, and strong also. They can also help each other. It became like that.

Baɪ	tui	xupi-məəri,	xupi-əsi-či	bi-či-ni	goanɪ.
just	so	play-SIM.PL	play-NEG.PRS.P-3PL	be-PST.P-3SG	certainly

Like that, playing was not simply just playing at all.

Arčokaan-sal=daa,	akoačɪ-maarɪ,	čaa	xəm
girl-PL=ADD	doll.VBZ-SIM.PL	that.ACC	all

otolɪ-ɪ	bi-či-či	goanɪ.
understand-PRS.P	be-PST.P-3PL	certainly

Girls also learned everything by playing with dolls (See Fig. 12 on page xii above).

Arčokaan-sal=daa	tui	xupi-i-či	bi-či-ni	goanɪ.
girl-PL=ADD	so	play-PRS.P-3PL	be-PST.P-3SG	certainly

Girls also played as follows:

Ənin-bəri,	daaɪ əkəsəl,	əikə-wəri
mother-REFL.PL	grand-female.PL	elder.sister-REFL.PL

ta-ɪ-wa-čɪ	— Čaa	xəm	tui	akoačɪ-maarɪ,
do-PRS.P-ACC-3PL	that.ACC	all	so	doll.VBZ-SIM.PL

otolɪ-ɪ	bi-či-či	goanɪ:
understand-PRS.P	be-PST.P-3PL	certainly

By playing with dolls, they understood all of their mother, grandmother and elder sister's tasks.

Goljon-ba	ɪwa-čɪ-orɪ-wa,	sɪa-orɪ-a
stove-ACC	heat-FR-PRS.IMPS.P-ACC	eat-PRS.IMPS.P-ACC

pujuu-či-uri-wə,	Xaɪ-wa=daa	ətəxi-uri,
cook-FR-PRS.IMPS.P-ACC	what-ACC=ADD	take.care-PRS.IMPS.P,

nuučikəənǰuəm	ətəxi-uri-wə,	ulpi-uri
children.ACC	take.care-PRS.IMPS.P-ACC,	sew-PRS.IMPS.P

— čaa	xəm	otolɪ-ɪ	bi-či-či	goanɪ.
that.ACC	all	understand-PRS.P	be-PST.P-3PL	certainly

Girls understood all things, such as making fire in a stove, making food, taking care of children, and sewing.

Gəə,	tui	nuučikəənǰuəm	uruuči-i	bi-či-či	goanɪ.
OK	so	children.ACC	bring.up-PRS.P	be-PST.P-3PL	certainly

People raised their children like this.

Gəə,	tui tamaarɪ,	nuučikəənǰuən,	əlkəǰiəni
Ok,	therefore	children	gradually

urə-məəri,	daaɪ	gurun	xoonɪ=daa	bi-i-wə-či,
grow-SIM.PL	large	people	how=ADD	live-PRS.P-ACC-3PL

xəm	otolɪ-ɪ	bi-či-či	goanɪ.
all	understand-PRS.P	be-PST.P-3PL	certainly

In this way, as children matured gradually, they understood all about how adults lived.

Mənə=dəə, daaɪ urə-məəri=ə, urə-məəri=ə, təi=məə
oneself=ADD large grow-SIM.PL=MIR grow-SIM.PL=MIR that=SML

osɪ-ɪča-maarɪ.
become-DES-SIM.PL

Growing up, they hoped to become like the adults by themselves.

Tui busəsi-i bi-či-či goanɪ.
so endeavor-PRS.P be-PST.P-3PL certainly

They tried hard for this.

Tui ta-mɪ daaɪ gurun, sagdan-go-paarɪ,
so do-SIM large people get.old-REV-COND.PL.IMPS

un-dii bi-či-či goanɪ:
say-PRS.P be-PST.P-3PL certainly

Thus, when they got old, the adults said the following:

«Gəə, bu-dii ǰuliə-lə-ni baa-xam puril-bə,
OK, die-PRS.P front-LOC-3SG get-PST.P.REFL children-ACC

uǰi-xən-bi puril-bə — xəm məən
raise-PST.P-REFL children-ACC all oneself

saa-xan-bɪ saa-waan-borɪ, xəm məən
know-PST.P-REFL know-CAUS-PRS.IMPS.P all oneself

otolɪ-xan-bɪ otolɪ-waan-borɪ.
understand-PST.P-REFL understand-CAUS-PRS.IMPS.P

"Well, before dying I must let my own children know all that I knew by myself, and make them understand all that I understood by myself.

Balǰɪ-xan-bɪ, bi-čin-bi, boatoačɪ-xan-bɪ,
live-PST.P-1SG be-PST.P-1SG, hunt-PST.P-1SG

sogǰama-sɪ-xan-bɪ boa-wa — xəm ičuən-buri, xəm
fish-DUR-PST.P-1SG world-ACC all show-PRS.IMPS.P all

saa-waan-borɪ.
know-CAUS-PRS.IMPS.P

I must show them and let them know all about world where I have lived, hunted, and fished.

Čaa	saa-rasɪ	osɪnɪ,	njoanɪ	xoonɪ	balǰɪ-ɪ,
that.ACC	know-NEG.PRS.P	if	he	how	live-PRS.P

buə	anaa	osɪ-go-očɪa-po=wa.
we	without	become-REV-COND-1PL=MIR

If he does not know this, how can he live his life after we pass away.

Təluŋgu-səl-bə,	nɪŋmaan-sal-ba=daa	— xəm	gusərə-uri.
legend-PL-ACC	fairy.tale-PL-ACC=ADD	all	say-PRS.IMPS.P

We must tell them all the legends and fairy tales.

Čaa	saa-rasɪ	osɪnɪ,	urə-i	gurun	buə
that.ACC	know-NEG.PRS.P	if	grow-PRS.P	people	we

kolɪ-po-wa,	buə	saa-xa-pu	ǰaka-sal-ba
custom-1PL-ACC	we	know-PST.P-1PL	affair-PL-ACC

saa-rasɪ	osɪ-ɪ.
know-NEG.PRS.P	become-PRS.P

If growing people do not know these things, they will forget our customs and what we have known.

Təi	orkɪn.	Buə	balǰɪ-ɪ-pu	xətuə-rii.»
that	bad	we	live-PRS.P-1PL	cut-PRS.P

This is bad. It makes our lifestyle disappear."

Tui	ta-mɪ,	əsi	buə	tui	ǰobo-ɪ-po	goanɪ.
so	do-SIM	now	we	so	work-PRS.P-1PL	certainly

Čawa təræk osɪgoaan-kɪča-maarɪ.

that.ACC just revitalize-DES-SIM.PL

This is why we are doing such work nowadays. We are now only hoping to revitalize this (See Figs. 6 and 7 on page ix–x above).

Əsi *učitel'*-səl=dəə tui un-dii-či goanɪ, xaɪ
now R. teacher-PL=ADD so say-PRS.P-3PL certainly indeed

pedagogika=daa naɪ goɪ goɪ golo
R. pedagogy=ADD person various ethic.group

pedagogika-nɪ=am=daa.
R. pedagogy-3SG=REPO=ADD

Nowadays teachers say as follows: pedagogy is also concerned with teaching various tribes.

Tui tamaarɪ əsi nuučikəənǰuən-bə tačɪo-čɪ-ɪ
therefore now children-ACC teach-DUR-PRS.P

gurun təi balapčɪ naɪ puril-bə uruuči-xə-ni
people that ancient person children-ACC bring.up-PST.P-3SG

ǰaka-sal-ba xəm ǰooŋgo-maarɪ, nuučikəənǰuəm
affair-PL-ACC all come.to.mind-SIM.PL children.ACC

tačɪo-čɪ-ɪ-čɪ goanɪ čawa.
teach-DUR-PRS.P-3PL certainly that.ACC

To do so, teachers nowadays teach children bearing in mind how children were taught long ago.

Gəə, təi, təi uləən goanɪ əsi.
OK that that good certainly now

Now this is very good.

Buə balǰɪ-ɪ-pu *Xabarowskii* *krai*-du=daa bi-i
we live-PRS.P-1PL R. Khabarovsk R. Krai-DAT=ADD be-PRS.P

əmbə əmbə *shkola*-du tui bi-i *shkola*-sal

rarely R. school-DAT so be-PRS.P R. school-PL

nuučikəənǰuən-bə tui uruuči-i gurun.
children-ACC so bring.up-PRS.P people

There are teachers who teach in this way at a small number of schools in Khabarovsk Krai, where we live now.

Gəə, banıxa, ələ. Mii goıda-mı gusərə-xən-bi.
OK thanks enough I last.long-SIM say-PST.P-1SG

Ələ bi-əsi?
enough be-NEG.PRS.P

OK. Thank you. I've said for a long time. Isn't this sufficient?

2.2. Birth rituals

Gəə,	xora-ɪ	əktə,	xaɪ=daa	niə-rii-du-ə-ni,
well	give.birth-PRS.P	female	indeed=ADD	go.out-PRS.P-DAT-OCM-3SG

səəksə-ni,	muə-ni	niə-rii-du-ə-ni,	saorɪ-a,
blood-3SG	water-3SG	go.out-PRS.P-DAT-OCM-3SG	*saori*-ACC

əgǰi-ə	saorɪ-a	bargɪ-ɪ	bi-či-či	goanɪ.
many-ACC	*saori*-ACC	prepare-PRS.P	be-PST.P-3PL	certainly

Well, when a pregnant woman gave birth to her child, they prepared lots of *saoris* (thin and soft wood chips. See Fig. 11 on page xii above) for her flowing blood and amniotic fluid out.

Totapɪ=tanɪɪ	aŋgo-oxan	čooro	doo-čɪ-a-nɪ
then=TOP	make-PST.IMPS.P	hut	inside-DIR-OCM-3SG

saorɪ-a	ɪra-ɪ,	xukunə-ǰi…	xukunə-ǰi	xuku-rəə;
saori-ACC	bring-PRS.P	bundle-INS	bundle-INS	wrap-ANT

təi	saorɪ-a	əgǰi-ə	buu-rii	bi-či-či	goan,
that	*saori*-ACC	many-ACC	give-PRS.P	be-PST.P-3PL	certainly

xao-čɪ-go-a-nɪ	təi	səəksə,	muə	niə-rii-du-ə-ni.
wipe-FR-PURP-OCM-3SG	that	blood	water	go.out-PRS.P-DAT-OCM-3SG

And then, to wipe the blood and amniotic fluid that flowed out, they wrapped the *saoris* in bundles and delivered to the hut.

Piktə	balǰɪ-očɪa-nɪ=daa	təi	piktə-wə=dəə	təi
child	be.born-COND-3SG=ADD	that	child-ACC=ADD	that

saorɪ-ǰɪ	xao-go-ɪ.
saori-INS	wipe-ITER-PRS.P

When a baby was born, it was also wiped with the *saoris*.

Saorɪ-a=tanɪɪ	baɪbɪɪ	moo-ǰɪ	aŋgo-asɪ	bi-či-či	goan.
saori-ACC=TOP	ordinary	wood-INS	make-NEG.PRS.P	be-PST.P-3PL	certainly

They did not make *saoris* from ordinary trees.

Saorɪ-a	aŋgo-ɪ,	tui	bi-i	moo-sal-ǰɪ
saori-ACC	make-PRS.P	that.way	be-PRS.P	wood-PL-INS

aŋgo-ɪ	bi-či-či	goan	saorɪ-wa.
make-PRS.P	be-PST.P-3PL	certainly	*saori*-ACC

They made *saoris* from some kinds of trees.

Xaɪ=daa	kolaan-sal,	xaɪ=daa	xəm	ənuu-wə
indeed=ADD	insect-PL	indeed=ADD	all	illness-ACC

aŋgo-ɪ	ǰaka-sal	agbɪn-dasɪ
make-PRS.P	thing-PL	appear-NEG.PRS.P

osɪ-go-a-nɪ,	təi	saorɪ	puŋku.
become-PURP-OCM-3SG	that	*saori*	wraparound

The *saoris* wraparound is used for the sake of making all the insects and the factors in illness disappear.

Təi	saorɪ=tanɪɪ	təi	ənuu-ku,	ənuu-wə
that	*saori*=TOP	that	illness-PROP	illness-ACC

aŋgo-ɪ	kolaan-sal-ba	xəm	waa-rɪɪ	bi-čin.
make-PRS.P	insect-PL-ACC	all	kill-PRS.P	be-PST.P

The *saoris* killed all the insects which carry disease.

Təi	bolookto,	busuəktə,	ačaŋkora	—	təi	moo-ǰɪaǰɪ
that	meadowsweet	willow	filbert		that	wood-ABL

saorɪ-a	saorɪ-raa,	əktə-du	buu-rii	bi-či-či	goan.
saori-ACC	whittle-ANT	female-DAT	give-PRS.P	be-PST.P-3PL	certainly

They made the *saoris* from those trees such as meadowsweets, willows, and filberts, and gave them to the woman.

Təi	xao-čɪ-orɪ	saorɪ=tanɪɪ	nəmdə-kuukəən-ǰi	uləən
that	wipe-FR-PRS.IMPS.P	*saori*=TOP	thin-EXDIM-INS	good

saorɪ	bi-či-či	goanɪ,	kičə-məəri,	səpərsi-əsi
saori	be-PST.P-3PL	certainly	make.efforts-SIM.PL	cut-NEG.PRS.P

osɪ-ɪ	goanɪ,	pujə	aŋgo-asɪ	osɪ-ɪ	goanɪ.
become-PRS.P	certainly	injury	make-NEG.PRS.P	become-PRS.P	certainly

The thinner the *saori*s for wiping are, the better, and those *saori*s which were made carefully do not cause cuts or any injuries on the contacted skin.

Təi	saorɪ-a	aŋgo-raa,	təi	xora-ɪ	əktə-či
that	*saori*-ACC	make-ANT	that	give.birth-PRS.P	woman-DIR

ɪra-ɪ	bi-či-či	goan	təi	čooro-čɪ.
carry-PRS.P	be-PST.P-3PL	certainly	that	hut-DIR

The *saoris* were made and taken to the woman in the hut.

Təi	čooro-do,	xora…	xora-orɪ	čooro-do,
that	hut-DAT	give.birth	give.birth-PRS.IMPS.P	hut-DAT

xusəni-səl,	nuuči	bi-mi=u,	daaɪ	bi-mi=u,
man-PL	small	be-SIM=CONC	large	be-SIM=CONC

bi-i-či	ačaasɪ	bi-čin.
be-PRS.P-3PL	not.appropriate	be-PST.P

Men, whether they were children or adults, were not to bc in the hut where a woman would give birth.

Xusə	gursəl-bə	xaal=daa	təi	čooro
man	people.PL-ACC	when=ADD	that	hut

doo-čɪ-a-nɪ	ii-wəən-dəsi	bi-čin.
inside-DIR-OCM-3SG	enter-CAUS-NEG.PRS.P	be-PST.P

Men were never allowed to enter the hut.

Xaɪmaarɪ	tui	ta-ɪ-čɪ	bi-či-n?
why	that.way	do-PRS.P-3PL	be-PST.P-3SG

Why did they do so?

Xusə	gursəl	ii-rii	osıni	(daaı	gursəl	tui	un-dii
male	people.PL	enter-PRS.P	if	adult	people.PL	that.way	say-PRS.P

bi-či-či	goanı),	uləən	waaıča-mı,	uləən	sogǰa...
be-PST.P-3PL	certainly	well	hunt-SIM	well	fish

sogǰama-sı-mı	aba-na-ı-nı=am=daa.
fish-DUR-SIM	not-VBZ-PRS.P-3SG=REPO=ADD

Elders said as follows: “If men enter the hut they can’t hunt and fish well anymore.”

Tui tamaarı	xusə	gursəl-bə	ii-wəən-dəsi	bi-či-či.
therefore	male	people.PL-ACC	enter-CAUS-NEG.PRS.P	be-PST.P-3PL

In that way, men were not allowed to enter the hut.

Waaıča-orı	xaǰon=daa	təi	čooro	doo-la-n...
hunt-PRS.IMPS.P	stuff=ADD	that	hut	inside-LOC-3SG

doo-la-nı	nəučə-wəsi.
inside-LOC-3SG	keep-NEG.PRS.IMPS.P

The hunting tools were not put in the hut, either.

Xusə	gursəl	xaalı=daa	təi	waaıča-orı	xaǰon-ba
man	people.PL	when=ADD	that	hunt-PRS.IMPS.P	stuff-ACC

təi	čooro	doo-čı-a-nı	ii-wəsi	bi-čin.
that	hut	inside-DIR-OCM-3SG	enter-NEG.PRS.IMPS.P	be-PST.P

Men and the hunting tools were never brought in the hut.

Təi=dəə	ačaası,	papon-ko	bi-čin.
that=ADD	not.appropriate	ban-PROP	be-PST.P

These were also prohibited.

Waaıča-orı	maal-kın	osı-ı-nı	goanı.
hunt-PRS.IMPS.P	die.out-PST.P	become-PRS.P-3SG	certainly

Game would die out.

Xaɪ, waaɪča-wasɪ osɪnɪ, xaɪ-wa=daa
indeed hunt-NEG.PRS.IMPS.P if what-ACC=ADD

waa-was... waa-wasɪ osɪ-ɪ-nɪ.
kill-NEG.PRS.IMPS.P catch-NEG.PRS.IMPS.P become-PRS.P-3SG

If they do not hunt anything, they will not gain anything.

Tui ta-mɪ čawa papola-ɪ bi-či-či.
that.way do-SIM that.ACC prohibit-PRS.P be-PST.P-3PL

By saying this, those were prohibited.

Əktəni xora-ɪ-do-a-nɪ, səəl-dii-ni osɪnɪ=tanɪɪ, təi
woman give.birth-PRS.P-DAT-OCM-3SG prick-PRS.P-3SG if=TOP that

əŋpə-ni=dəə, njoanǰɪ-a-nɪ gəsə bi-i
mother.in.law-3SG=ADD she.INS-OCM-3SG together be-PRS.P

mama=daa bələči-i bi-čin goanɪ.
elderly.woman=ADD help-PRS.P be-PST.P certainly

During childbirth, when contractions came for the woman, her mother-in-law, and the midwife who was with her helped her.

Əlkəǰiəni əktəni, xora-mɪ, təə-si-mi xora-ɪ
gradually woman give.birth-SIM sit-DUR-SIM give.birth-PRS.P

bi-čin, njaŋgaa=daa.
be-PST.P a.little=ADD

She sat down and gave birth quietly and gradually.

Akpan-dasɪ bi-čin.
lie.down-NEG.PRS.P be-PST.P

She did not lie down.

Təə-si-rəə, təə-rəə, tui njaŋgaa, əmutuu
sit-DUR-ANT sit-ANT that.way a.little as.if

darama-do-a-nɪ xaɪ=daa bi-i=dəə, pɪanǰɪko

backbone-DAT-OCM-3SG what=ADD be-PRS.P=ADD sofa
bi-i=dəə, tui təə-rii bi-či-ni goan.
be-PRS.P=ADD that.way sit.up-PRS.P be-PST.P-3SG certainly

She sat down as if there were a sofa on her back.

Təi səəl-dii-du-ə-ni=tənii, mama=tanɪɪ əlkəə
that prick-PRS.P-DAT-OCM-3SG=TOP elderly.woman=TOP quietly
darama-la-nɪ bəgǰi-ǰi-ji tui njaŋ... njaŋgaa ana-ɪ
back-LOC-3SG leg-INS-REFL that.way a.little a.little push-PRS.P
bi-čin goanɪ.
be-PST.P certainly

When the contractions started, the midwife quietly pushed the woman's back gently with her own foot.

Ana-ɪ-do-ji=tanɪɪ, un-dii bi-či-ni goan:
push-PRS.P-DAT-REFL=TOP say-PRS.P be-PST.P-3SG certainly
— Gəə, xoonɪ=daa bələči-ruu.
well how=ADD help-2SG.IMP

While pushing with her foot, the midwife said as follows: "Please help us somehow.

Xoonɪ=daa xora-ɪ-wa-nɪ bələči-ruu=əm=dəə.
how=ADD give.birth-PRS.P-ACC-3SG help-2SG.IMP=REPO=ADD

Please help her delivery by some means.

Aja, xoonɪ=daa bələči-ruu turgəsuən xora-go-a-nɪ.
good, how=ADD help-2SG.IMP quickly give.birth-PURP-OCM-3SG

Please help her give birth more quickly.

Piktə-ni=dəə uləən-ǰi balǰɪ-go-a-nɪ, bələči-ruu, —
child-3SG=ADD good-INS be.born-PURP-OCM-3SG help-2SG.IMP
un-dii bi-či-ni goan.

say-PRS.P	be-PST.P-3SG	certainly

Please help the baby that it may be born safely.”

Tui	bələči-i	bi-či-ni	goan	təi	njoanǰɪ-a-nɪ
that.way	help-PRS.P	be-PST.P-3SG	certainly	that	she.INS-OCM-3SG

gəsə	bi-i	əktə=dəə,	əŋpə-ni=dəə.
together	be-PRS.P	female=ADD	mother.in.law-3SG=ADD

The midwife and her mother-in-law helped the mother like this.

Piktə	balǰɪ-očɪa-nɪ=tanɪɪ,	təi	uləən,	nəmik…	nəmi,
child	be.born-COND-3SG=TOP	that	good	very.thin	thin

uləən	saorɪ-oxan	saorɪ-ǰɪ	piktə	xao-raa,
well	whittle-PST.IMPS.P	*saori*-INS	child	wipe-ANT

xuku-rəə,	duri-du	nəə-rii	bi-či-či	goan.
wrap-ANT	baby.bed-DAT	put-PRS.P	be-PST.P-3PL	certainly

When the baby was born, after being wiped with and wrapped in thin and well-whittled *saoris*, they put it in the baby bed.

Təi	duri=tənii	talo-ǰɪ	aŋgo-oxan,	uləən
that	baby.bed=TOP	birch.bark-INS	make-PST.IMPS.P	well

pujuu-wu-xən.	Talo-ǰɪ.
cook-TR-PST.P	birch.bark-INS

The baby bed was made of birch bark which was sufficiently boiled.

Nəmi-kuukəən	uləən	talo-ǰɪ	aŋgo-ɪ-čɪ	goanɪ=a
thin-EXTR	good	birch.bark-INS	make-PRS.P-3PL	certainly=MIR

təi	tənii	balǰɪ-xa-nɪ	piktə	nəə-gu-əri.
that	just	be.born-PST.P-3SG	child	put-PURP-REFL.PL

They made a baby bed of very thin and good birch bark to lay the newborn baby on.

Aɪ,	əktə=tənii,	ɪlaan	aoŋga-pɪ,	ǰului
R. oh	female=TOP	three	spend.a.night-COND.IMPS	first

əər-du-ji	məəpi	sɪlko-go-ɪ
time-DAT-REFL	oneself.ACC	wash-ITER-PRS.P

bi-či-ni	goan,	ɪlaan	aoŋga-pɪ.
be-PST.P-3SG	certainly	three	spend.a.night-COND.IMPS

After three days, the woman washes herself first.

Xora-xam	xaɪ,	xaǰon-bɪ,	məəpi=dəə
give.birth-PST.P.REFL	what	clothes-REFL	oneself.ACC=ADD

xao-čɪ-go-ɪ	muə-ǰi	uləən-ǰi.
wash-FR-ITER-PRS.P	water-INS	good-INS

Ilaan	ao…	aon	sii-učiə-ni=ə=dəə.
three	day	day	pass-COND-3SG=MIR=ADD

And she washes her underwear clean with water after three days.

Piktə	balǰɪ-očɪa-nɪ=tanɪɪ,	xuimu-wə-ni	čaalɪ-go-arɪ,	əktəni
child	be.born-COND-3SG=TOP	navel-ACC-3SG	cut-PURP-REFL.PL	woman

gɪrsoo-wa-nɪ,	balana	əktəni	gɪrsoo-ǰɪ-a-nɪ
knife.for.sewing-ACC-3SG	long.ago	woman	knife.for.sewing-INS-OCM-3SG

xuimu-ə-ni	čaalɪ-ɪ	bi-či-či	goan.
navel-ACC-3SG	cut-PRS.P	be-PST.P-3PL	certainly

In the old days, if a baby was born, they cut the umbilical cord with the woman's knife for sewing.

Totapɪa,	təi	xaǰa	agbɪn-bo-očɪa-nɪ=tanɪɪ,	xaǰa-ǰɪ
later	that	scissors	appear-TR-COND-3SG=TOP	scissors-INS

xaǰa-la-ɪ	bi-či-či.
scissors-VBZ-PRS.P	be-PST.P-3PL

A little later, after the scissors appeared, they cut it with scissors.

Təi xuimu-kəən-bə=tənii, xaǰa-la-raa, gɪrsoo-ǰi

that navel-DIM-ACC=TOP scissors-VBZ-ANT knife.for.sewing-INS

čaalı-raa=tanıı, uləən boso-kaan-ǰı=daa, xaı,
cut-ANT=TOP good cloth-DIM-INS=ADD indeed

sogbo-kaan-ǰı=daa (nəmdə-kuukəən, uju-xən uləən-ǰi),
fish.skin-DIM-INS=ADD thin-EXTR braid-PST.P good-INS

čaa xuku-rəə=tənii, uləən nəə-rii bi-či-či goan.
that.ACC wrap-ANT=TOP well put-PRS.P be-PST.P-3PL certainly

After cutting umbilical cord with the knife for sewing, they wrapped in a clean cloth or a good, thin and well-braided fish skin and preserved it.

Balana təi xora-xan əktə təi piktə-ji xuimu-wə-ni,
long.ago that give.birth-PST.P female that child-REFL navel-ACC-3SG

uləən xuku-rəə=tənii, xaı-kaan-do, somalaakaan-do
well wrap-ANT=TOP what-DIM-DAT pouch.DIM-DAT

nəə-rəə=tənii, xukuən-či, xukuən-či ulpi-i
put-ANT=TOP bag-DIR bag-DIR sew-PRS.P

bi-či-ni goanı.
be-PST.P-3SG certainly

In the old days, the mother carefully wrapped the umbilical cord of her own baby, put it in a pouch, and sewed into a bag.

Təi xuimu-kəən, tul tul čado bi-mi,
that navel-DIM always then be-SIM

xolgo-ı-nı goan uləən-ǰi.
dry-PRS.P-3SG certainly good-INS

The umbilical cord remained then, and completely dried.

Xaıgojı tui ta-ı-čı bi-či-ni?
why that.way do-PRS.P-3PL be-PST.P-3SG

Why did they do this?

Təi	piktə	xuimu-kəən-bə-ni,	tui	əsəli-rəə,
that	child	navel-DIM-ACC-3SG	that.way	put-ANT

nəuči-uri	osını,	guči	piktə	baa-orı=a,
store-PRS.IMPS.P	if	again	child	get-PRS.IMPS.P=MIR

un-dii	bi-či-či	goanı.
say-PRS.P	be-PST.P-3PL1	certainly

They said that she would be able to have another baby by preserving the umbilical cord of her baby.

Əm	piktə	baa-raa,	xoǰı-wası;	guči guči
one	child	get-ANT	finish-NEG.PRS.IMPS.P	again.and.again

piktə	baa-orı.
child	get-PRS.IMPS.P

That is, she will have more babies successively, not ending with just one.

Balana	əgǰi	piktə	baa-orı	uləən	bi-či-ni	goanı.
long.ago	many	child	get-PRS.IMPS.P	good	be-PST.P-3SG	certainly

It was good to have many children in the old days.

Tui tamaarı	təi	xuimu-kəən-bə	tui	nəə-rii
therefore	that	navel-DIM-ACC	that.way	put-PRS.P

bi-či-či	goan	čado.
be-PST.P-3PL	certainly	then

In those days, they preserved the umbilical cord in that way.

Təi	čaalı-oxan	xuimu-kəən-bə=tənii	naanaı
that	cut-PST.IMPS.P	navel-DIM-ACC=TOP	Nanai

«čuŋguru=əm»	gərbiə-si-i	bi-či-ni.
fallen.away.navel=REPO	call-DUR-PRS.P	be-PST.P-3SG

«Čuŋguru»,	«čuŋguru»,	un-dii	bi-či-či	goan.
fallen.away.navel	fallen.away.navel	say-PRS.P	be-PST.P-3PL	certainly

This umbilical cord that was cut was called *čuŋguru* in Nanai.

Xaɪ-wa, əktə təi čaalɪ-oxan xuimu duə-wə-ni,
what-ACC woman that cut-PST.IMPS.P navel end-ACC-3SG

xaɪ-ǰɪ uji-i-či goanɪ kupən-ǰi=dəə, sirxə...
what-INS tie-PRS.P-3PL certainly thread-INS=ADD twine

Nəmdəkuu sirxə-kəən-ǰi=dəə uji-i-či.
thin twine-DIM-INS=ADD tie-PRS.P-3PL

They tie the end of the navel with thread or very thin strings.

A, uji-i-wəri ǰuliə-lə-ni=tənii, xaɪ-ǰɪ, waaraŋkola-ǰɪ,
R. but tie-PRS.P-REFL.PL front-LOC-3SG=TOP what-INS acacia-INS

waaraŋkola moo-kaan-ba-nɪ nɪlčalɪ-raa, təi nɪlčalɪ-oxan-ǰɪ,
acacia tree-DIM-ACC-3SG crush-ANT that crush-PST.IMPS.P-INS

nɪlčalɪ-oxan waaraŋkola moo-wa-nɪ=tanɪɪ nəə-rii-či
crush-PST.IMPS.P acacia tree-ACC-3SG=TOP put-PRS.P-3PL

bi-či-ni goan təi pujə-du-ə-ni.
be-PST.P-3SG certainly that injury-DAT-OCM-3SG

Gɪrsoo-ǰɪ xaɪ-woxan, čaalɪ-oxan xuimu
knife.for.sewing-INS do.what-PST.IMPS.P cut-PST.IMPS.P navel

duə-du-ə-ni təi waaraŋkola.
end-DAT-OCM-3SG that acacia

Before tying it, they put the crushed powder of acacia, a kind of willow on the wound, that is, the end of the umbilical cord which has been cut with a sewing knife.

Təi=tənii, əmun ǰuər aoŋga-mɪ, xəm xoo-go-ɪ
that=TOP one two spend.a.night-SIM all heal-REV-PRS.P

bi-čin goanɪ.
be-PST.P certainly

After a day or two, all the wound healed up.

Xaɪ=daa	aba-na-go-mɪ.
what=ADD	not-VBZ-ITER-SIM

All disappeared.

Tui	okčɪ-čɪ-ɪ	bi-či-či	goanɪ	əktə-wə,
that.way	cure-FR-PRS.P	be-PST.P-3PL	certainly	female-ACC

xora-xan	əktə-wə.
give.birth-PST.P	female-ACC

They used to cure women who had given birth in that way.

Guči=tənii	uləən	osɪ-ɪ=nuu,	xoonɪ	osɪ-ɪ=nuu
again=TOP	good	become-PRS.P=Q	how	become-PRS.P=Q

təi	balǰɪ-xan	piktə,	ənini,	təi	piktə	balǰɪ-očɪa-nɪ.
that	be.born-PST.P	child	mother.3SG	that	child	be.born-COND-3SG

Furthermore, if a baby is born, will the new-born baby and its mother be healthy and how will they turn out?

Təi	ǰuulgəən-bə-ni	saa-go-arɪ,	saman-sal=tanɪɪ	təi
that	fortune-ACC-3SG	know-PURP-REFL.PL	shaman-PL=TOP	that

əktə-wə	tui	bi-i	kolɪ-ǰɪ	pərgə-wəən-dii
female-ACC	that.way	be-PRS.P	custom-INS	try-CAUS-PRS.P

bi-či-či	goan.
be-PST.P-3PL	certainly

It was customary for shamans to make her try in order to know the fortunes of the mother and child.

«Solbon»	təi	gərbu-ni.
fortune-telling.ritual	that	name-3SG

Təi	«solbon».
that	fortune-telling.ritual

This was called *solbon*, that is, fortune-telling ritual.

Solbon=tanıı,	xaı-wa,	kəŋgi...
fortune-telling.ritual=TOP	what-ACC	felly

(xaı	goanı=a,	təi	gərbu-ni	xamačaa	bi-či-ni=nuu?)
what	certainly=MIR	that	name-3SG	which	be-PST.P-3SG=Q

(What was its name?)

Kərgiən,	təi	kərgiən	ǰaka-wa	moo-ǰı	aŋgo-orı
felly	that	felly	thing-ACC	tree-INS	make-PRS.IMPS.P

bi-či-ni	goanı,	kərgiən,	tuŋdə	moo-ǰı-a-nı.
be-PST.P-3SG	certainly	felly	willow	tree-INS-OCM-3SG

For this ritual, a wheel made of willow was prepared.

Aŋgo-raa=tanıı,	təi	kərgiən-dulə	əjə-ǰiəǰi	doo-čı
make-ANT=TOP	that	felly-LOC	near-ABL	inside-DIR

ii-wəən-də,	tui	pərgə-i	bi-či-či	goan.
enter-CAUS-PRS	that.way	try-PRS.P	be-PST.P-3PL	certainly

After that, they made the woman go through the wheel.

Təi	əktə	təi	kərgiən	doo...	dookıa-la-nı,	əm
that	female	that	felly	inside	inside-LOC-3SG	not

toŋgala-mı,	tui	uləən-ǰi	ii-rii-nı	osını,	gəə,	təi
touch-SIM	that.way	good-INS	enter-PRS.P-3SG	if	well	that

ǰuulgəəni	uləən	osı-ı-nı	goan.
fortune.3SG	good	become-PRS.P-3SG	certainly

If she goes into the wheel without touching anything, the mother and child will have good fortune.

A,	ii-rii-du-ji,	təi	kərgiən	ǰə...	aaŋgıa-la-jı=daa,
R. but	enter-PRS.P-DAT-REFL	that	felly	left	right-LOC-REFL=ADD

ǰəuŋgiə-lə-ji=dəə	toŋgala-ı-nı	osını,	gəə,	aso	uləən
left-LOC-REFL=ADD	touch-PRS.P-3SG	if	well	so.much	good

bi-əsi təi ǰuulgəən-či.

be-NEG.PRS.P that fortune-3PL

If she touches the right or left part of the wheel, they will not be so fortunate.

Təi əktə=dəə, piktə=dəə ǰuulgəəni.
that female=ADD child=ADD fortune.3SG

That was a fortune of the woman and the baby.

Čaa=tanɪɪ saman gurun ta-ɪ bi-či-či goanɪ.
that.ACC=TOP shaman people do-PRS.P be-PST.P-3PL certainly

Shamans performed the ritual.

Baɪbɪɪ gurun ta-asɪ bi-či-ni balana.
ordinary people do-NEG.PRS.P be-PST.P-3SG long.ago

In the old days, ordinary persons did not perform it.

Gəə, čawa ta-ɪ=daa aja, ta-asɪ=daa aja.
well that.ACC do-PRS.P=ADD good do-NEG.PRS.P=ADD good

It was all right to perform it or not.

Naɪ gələ-i-ni osɪnɪ, ta-ɪ, gələ-əsi-ni osɪnɪ,
person want-PRS.P-3SG if do-PRS.P want-NEG.PRS.P-3SG if
ta-asɪ=daa aja.
do-NEG.PRS.P=ADD good

At that time, it was performed if people wanted to and it was all right not to perform it if they did not want to.

ǰoog-čɪ ii-wu-gu-pəəri, ǰoog-čɪ
house-DIR enter-TR-REV-COND.PL.IMPS house-DIR
ii-wu-gu-pəəri, təi əktə-du čuu uləən bəun-bə
enter-TR-REV-COND.PL.IMPS that female-DAT very good place-ACC

buu-rii bi-či-či goan, təi xora-xan əktə-du.
give-PRS.P be-PST.P-3PL certainly that give.birth-PST.P female-DAT

Čuu njama bəun-bə.
very warmish place-ACC

After the woman was taken home, they offered her a very good, that is, warm place.

Təi bəun=tənii golǰon ǰakpa-do-a-nɪ bi-i nakan.
that place=TOP stove next-DAT-OCM-3SG be-PRS.P heated.floor

Təi čuu uləən xulǰii nakan.
that very good warm heated.floor

That place is the heated floor (*ondol*) next to the stove in the house.

Čado, čaa..., əktə-wə, piktə-wə-ni osɪ-waan-dɪɪ
then that female-ACC child-ACC-3SG become-CAUS-PRS.P

bi-či-či goanɪ.
be-PST.P-3PL certainly

They gave that place to the woman and the baby as their own space.

Xaɪmaarɪ tui ta-ɪ-čɪ?
why that.way do-PRS.P

Why do they do so?

Gəə, təi naɪ un-dii-ni goan: xora-xan əktə
well that person say-PRS.P-3SG certainly give.birth-PST.P female

njaaloon, njaaloon.
raw raw

It is said that the women after childbirth are sensitive.

doo-nɪ turgəsuən xoo-go-go-a-nɪ, turgəsuən

inside-3SG	quickly	be.cured-REV-PURP-OCM-3SG	quickly

aja-na-go-go-a-nɪ,	kusun-ku
good-VBZ-REV-PURP-OCM-3SG	strong-PROP

osɪ-go-go-a-nɪ,	təi	əktə,	čaa,	njama
become-ITER-PURP-OCM-3SG	that	female	that.ACC	warmish

boa-do	nəə-rii.
place-DAT	put-PRS.P

The mother is to be at a warm place so that she may have her internal wounds cured quickly and recover quickly and become strong.

Guči=tənii	tul tul	əuxəxim	omɪ-nasɪ-waan-dɪɪ.
again=TOP	always	angelica.ACC	drink-REP-CAUS-PRS.P

She is always made to drink angelica juice.

Əuxəxin,	təi	əuxəxin=tənii	təi	xora-xan	əktəni
angelica	that	angelica=TOP	that	give.birth-PST.P	female

doo-nɪ	pujə-ku,	un-dii	bi-či-či	goanɪ	balana.
inside-3SG	injury-PROP	say-PRS.P	be-PST.P-3PL	certainly	long.ago

In the old days, they said that it dissolved the internal wounds of the body of a woman after she gave birth.

Təi	pujə-wə-ni=dəə	turgən	xoo-go-waan-dɪɪ-ni
that	injury-ACC-3SG=ADD	fast	be.cured-REV-CAUS-PRS.P-3SG

goan,	tul tul	əuxəxin-bə	omɪ-nasɪ-mɪ.
certainly	always	angelica-ACC	drink-REP-SIM

If she always drinks angelica juice, her injuries are cured quickly.

Guči=tənii	təi	njama	boa	piktə-du=dəə	uləən	goan.
again=TOP	that	warmish	place	child-DAT=ADD	good	certainly

That warm place is also good for the baby.

Nuuči-kuukəən	piktə	duri-kəən-du	bi-i,	njama-du
small-EXTR	child	baby.bed-DIM-DAT	be-PRS.P	warmish-DAT

uləən	ao-rɪɪ,	ənusi-ədəəsi=ə.
well	sleep-PRS.P	illness.VBZ-NEG.PRS.P=MIR

If the newborn baby is in the baby bed, it slept well in the warm place, and did not get sick.

Tui	nəučə-i	bi-či-či	goan.
that.way	keep-PRS.P	be-PST.P-3PL	certainly

We protected the mother and her baby in that way.

J̌oan	ini	sii-učiə-ni=tənii	guči	təi	xora-xan-bɪ
ten	day	pass-COND-3SG=TOP	again	that	give.birth-PST.P-REFL

xaǰon-bɪ	təi	əktə	xəm	sɪlko-go-ɪ.
stuff-REFL	that	female	all	wash-ITER-PRS.P

Xəm	sɪlko-go-ɪ.
all	wash-ITER-PRS.P

After ten days, she washes again all the materials that was used for childbirth.

Təi	əktə,	təi	xora-xam	xaǰon-bɪ	xəm
that	woman	that	give.birth-PST.P.REFL	stuff-REFL	all

sɪlko-go-raa,	xəm	xolgɪ-čɪ-go-raa,	uləən-ǰi	namo-go-raa,
wash-ITER-ANT	all	dry-FR-ITER-ANT	good-INS	fold-ITER-ANT

xuku-rəə,	goɪ	boa-do	nəə-rii.
wrap-ANT	other	place-DAT	put-PRS.P

She dries up, carefully folds, wraps, and puts the childbirth materials, which she washed herself, in another place.

Xusəni	ičə…	ičə-əsi-ni	goan.
man	see	see-NEG.PRS.P-3SG	certainly

Men should not see them.

Təi xaǰon-ba xusənəj-jə ičə-wəən-buwəsi=ə, un-dii.
that thing-ACC man-ACC see-CAUS-NEG.PRS.IMPS.P=MIR say-PRS.P

It is said that she should not show them to a man.

Xoro-xan-ba… xoro-xan xaǰon-ba xusə… xusəni
remove-PST.P-ACC remove-PST.P thing-ACC man male

ičə-i osɪnɪ, waaɪčaŋko-nɪ orkɪn osɪ-ɪ=a, un-dii.
see-PRS.P if game-3SG bad become-PRS.P=MIR say-PRS.P

It is said that if a man see the childbirth materials, he will not be very good at hunting.

Tui tamaarɪ əktəni xaǰon-ba-nɪ, xora-xan əktəni
therefore woman stuff-ACC-3SG give.birth-PST.P woman

xaǰon-ba-nɪ xusənəj-ə xaal=daa ičə-wəən-dəsi bi-čin.
stuff-ACC-3SG man-ACC when=ADD see-CAUS-NEG.PRS.P be-PST.P

Therefore, men was never allowed to see the childbirth materials of the woman who gave birth.

Totapɪa guči modan xora-ɪ osɪnɪ, təi xaǰom
later again time (turn) give.birth-PRS.P if that stuff.ACC

tətu-gu-i=dəə aja.
wear-ITER-PRS.P=ADD good

In the later, when she gives birth again, she can wear the same materials again.

Tui=dəə.
that.way=ADD

That is the way it goes.

Xora-xan əktə xaɪgoanɪ, xao-čɪ-go-a-nɪ təi
give.birth-PST.P female for.what wash-FR-PURP-OCM-3SG that

niə-rii ǰaka-wa, nəučə-gu-ə-ni=tənii, xaɪ-wa,

go.out-PRS.P	thing-ACC	keep-PURP-OCM-3SG=TOP	what-ACC

saorɪ-wa,	xaɪ-ǰɪ,	siŋəəktə...	siŋəəktə
saori-ACC	what-INS	flowering.cherry	flowering.cherry

moo-ǰɪ-a-nɪ	saorɪ-ɪ	bi-či-či	goan.
tree-INS-OCM-3SG	whittle-PRS.P	be-PST.P-3PL	certainly

They made *saoris* by planing flowering cherry trees thin so that they might check the flow and wipe the blood of the woman who had given birth.

Təi	siŋəəktə	moo-nɪ=tanɪɪ	puuni	təŋ	uləən.
that	flowering.cherry	tree-3SG=TOP	scent.3SG	very	good

Təŋ	uləən.
very	good

The flowering cherry has a nice fragrance.

Baɪ	ǰoog-do	naɪ	tuə	saorɪ-do-a-nɪ,
just	house-DAT	person	winter	*saori*-DAT-OCM-3SG

puuŋgiči-mi=tənii,	naɪ	doo-nɪ	səək	ənə-i.
smell-SIM=TOP	person	inside-3SG	easily	go-PRS.P

If someone smells the flowering cherry at home in the winter, the smell easily spreads through his body.

Daaɪ	gursəl	un-dii	bi-či-či	goan,	təi	siŋəəktə
large	people.PL	say-PRS.P	be-PST.P-3PL	certainly	that	flowering.cherry

moo-nɪ	okto-nɪ	əgǰi=əm=dəə.
tree-3SG	medicine-3SG	many=REPO=ADD

Elders said that the flowering cherry tree had a lot of antiseptic properties.

xaɪ=daa	pujə-du	nəə-rii	osɪnɪ,	xəm	turgən
what=ADD	injury-DAT	put-PRS.P	if	all	fast

xoo-go-ɪ=am=daa.

be.cured-REV-PRS.P=REPO=ADD

They treat any injury quickly when applied.

Tui tamaarı təi siŋəəktə moo-wa-nı bolo
therefore that flowering.cherry tree-ACC-3SG autumn

əgǰi-ə bargı-ı bi-či-či goan, tuə
many-ACC prepare-PRS.P be-PST.P-3PL certainly winter

saorı-go-arı. Tuə saorı-go-arı.
whittle-PURP-REFL.PL winter whittle-PURP-REFL.PL

Therefore, they prepared a lot of flowering cherries in autumn to whittle them in the winter.

Gəkči-učiə-ni=tənii saorı-orı uləən goan.
freeze-COND-3SG=TOP whittle-PRS.IMPS.P good certainly

When the pieces froze, they were easier to whittle.

ǰoa saorı-orı maŋga. Xəm xolgokto.
summer whittle-PRS.IMPS.P difficult all dried

In the summer, they were difficult to whittle, because all of them dried up.

A, gəkčiun-bə, təi suuktu-səl xəm gəkči-učiə-či=tənii,
R. but frost-ACC that branch-PL all freeze-COND-3PL=TOP

kučəən-ǰi saorı-orı-do mənə təi saorı
knife-INS whittle-PRS.IMPS.P-DAT oneself that *saori*

ačoa-rıı=maa bi-i.
be.removed-PRS.P=SML be-PRS.P

If the branches of the trees are frozen, when they are whittled thin with a blade, it is as if the *saoris* came off by themselves.

Xora-xan əktə ǰapa-čı-ı-nı saorı — uləən
give.birth-PST.P female keep-FR-PRS.P-3SG *saori* well

saorɪ-ɪ	bi-či-ni	okto-ko,	uləən,	kičə-mi
whittle-PRS.P	be-PST.P-3SG	medicine-PROP	good	be.diligent-SIM

aŋgo-oxan	saorɪ.
make-PST.IMPS.P	*saori*

Saoris that protected the woman who had given birth were medicines which were elaborately whittled, and those made with great effort.

Təi	uləən	bi-či-ni.
that	good	be-PST.P-3SG

That was very good.

Xora-xan	əktə	kuun-bə-ni	təŋ	masɪ-ǰɪ
give.birth-PST.P	female	breast-ACC-3SG	very	hard-INS

kičə-i-či	bi-čin	goanɪ.
be.diligent-PRS.P-3PL	be-PST.P	certainly

They had the breast of the woman who had given birth work very diligent.

Balana	balǰɪ-xan	piktə	əm	səə,	ǰuə	səə,	ɪlaan
long.ago	be.born-PST.P	child	one	year	two	year	three

səə	ɪsɪ-ɪ=daa,	tul tul	ənin-bi	kuun-bə-ni
year	arrive-PRS.P=ADD	always	mother-REFL	breast-ACC-3SG

kuuči-i	bi-či-ni.
suck-PRS.P	be-PST.P-3SG

In the old days, Nanai babies always sucked breast milk of their own mother until three years old.

Daaɪ-nɪ	sɪa-rɪɪ-wa-nɪ	sɪa-rɪɪ=daa,	xaɪs	piktə-wə-əri
adult-3SG	eat-PRS.P-ACC-3SG	eat-PRS.P=ADD	still	child-ACC-REFL.PL

kuwuu-rii	bi-či-či	goan.
feed-PRS.P	be-PST.P-3PL	certainly

They nursed their babies until they were able to eat the adult food.

Əktəni kuuni xaɪ-ko, okto=maa bi-ə=m=dəə.
woman breast.3SG what-PROP medicine=SML be-PRS=REPO=ADD

It is said that mother's milk is like any other medicine.

Piktə ənu-lu-xən=dəə, təi ə-ə... əktə
child get.ill-INCH-PST.P=ADD that woman female

kuun-bə-ni ənin-bi kuun-bə-ni kuuči-mi,
breast-ACC-3SG mother-REFL breast-ACC-3SG suck-SIM

turgən xora-go-ɪ, turgən aja-na-go-ɪ.
fast stay.alive-ITER-PRS.P fast good-VBZ-REV-PRS.P

Even when babies are sick, by sucking breast milk, they break away and recover quickly from disease.

Tui tamaarɪ=tanɪɪ, təi kuun-bə-ni tul tul
therefore=TOP that breast-ACC-3SG always

moŋgɪ-čɪ-ɪ bi-či-či goanɪ.
massage-FR-PRS.P be-PST.P-3PL certainly

Therefore, they always kneaded her breasts.

Təi uləən xaɪ-go-go-a-nɪ, xaɪ, ku...
that sufficiently do.what-ITER-PURP-OCM-3SG indeed breast

kuuni daoko osɪ-go-go-a-nɪ.
breast.3SG loaded become-ITER-PURP-OCM-3SG

They replenish her breast sufficiently with milk.

Ənuu maŋga-nɪ goanɪ təi moŋgɪ-čɪ-ɪ-čɪ.
illness serious-3SG certainly that knead-FR-PRS.P-3PL

When they knead her breast, she feels sharp pain.

Daaɪ gurun moŋgɪ-čɪ-ɪ-čɪ goan.
large people knead-FR-PRS.P-3PL certainly

Older women knead her breast.

Əŋpə-ni, daaɪ-ǰɪma əkəsəl bi-i osɪnɪ, təi
mother.in.law-3SG big-SEL woman.PL be-PRS.P if that

daaɪ-ǰɪma əkəsəl kusun-ǰi-əri moŋgɪ-čɪ-ɪ-čɪ.
big-SEL woman.PL power-INS-REFL.PL knead-FR-PRS.P-3PL

If she is her mother-in-law or an older woman, she kneads the breasts with all her might.

Moŋgɪ-čɪ-ɪ-čɪ goan. čawa.
knead-FR-PRS.P-3PL certainly that.ACC

They knead it frequently.

Əktə=tənii, xaɪ, ənusi-i-du-ə-ni=kəs,
female=TOP indeed illness.VBZ-PRS.P-DAT-OCM-3SG=EMP

miŋguči-i-ni goanɪ.
moan-PRS.P-3SG certainly

The woman moans when she feels pain.

Totamɪ buə gɪan-dola-po-wa əktəni, miŋguči-i=dəə,
therefore we rule-LOC-1PL-OCM female moan-PRS.P=ADD

əlkə əlkə ǰɪlgan-bɪ niə-wəən-buri.
very.quietly voice-REFL go.out-CAUS-PRS.IMPS.P

Therefore, according to our rule, even if she moans, she should let her voice out quietly.

ǰɪlgan-bɪ daaɪ-ǰɪ niə-wəən-buri — soron-borɪ=a,
voice-REFL large-INS go.out-CAUS-PRS.IMPS.P sin-PRS.IMPS.P=MIR

un-dii, ačaasɪ=a, un-dii.
say-PRS.P not.appropriate=MIR say-PRS.P

It is said that emitting her voice aloud is not allowed, because to do so is to commit a crime.

Boa-la xoonɪ=daa xəm bi-i ǰaka-sal bi-i.
outside-LOC how=ADD all be-PRS.P thing-PL be-PRS.P

Outside whatever exists, and things exist.

Təi doolǰɪ-paarɪ=tanɪɪ, ǰuki-či-i goan.
that hear-COND.PL.IMPS=TOP bewitch-FR-PRS.P certainly

If they hear it, she would be possessed by them.

Totamɪ əktə-du=dəə orkɪn osɪ-ɪ, piktə-du=dəə
therefore female-DAT=ADD bad become-PRS.P child-DAT=ADD

orkɪn osɪ-ɪ.
bad become-PRS.P

If so, that situation will have a bad influence on herself and her baby.

Totamaarɪ ǰɪlgan-bar aso niə-wəən-dəsi
so voice-REFL.PL so.much go.out-CAUS-NEG.PRS.P

bi-či-či.
be-PST.P-3PL

Therefore, they did not let their own voices out loudly.

Piktə-du, əkəsəl tul tul təi piktə ičə-ndə-su-i,
child-DAT woman.PL always that child see-INT-DUR-PRS.P

kičə-i ta-ɪ bi-či-či goan.
try-PRS.P do-PRS.P be-PST.P-3PL certainly

Women always tried to keep seeing their baby.

Piktə ənu-lu-əsi osɪ-go-a-nɪ,
child get.ill-INCH-NEG.PRS.P become-PURP-OCM-3SG

səwəkəən-gu-ə-ni	aŋgo-ɪ,	suu-kəəŋ...
sewen.DIM-DSG-OCM-3SG	make-PRS.P	talisman-DIM

suu-kəən-gu-ə-ni	aŋgo-ɪ.
talisman-DIM-DSG-OCM-3SG	make-PRS.P

She makes *sewens* (figures for spirits) and talismans lest the baby get ill.

Moo-ǰɪ,	talo-ǰɪ,	boso-ǰɪ	xaɪ=daa	xəm
tree-INS	birch.bark-INS	cloth-INS	what=ADD	all

səwən-səl-bə-ni,	suu-wə-ni	aŋgo-raa,
sewen-PL-ACC-3SG	talisman-ACC-3SG	make-ANT

poaɪ-kta-waan-ɪ=tanɪɪ	tuŋgən-du-ə-ni,	moŋgon-do-a-nɪ
pad-DISTR-CAUS-PRS.P=TOP	chest-DAT-OCM-3SG	neck-DAT-OCM-3SG

tətuə-n...	tətuə-ni=dəə,	tuŋgən-du-ə-nɪ	nəučə-i.
dress-3SG	clothes-3SG=ADD	chest-DAT-OCM-3SG	keep-PRS.P

The mother keeps the *sewens* and a talisman, which are made with birch bark and fabrics, padding them on her chest, neck, and clothes.

Poaɪ-kta-waan-ɪ=tanɪɪ,	piktə	tul tul	dolbo	soŋgo-ɪ-nɪ
pad-DISTR-CAUS-PRS.P=TOP	child	always	night	cry-PRS.P-3SG

osɪɪ=tanɪɪ,	un-dɪɪ	bi-či-či	goan,	gəə,	xaɪ=daa
if=TOP	say-PRS.P	be-PST.P-3PL	certainly	well	indeed=ADD

ǰuki-i-ni,	biǰərə=m.
bewitch-PRS.P-3SG	likely=REPO

They said that a baby who always cried in the night, though she did so, might be possessed by demons.

Təi	piktə	ao-radaasɪ=a.
that	child	sleep-NEG.PRS.P=MIR

Such a baby does not sleep.

Təi piktə tul tul soŋgo-ɪ.
that child always cry-PRS.P

The baby always cries.

Čado=tanɪɪ bəjun-səl xujə-səl-bə-ni, bəjun-səl xuktə-səl-bə-ni
then=TOP elk-PL horn-PL-ACC-3SG elk-PL tooth-PL-ACC-3SG

(xaɪ, xaɪ-sal-ba-nɪ goanɪ), təi xosakta-sal-ba-nɪ —
indeed what-PL-ACC-3SG certainly that nail-PL-ACC-3SG

čaa uləən xəm xaɪ-raa, kučəən-ǰi sɪdo-raa=tanɪɪ,
that.ACC well all do.what-ANT knife-INS scrape-ANT=TOP,

xaɪ-ǰɪ, əmuə-ni ujə-lə-ni loo-rɪɪ bi-či-či goan.
what-INS cradle-3SG top-LOC-3SG hang-PRS.P be-PST.P-3PL certainly

Təi kupə-kəən-du, sirxə-kəən-du=dəə.
that thread-DIM-DAT, twine-DIM-DAT=ADD

At that time, they hung elk's horns, teeth, and nails, which had been scraped with a knife, on its cradle (See Fig. 9 on page xi above) hung with thread and string.

Kupi-gu-ə-ni, təi piktə-kəən-bə ətuu-gu-ə-ni.
show-PURP-OCM-3SG that child-DIM-ACC protect-PURP-OCM-3SG

The purpose was to show them to the baby as a kind of mobile on the one hand, and protect it on the other.

Dolbo maŋga soŋgo-ɪ-do-a-nɪ=tanɪɪ, ənuu... ənuu-ku=ə,
night hard cry-PRS.P-DAT-OCM-3SG=TOP illness illness-PROP=MIR

un-dii-či bi-či-ni goan, — xaɪ=daa ǰuki-i-ni,
say-PRS.P-3PL be-PST.P-3SG certainly indeed=ADD bewitch-PRS.P-3SG

biǰərə=m=dəə.
likely=REPO=ADD

They said that the baby was ill, if the baby cried severely in the night, and might be possessed.

Əmuə-du-ə-ni,	təi	piktə	ao-rɪɪ-nɪ	xaǰon
cradle-DAT-OCM-3SG	that	child	sleep-PRS.P-3SG	stuff

pəgiə-lə-ni,	xoldokaan-do-a-nɪ,	čiptuni…	čiptuni
bottom-LOC-3SG	side.DIM-DAT-OCM-3SG	pillow	pillow.3SG

pəgiə-lə-ni=dəə	nəə-rii	bi-či-či	goan	niču…
bottom-LOC-3SG=ADD	put-PRS.P	be-PST.P-3PL	certainly	small

nuučiku	kučəən-bə,	ǰəjəku	ǰaka-wa,	paloa-wa.
small	knife-ACC	blade	thing-ACC	hammer-ACC

They put sharp things such as daggers or hammers under and beside the baby's cradle and bedding, and under the pillow.

Xaɪ=daa	ambaan-sal	ǰuki-i-ni	osɪnɪ,	dolbo	təi
indeed=ADD	demon-PL	bewitch-PRS.P-3SG	if	night	that

kučəən,	təi	paloa=tanɪɪ	təi	piktə	xorɪ-čɪ-mɪ,	təi
knife	that	hammer=TOP	that	child	save-FR-SIM	that

ambaan-sal	ǰɪǰan-dɪɪ-do-a-čɪ,	kučəəli-i,	paloa-ǰɪ
demon-PL	approach-PRS.P-DAT-OCM-3PL	pierce-PRS.P	hammer-INS

paloa-la-ɪ	ta-ɪ-čɪ	goan,	xorɪ-čɪ-mɪ	təi	piktə-wə.
hammer-VBZ-PRS.P	do-PRS.P-3PL	certainly	save-FR-SIM	that	child-ACC

If demons possess the baby, those things such as the knife and the hammer keep the baby safe in the night. When the demons approach, the knife and the hammer attack them to protect the baby.

Gəə,	tui	un-dii	bi-či-či	goan	təi	piktə	ajaǰɪɪ
well	that.way	say-PRS.P	be-PST.P-3PL	certainly	that	child	well

bi-gu-ə-ni.
be-PURP-OCM-3SG

They said that they would have the baby be well.

Guči=tənii	baar-bɪ	ɪsɪ-očɪa-nɪ=a=daa,	piktə
again=TOP	one.year-REFL	arrive-COND-3SG=MIR=ADD	child

xaǰon-ba-nɪ	sɪlko-raa,
stuff-ACC-3SG	wash-ANT

boa-la	loo-rɪɪ-čɪ	xolgo-go-a-nɪ.
outside-LOC	hang-PRS.P-3PL	dry-PURP-OCM-3SG

After the baby was a year old, they washed and hung the baby's things outside to dry.

Siksəŋgiələə,	xolgo-xan=daa,	əčiə	xolgo-a=daa,
evening	dry-PST.P=ADD	not	dry-INF=ADD

təi	xaǰon-ba	xəm	ačo-orɪ-a	gələ-i.
that	clothes-ACC	all	remove-PRS.IMPS.P-ACC	need-PRS.P

In the evening, whether the things are dry or not, they should be brought into the house.

Totaraa,	ǰoog-čɪ	ii-wu-gu-rəə,	ǰoog-do
and.then	house-DIR	enter-TR-REV-ANT	house-DAT

xolgɪ-čɪ-orɪ-a	gələ-i.
dry-FR-PRS.IMPS.P-ACC	need-PRS.P

She should bring into the house and dry them.

Baar-bɪ	əčiə	ɪsɪ-go-ɪ	piktə	xaǰon-ba-nɪ	boa-la
year-REFL	not	arrive-ITER-PRS.P	child	stuff-ACC-3SG	outside-LOC

naŋgala-go-wasɪ=a,	un-dii	bi-či-ni	balana,
leave-ITER-NEG.PRS.IMPS.P=MIR	say-PRS.P	be-PST.P-3SG	long.ago

—	ambaan	ǰuki-i=jəm.
	demon	bewitch-PRS.P=REPO

In the old days, they said that the stuff of a baby who was not yet a year old should not be left outside, because demons would bewitch it.

Təi	xaǰon-dola	ambaan,	nuuči...	nuuči	piktə
that	stuff-LOC	demon	small	small	child

təi	xaǰon	tətu-gu-učiə-ni,	nuuči	piktə-či	ǰuki-rəə,
that	stuff	dress-ITER-COND-3SG	small	child-DIR	bewitch-ANT

ənu-lu-wəən-dii,	waa-rɪɪ	ta-ɪ.
get.ill-INCH-CAUS-PRS.P	kill-PRS.P	do-PRS.P

If a baby wears something that was left outside, it will be possessed by demons which was in it, and then become ill or be killed.

Totamɪ	təi	xaǰom	nəə	ǰoog-čɪ	ii-wu-gu-rii-ə
therefore	that	stuff.ACC	certainly	house-DIR	enter-TR-REV-PRS.P-ACC

gələ-i	bi-či-či	goan.
need-PRS.P	be-PST.P-3PL	certainly

Therefore, they should bring the baby's things into the house.

Nuuči	əkəsəl	poaldoanɪ	saa-rasɪ-wa-nɪ=tanɪɪ,
small	woman.PL	sometimes	understand-NEG.PRS.P-ACC-3SG=TOP

čaa	əŋpə-ni	ičəǰə-i	bi-či-ni	goanɪ.
that.ACC	mother.in.law-3SG	watch-PRS.P	be-PST.P-3SG	certainly

If young women did not know what to do at times, her mother-in-law observed her.

Əŋpə-ji	un-dii-wə-ni,	čaa	xəm
mother.in.law-REFL	say-PRS.P-ACC-3SG	that.ACC	all

dosɪǰa-orɪ-a	gələ-i.
listen-PRS.IMPS.P-ACC	need-PRS.P

All the women have to listen to what their mother-in-law said.

Daaɪ	əktə	un-dii-wə-ni	ǰoog-do	nuuči	əktə	nəə
big	woman	say-PRS.P-ACC-3SG	house-DAT	small	woman	certainly

dosɪǰa-orɪ-a	gələ-i.
listen-PRS.IMPS.P-ACC	need-PRS.P

In the house, young women should listen to what older women

said.

Xəsə-wə-ni xaal=daa čaalɪ-wasɪ.
language-ACC-3SG when=ADD cut-NEG.PRS.IMPS.P
Young women does not cut off older women's saying.

Nuuči piktə xaǰon-ba-nɪ ǰoog-čɪ ii-wu-gu-rii
small child stuff-ACC-3SG house-DIR enter-TR-REV-PRS.P
bi-čin.
be-PST.P
She have the small baby's things brought into the house.

Tui=dəə.
that.way=ADD
That is the way it goes.

Totapɪ=tanɪɪ, guči xaɪ-wa aŋgo-ɪ bi-čin, tui
after.that=TOP again what-ACC make-PRS.P be-PST.P that.way
soŋgo-ɪ piktə osɪ-očɪa-nɪ?
cry-PRS.P child become-COND-3SG
What else did she do if the baby cried severely?

Poaldoanɪ un-dii bi-či-či goan, təi piktə=kəə,
sometimes say-PRS.P be-PST.P-3PL certainly that child=CNTR
saɪnaa, adoo-ko bi-či-ni, biǰərə=m=dəə.
perhaps twins-PROP be-PST.P-3SG likely=REPO=ADD
They sometimes said that the baby might be a twin.

Adoo-jɪ gələ-gu-m, soŋgo-ɪ-nɪ, biǰərə=m.
twins-REFL seek-REV-SIM cry-PRS.P-3SG likely=REPO
They said that it might be crying to seek out the other twin.

Čado=tanɪɪ	adoo-go-a-nɪ	aŋgo-go-ɪ	bi-či-či
at.that.time=TOP	twins-DSG-OCM-3SG	make-REV-PRS.P	be-PST.P-3PL

goan.
certainly

Moo-ǰɪ,	talo-ǰɪ,	sii…	(xaɪ-ǰɪ),	naokta-ǰɪ
wood-INS	birch.bark-INS	you	what-INS	soft.grass-INS

aŋgo-ɪ	bi-či-či	goanɪ.
make-PRS.P	be-PST.P-3PL	certainly

In that case, they made a twin with wood, birch bark and soft grass.

Totaraa	ǰakpa-do-a-nɪ	nəə-rii	bi-či-či	goan.
and.then	next-DAT-OCM-3SG	put-PRS.P	be-PST.P-3PL	certainly

Then they put it next to the baby.

Təi	əmuə-du-ə-ni=tul,	piktə	ǰakpa-do-a-nɪ,
that	cradle-DAT-OCM-3SG=EXCL	child	next-DAT-OCM-3SG

ǰɪa-go-a-nɪ,	adoo-go-a-nɪ	nəə-rii	bi-či-či	goan.
friend-DSG-OCM-3SG	twins-DSG-OCM-3SG	put-PRS.P	be-PST.P-3PL	certainly

They put it beside the baby in the cradle as a friend and a twin.

Gəə,	čado	tərək	osɪ-ɪ-nɪ	osɪnɪ,	adoo-jɪ	gələ-gu-mi
well	then	exactly	become-PRS.P-3SG	if	twins-REFL	ant-REV-SIM

soŋgo-xa-nɪ	osɪnɪ,	soŋgo-asɪ	osɪ-go-ɪ	piktə.
cry-PST.P-3SG	if	cry-NEG.PRS.P	become-REV-PRS.P	child

If it was the case that the baby was crying to seek out its twin, it stopped crying.

Uləən	ao-rɪɪ	osɪ-go-ɪ,	sim	osɪ-go-ɪ.
well	sleep-PRS.P	become-REV-PRS.P	quietly	become-REV-PRS.P

It falls asleep fast and quiet.

Gəə, čaa agda-nasɪ-ɪ-čɪ goan:
well that.ACC rejoice-REP-PRS.P-3PL certainly
Being pleased with it, they say,

— Gəə, tərək ta-xa-pu, tərək bi-i.
well just do-PST.P-1PL just be-PRS.P
"OK, what we did is right!

Təi, saɪnaa, piktə-pu adoo-ko bi-či-ni.
that perhaps child-1PL twins-PROP be-PST.P-3SG
Our baby might have been a twin.

Balǰɪ-m=tanɪɪ, əmuučəkəən balǰɪ-xa-nɪ.
be.born-SIM=TOP alone.DIM be.born-PST.P-3SG
It was born alone.

Adoo-nɪ xaɪdo=daa dərəǰi-xə-ni.
twins-3SG where=ADD stay-PST.P-3SG
Its twin must have fallen behind somewhere."

Tui=dəə.
that.way=ADD
That is the way it goes.

Tui un-dii bi-či-či goan.
that.way say-PRS.P be-PST.P-3PL certainly
They said so.

Piktə balǰɪ-očɪa-nɪ, təi mədəə-wə aso naɪ-a
child be.born-COND-3SG that message-ACC so.much person-ACC
doolǰɪ-waan-dasɪ bi-či-či.

hear-CAUS-NEG.PRS.P be-PST.P-3PL

They did not let other people know the news when a new baby was born.

Xaımaarı?
why

Why?

Daaı	gursəl=dəə	tui	un-dii	bi-či-či	goan,
big	people.PL=ADD	that.way	say-PRS.P	be-PST.P-3PL	certainly

The elders said as follows:

ǰəəri-wəsi=əm=dəə	piktə	balǰı-ı-wa-nı.
spread-NEG.PRS.IMPS.P=REPO=ADD	child	be.born-PRS.P-ACC-3SG

“The news that a baby was born should not be spread.

ǰəəri-i-du-ə-si	naı=ragda	doolǰı-ası-ni	goanı.
spread-PRS.P-DAT-OCM-2SG	person=LIM	hear-NEG.PRS.P-3SG	certainly

If you spread the news, it is not the case only those people hear it.

Ui=dəə	xəm	doolǰı-ı,	xaı=daa	xəm	doolǰı-ı.
who=ADD	all	hear-PRS.P	indeed=ADD	all	hear-PRS.P

Everyone hears everything.

Poaldoanı	orkın	gurun=dəə	doolǰı-ı.
sometimes	bad	people=ADD	hear-PRS.P

Sometimes bad people also hear it.

Sı...	d...	Ui=dəə	xəm	sıan-ko.
ear	inside	who=ADD	all	ear-PROP

Everyone has ears.

Sɪan doo-čɪ-a-nɪ ii-rii.
ear inside-DIR-OCM-3SG enter-PRS.P

It can reach everyone's ear."

Tui ta-mɪ əgǰi naɪ-a saa-waa…
that.way do-SIM many person-ACC know-CAUS

saa-waan-bowasɪ bi-čin. Saa-waan-bowasɪ bi-čin.
know-CAUS-NEG.PRS.IMPS.P be-PST.P know-CAUS-NEG.PRS.IMPS.P be-PST.P

For that reason, they made the news not known to many people.

Guči=tənii, piktə urə-gu-ə-ni, ənusi-əsi, bu…
again=TOP child grow-PURP-OCM-3SG illness.VBZ-NEG.PRS.P die

bu-dəsi osɪ-go-a-ni=tanɪɪ, gərbu-gu-ə-ni ambaan
die-NEG.PRS.P become-PURP-OCM-3SG=TOP name-DSG-OCM-3SG fairly

goɪda-maarɪ buu-rəsi bi-či-či goan.
last.long-SIM.PL give-NEG.PRS.P be-PST.P-3PL certainly

Furthermore, they did not give its name to the child until a considerable time went by so that the baby might grow, and not become sick or be killed.

Gərbiə-si-əsi-či bi-čin. Baɪ tui gərbiə-si-i-či
call-DUR-NEG.PRS.P-3PL be-PST.P just that.way call-DUR-PRS.P-3PL

bi-čin: nəku, poja.
be-PST.P child baby

They did not call the baby by its name, but just as child or baby.

Tui gərbiə-si-i bi-čin.
that.way call-DUR-PRS.P bi-PST.P

They called it in that way.

Totapɪ=tanɪɪ, gərbu-gu-ə-ni buu-rii=dəə,
after.that=TOP name-DSG-OCM-3SG give-PRS.P=ADD

daaɪ gursəl gərbu... gərbu-ə buu-wəən-dii bi-čin.
big people.PL name name-ACC give-CAUS-PRS.P be-PST.P

After that, they called it as its name which elders gave the baby.

Gərbu-ə=tənii goɪda-mɪ balǰɪ-ɪ sagǰɪ gurun gərbu-wə-ni,
name-ACC=TOP last.long-SIM live-PRS.P old people name-ACC-3SG

bui-kin gurun, daaɪ, goɪda-mɪ bi-čin gurun.
die-PST.P people grown-up be.long-SIM be-PST.P people

The baby was given the name of someone who lived a long life, such as an old man who lived a long life, the deceased, or an adult.

Guči=tənii, ɪlɪočɪ-maar=tanɪɪ,
again=TOP save.a.child's.life-SIM.PL=TOP

təi piktə-du xaɪ=daa xəm kolaan-sal gərbu-wə-ni,
that child-DAT indeed=ADD all insect-PL name-ACC-3SG

ɪrbasɪ-orɪ ǰaka-sal gərbu-wə-ni buu-rii
dislike-PRS.IMPS.P thing-PL name-ACC-3SG give-PRS.P

bi-či-či goanɪ.
be-PST.P-3PL certainly

Baɪ təi piktə-wə-əri xorɪ-čɪ-maarɪ, bu-dəsi,
just that child-ACC-REFL.PL save-FR-SIM.PL die-NEG.PRS.P

ənusi-əsi osɪ-go-a-nɪ.
illness.VBZ-NEG.PRS.P become-PURP-OCM-3SG

While the ritual to save the child's life was held, they gave the child its name after any insects or things that were disliked so that they might protect the child, he might not die or get sick.

Tui buu-rii bi-či-či goanɪ poanɪ, xaɪ, puril
that.way give-PRS.P be-PST.P-3PL certainly some indeed children

tui bi-i gərbu-səl-ǰi xamačaa=daa Xərə-kəən,

that.way be-PRS.P name-PL-INS what=ADD frog-DIM

guči=tənii, guči, xaɪ, ɪnoksa, xaɪ=daa xəm tui
again=TOP again what snot what=ADD all that.way

bi-i, xaɪ, gara — tui bi-i gərbu-səl-bə
be-PRS.P what little.branch that.way be-PRS.P name-PL-ACC

buu-rii bi-či-či goan.
give-PRS.P be-PST.P-3PL certainly

They gave him any name like frog, nasal discharge, tree branch and so on.

Ilɪočɪ-maarɪ, tui gərbiə-si-i bi-či-či.
save.a.child's.life-SIM.PL that.way call-DUR-PRS.P be-PST.P-3PL

While the ritual to save the child's life was held, they called him such names.

Totapɪ guči=tənii piktə balǰɪ-ɪ-nɪ ǰuliə-lə-ni
after.that again=TOP child be.born-PRS.P-3SG front-LOC-3SG

xaǰon-go-a-nɪ xaɪ-wa=daa bargɪ-asɪ bi-čin.
stuff-DSG-OCM-3SG what-ACC=ADD prepare-NEG.PRS.P be-PST.P

Furthermore, before the baby was born, the mother prepared nothing.

Tui un-dii bi-či-či goan balana, ǰuləsi
that.way say-PRS.P be-PST.P-3PL certainly long.ago forward

bargɪ-wasɪ=am.
prepare-NEG.PRS.IMPS.P=REPO

In the old days, they said, "The mother should not prepare anything in advance.

Təi balǰɪ-ɪ-wa-nɪ kočalɪ-orɪ=am=daa, təi
that be.born-PRS.P-ACC-3SG hinder-PRS.IMPS.P=REPO=ADD that

xaǰon-ba ǰuləsi bargɪ-orɪ osɪnɪ.

stuff-ACC forward prepare-PRS.IMPS.P if

If the mother prepare the baby's things in advance, it will hinder the birth.

Korpɪ-orɪ=am,	baľǰɪ-očɪa-nɪ=a	aŋgo-ɪ=daa,
be.in.time-PRS.IMPS.P=REPO	be.born-COND-3SG=MIR	make-PRS.P=ADD

xaɪ,	xaɪ	əgǰi	xaǰon-go-jɪ	gələ-rəə	baɪ	əsii
indeed	indeed	many	stuff-DSG-REFL	need-ANT	just	just.now

baľǰɪ-xan	piktə-kəən,	nuuči-kuukəən.
be.born-PST.P	child-DIM	small-EXTR

Though a lot of stuff for the small newborn baby was needed, the mother should make it just in time, soon after the baby is born.

Baľǰɪ-očɪa-nɪ=a	aŋgo-orɪ=am=daa.
be.born-COND-3SG=MIR	make-PRS.IMPS.P=REPO=ADD

The mother should make it right after the baby is born."

Tui	un-dii	bi-či-či	goan.
that.way	say-PRS.P	be-PST.P-3PL	certainly

They said so.

Ilɪočɪ-maar=tanɪɪ,	tui…	tui	ta-ɪ
save.a.child's.life-SIM.PL=TOP	that.way	that.way	do-PRS.P

bi-či-či	goan.
be-PST.P-3PL	certainly

Upholding the ritual to save a child's life, they did so.

Xaɪdo…	ǰooŋkan-do	puril	baľǰɪ-ɪ	—	bu-dii,
where	family-DAT	children	be.born-PRS.P		die-PRS.P

baľǰɪ-ɪ	—	bu-dii.
be.born-PRS.P		die-PRS.P

In some families, babies died right after they are born.

Baljɪ-ɪ — bu-dii ta-ɪ... ta-ɪ osɪnɪ, təi
be.born-PRS.P die-PRS.P do-PRS.P do-PRS.P if that

əktə=tənii, piktə-gu-ji baa-mɪ, goɪ gurun-du buu-rii
female=TOP child-DSG-REFL get-SIM other people-DAT give-PRS.P

bi-či-ni goanɪ.
be-PST.P-3SG certainly

In that case, the woman who gave birth gave her baby to someone else.

Təi gurun puril-ni xəm ujuun, xəm uləən
that people children-3SG all alive all well

urə-i-či osɪnɪ, təi gurun-bə təi piktə
grow-PRS.P-3PL if that people-ACC that child

uǰi-wəən-dii-či bi-či-ni goan.
bring.up-CAUS-PRS.P-3PL be-PST.P-3SG certainly

If all of the babies of that person grew up safe and sound, they left the person to raise the baby.

Ilaan, duin səə ɪsɪ-očɪa-nɪ=a tui
three four age arrive-COND-3SG=MIR that.way

uǰi-pəəri=məə, ənin-du-ə-ni buu-gu-i-či.
bring.up-COND.PL.IMPS=CON mother-DAT-OCM-3SG give-REV-PRS.P-3PL

If the child is three or four years old, the other person, who raised him returns the child to his mother.

Tui=dəə.
that.way=ADD

That is the way it goes.

Ənin-du-ə-ni, amɪn-do-a-nɪ=daa.

mother-DAT-OCM-3SG father-DAT-OCM-3SG=ADD

He returns the child to his mother or his father.

Tui	xorɪ-čɪ-ɪ	bi-či-či.
that.way	help-FR-PRS.P	be-PST.P-3PL

They helped with childcare in this way.

Guči=tənii	uləən,	gookoǰɪ	urə-i	puril,	xaɪ-wa-nɪ,
again=TOP	well	politely	grow-PRS.P	children	what-ACC-3SG

əmuə-wə-ni,	gələ-i	bi-či-či	goan.
cradle-ACC-3SG	ask-PRS.P	be-PST.P-3PL	certainly

They also asked for the cradle of children who grew up healthily.

Təi	əmuə-du	məən	piktə-ji	nəə-rəə,	gəə,
that	cradle-DAT	oneself	child-REFL	put-ANT	well

ɪŋsoo-rɪɪ-čɪ	goanɪ,	baɪ	xaɪ,	xaɪ-do,	əm	aɪŋanɪ-do=daa,
lend-PRS.P-3PL	certainly	just	what	what-DAT	one	year-DAT=ADD

urə-i-či	əniə=dəə	təi	goropčɪ	əmuə-wə.
grow.up-PRS.P-3PL	mother=ADD	that	long	cradle-ACC

They lend the mother the cradle so long which she puts her children in until they are one year old.

Təi	əmuə-du	balǰɪ-xan	piktə	nəə-rəə,	tui
that	cradle-DAT	be.born-PST.P	child	put-ANT	that.way

uruuči-i-či	bi-čin.
raise-PRS.P-3PL	be-PST.P

They put the newborn baby in the cradle and raised it in that way.

Təi=dəə	ɪlɪočɪ-ɪ-čɪ	bi-čin	goan.
that=ADD	save.a.child's.life-PRS.P-3PL	be-PST.P	certainly

They save a child's life in that way.

Totapɪa	buu-gu-i	bi-či-či	goan.
later	give-REV-PRS.P	be-PST.P-3PL	certainly

In the later they return it.

Poaldoanɪ	təi	əmuə-wə	goɪ goɪ	ǰooŋkan	ǰapa-ɪ
sometimes	that	cradle-ACC	various	family	take-PRS.P

bi-či-či	goanɪ,	məən	puril-bəri	uǰi-gu-əri.
be-PST.P-3PL	certainly	oneself	children-REFL.PL	bring.up-PURP-REFL.PL

At times, many families borrowed that cradle to raise their children.

Əi	səəgǰən	gɪanɪ	ɪsɪ-očɪa-nɪ=a=daa,
this	red	rule.3SG	arrive-COND-3SG=MIR=ADD

təi	*muzhej*-du	ǰobo-ɪ	gursəl=tənii	baa-rɪɪ
that	R. museum-DAT	work-PRS.P	people.PL=TOP	take-PRS.P

bi-či-či	goanɪ	təi	balapčɪ	xaɪ-wa,	əmuə-wə.
be-PST.P-3PL	certainly	that	ancient	what-ACC	cradle-ACC

After Russian government came to the power, workers took the old cradle to the museum.

Totaraa,	*muzhej*-du	nəə-gu-əri,	gələ-i
and.then	R. museum-DAT	put-PURP-REFL.PL	need-PRS.P

bi-či-či	goan.
be-PST.P-3PL	certainly

At that time, they needed exhibits for the museum.

Əsi,	buə	bi-i-du-pu-ə=dəə,	buə	*muzhej*-du-pu-ə
now	we	live-PRS.P-DAT-1PL-OCM=ADD	we	R. museum-DAT-1PL-OCM

taja-čɪ	bi-i	əmuə-səl	bi-i.
that.place-DIR	be-PRS.P	cradle-PL	be-PRS.P

The cradles are now in our museum.

Naɪ,	balana	aŋgo-ɪ=daa,	uləən	aŋgo-ɪ
person	long.ago	make-PRS.P=ADD	well	make-PRS.P

bi-či-či	goanɪ:
be-PST.P-3PL	certainly

masɪ,	ɪlga-ko,	gučkuli,	namčɪan	əmuə-kəən-səl-bə.
strong	picture-PROP	pretty	comfortable	cradle-DIM-PL-ACC

In the old days, people made strong, splendid, pretty, and comfortable cradles.

Puril-bəri	uǰi-məəri,	tui	kičə-i
children-REFL.PL	bring.up-SIM.PL	that.way	be.diligent-PRS.P

bi-či-či	goan.
be-PST.P-3PL	certainly

They were so diligent in raising their children.

Xaɪ=daa,	piktə-ji	ətəxi-mi=tənii,	əmuə	əmusi-i=dəə.
what=ADD	child-REFL	take.care-SIM=TOP	cradle	move.gently-PRS.P=ADD

While taking care of their children, they rocks the cradle.

Piktə	čado	bi-i-wə-ni=rəgdə	əmusi-uri	aja.
child	then	lie-PRS.P-ACC-3SG=LIM	move.gently-PRS.IMPS.P	good

At that time it was all right only to lay the baby and rock it.

Piktə	oŋasa-a	goanɪ,	piktə	soŋgo…	soŋgo-asɪ
child	sleep-PRS	certainly	child	cry	cry-NEG.PRS.P

osɪ-ɪ	goanɪ.
become-PRS.P	certainly

The baby falls asleep without crying.

Piktə nakan-du nəə-rəə, əmuə gəun-du-ə-ni,
child heated.floor-DAT put-ANT cradle empty-DAT-OCM-3SG

gəun əmuə-wə əmusi-wəsi.
empty cradle-ACC move.gently-NEG.PRS.IMPS.P

If the baby is laid on the heated floor, the empty cradle is not rocked.

Čaa un-dii bi-či-l, kısıako=am, ačaası.
that.ACC say-PRS.P be-PST.P-3PL misfortune=REPO not.appropriate

They said that this was unlucky and prohibited it.

«Xaı-wa əmusi-i-su gəun əmuə-wə? Piktə bu-dii!»
what-ACC move.gently-PRS.P-2PL empty cradle-ACC child die-PRS.P

"Do you rock an empty cradle? The child will die!"

Totamı kamalı-ı bi-či-či goan gəun əmuə-wə
therefore forbid-PRS.P be-PST.P-3PL certainly empty cradle-ACC

əmusi-uri-wə.
move.gently-PRS.IMPS.P-ACC

Therefore, they forbade to rock an empty cradle.

Təi papon-ko xəm bi-čin čado.
that ban-PROP all be-PST.P then

It was completely banned.

Čawa ta-ası bi-čin.
that.ACC do-NEG.PRS.P be-PST.P

Nobody did so.

Guči=tənii, puril-bəri ılıočı-maarı, əgǰi
again=TOP children-REFL.PL save.a.child's.life-SIM.PL many

puril-ku, ajaǰɪɪ urə-i puril-ku gurun-dulə,
children-PROP well grow.up-PRS.P children-PROP people-LOC

sagǰɪ gurun-dulə gələ-i bi-či-či goan nadaan,
old people-LOC request-PRS.P be-PST.P-3PL certainly seven

xujun pasɪ-kaan-sal boso-kaan-sal-ba.
nine piece-DIM-PL cloth-DIM-PL-ACC

Also, when holding the ritual to save a child's life for their own child, they requested seven, nine pieces of cloth from those who had many children who grew up well, or from older people.

Əsi bi-i-du-əri, boso-kaam gələ-i.
now live-PRS.P-DAT-REFL.PL cloth-DIM.ACC need-PRS.P

Now we need a piece of cloth.

Balan=tanɪɪ, xaɪ, tətuə-wə sogbo-ǰɪ aŋgo-ɪ.
long.ago=TOP indeed clothing-ACC fish.skin-INS make-PRS.P

In the old days, clothing was made from fish skin.

Sogbo pasɪ-kaan-sal-ba-nɪ gələ-i bi-či-či goan.
fish.skin piece-DIM-PL-ACC-3SG seek-PRS.P be-PST.P-3PL certainly

They asked for pieces of fish skin.

Təi pasɪ-kaan-sal-ǰɪ təi balǰɪ-xan piktə
that piece-DIM-PL-INS that be.born-PST.P child

tətuə-kəən-gu-ə-ni aŋgo-ɪ bi-či-či goan.
clothing-DIM-DSG-OCM-3SG make-PRS.P be-PST.P-3PL certainly

Using those pieces, they made clothes for the baby who had been born.

Tui un-dii bi-či-či goan, əi tətuə-kəən — təi
that.way say-PRS.P be-PST.P-3PL certainly this clothing-DIM that

piktə xorɪ-čɪ-ɪ tətuə-kəəm=dəə.

child protect-FR-PRS.P clothing-DIM.REPO=ADD

They said that the pieces in those clothes protected the baby.

Təi	tətuə-kəən-bə	goıda-m	baljı-xan	gurun
that	clothing-DIM-ACC	last.long-SIM	be.born-PST.P	people

tətuə-ni	pası-sal-ǰı-a-nı	aŋgo-oxan.
clothing-3SG	piece-PL-INS-OCM-3SG	make-PST.IMPS.P

They made the baby's clothes with pieces of cloth from people who had lived a long time.

Njoambanı	ətuu-rii	təi	tətuə.
he.ACC	guard-PRS.P	that	clothing

The clothes protects the baby.

Njoambanı,	urə-i-wə-ni,	ajaǰıı	bi-i-wə-ni,
he.ACC	grow-PRS.P-ACC-3SG	well	be-PRS.P-ACC-3SG

bələči-i-ni=əm=dəə.
help-PRS.P-3SG=REPO=ADD

It is said that the clothes help him grow safe and sound.

Tui	purig-bəri	xorı-čı-ı	bi-či-či	goanı
that.way	children-REFL.PL	protect-FR-PRS.P	be-PST.P-3PL	certainly

tul tul	bu-dii	gurun,	puril...	puril-ku	gurun.
always	die-PRS.P	people	children	children-PROP	people

Although they kept their children in that way, the children used to die.

Mii=dəə	saa-rıı	bi-čin-bi	goan.
I=ADD	know-PRS.P	be-PST.P-1SG	certainly

I know such a person.

Mii ǰıa-jı bi-čin, minǰi gəsə urə-xən, minǰi

I friend-1SG be-PST.P I.INS together grow-PST.P I.INS

gəsə tačıočı-xan əktə-kəən.
together study-PST.P woman-DIM

I have a female friend who grew up and studied with me.

Təi ənini ǰoan njuŋgun piktə baa-xa-nı.
that mother.3SG ten six child get-PST.P-3SG

Her mother gave birth to sixteen children.

Təi ǰoan njuŋgun-dulə təəm əmukəə-kəən təi
that ten six-LOC only one-DIM that

əktə=kəə=rəgdə xora-xa-nı.
woman=CNTR=LIM survive-PST.P-3SG

My friend was the only daughter who survived among them.

Vot. Gəə, tui bi-i gursəl tui ılıočı-ı
R. well well so be-PRS.P people.PL so save.a.child's.life-PRS.P

bi-či-či goanı puril-bəri.
be-PST.P-3PL certainly children-REFL.PL

In this way, such people held the ritual to save the life of their child.

Guǰiələ, tui ta-maarı piktə... piktə-či-əri uləən
poor so do-SIM child child-DIR-REFL.PL well

xaı-rıı bi-či-či goanı, kərəli-i bi-či-či.
do.what-PRS.P be-PST.P-3PL certainly take.care.of-PRS.P be-PST.P-3PL

Though they were poor, they took good care of their children by doing so.

Guči=tənii tui bi-i ərdən ta-xa... ta-ı
again=TOP so be-PRS.P custom do-PST.P do-PRS.P

bi-či-či goan.

be-PST.P-3PL certainly

They had also the following custom.

Goɪda-mɪ balǰɪ-xan gurun sagǰɪ mamaarɪ-sal, sagǰɪ

last.long-SIM live-PST.P people old grandmother-PL old

mapaarɪ-sal nuktə-lə-ni njaŋgaa čaalɪ-ɪ bi-či-či

grandfather-PL hair-LOC-3SG a.little cut-PRS.P be-PST.P-3PL

goan. Nuktə-kəən-bə-ni.

certainly hair-DIM-ACC-3SG

They cut off a little bit of hair of long-lived people, old grandmother, or old grandfather.

Totaraa təi nuktə-kəən-bə=tənii, xuku-rəə, xaɪ,

and.then that hair-DIM-ACC=TOP wrap-ANT indeed

somalaakaan doo-la-nɪ nəə-rəə, ulpi-gu-i.

pouch.DIM inside-LOC-3SG put-ANT sew-ITER-PRS.P

Then the hair is wrapped and put in a small pocket, and sewed.

Təi somalaakaan-ba=tanɪɪ piktə tətuə-či-ə-ni

that pouch.DIM-ACC=TOP child clothing-DIR-OCM-3SG

ulpi-gu-i.

sew-ITER-PRS.P

The pocket was sewed onto a child's clothes.

Təi tətuə-kəən-ǰi=tənii təi piktə tul tul

that clothing-DIM-INS=TOP that child always

təi sagǰɪ gurun nuktə-kəəni pasɪ-sal-ba-nɪ olbɪačɪ-ɪ.

that old people hair-DIM.3SG piece-PL-ACC-3SG carry-PRS.P

By wearing these clothes, the child always has the hair of an older person on himself.

Tui un-dii bi-či-či goan:

that.way say-PRS.P be-PST.P-3PL certainly

They said as follows:

— Boa ičə-i. Təi sagǰɪ gurun nuktə-ni təi piktə
heaven see-PRS.P that old people hair-3SG that child

ətuu-rii.
protect-PRS.P

"The heaven sees it, and the hair of the old protects him.

xaɪ=daa orkɪn — ǰaka-sal ǰuki-əsi
indeed=ADD bad thing-PL bewitch-NEG.PRS.P

osɪ-ɪ goanɪ.
become-PRS.P certainly

The wicked will not bewitch the child.

Njoambanɪ kərəli-i-ni goan təi sagǰɪ
he.ACC take.care.of-PRS.P-3SG certainly that old

gurun xaɪ-nɪ, nuktə-səl-ni.
people what-3SG hair-PL-3SG

The hair of the old person protects the child."

Guči=tənii tui bi-i ərdən bi-či-ni goanɪ.
again=TOP that.way be-PRS.P custom be-PST.P-3SG certainly

They also had the following custom.

Balana boatoŋgo-sal, mapa waa-raa, xaɪ-pɪ,
long.ago hunter-PL bear catch-ANT do.what-COND.IMPS

ǰɪlɪ-wa-nɪ sɪa-paarɪ=tanɪɪ, təi ǰɪlɪ-nɪ gɪrmaksa-wa-nɪ
head-ACC-3SG eat-COND.PL.IMPS=TOP that head-3SG bone-ACC-3SG

xolgɪ-čɪ-ɪ-čɪ goan.
dry-FR-PRS.P-3PL certainly

In the old days, if hunters caught a bear, they ate its head and hung to dry its skull.

Xolgɪ-čɪ-raa=tanɪɪ,	təi	mapa	ǰɪlɪ-ǰɪ-a-nɪ	puril-bəri
dry-FR-ANT=TOP	that	bear	head-INS-OCM-3SG	children-REFL.PL

uruuči-i-či	goan.
raise-PRS.P-3PL	certainly

After it was dried, they raised their children with the bear's head.

Təi	(xaɪ-wa,	xaɪ)	xoto-wa-nɪ,	mapa	xoto-nɪ
that	what-ACC,	what	brainpan-ACC-3SG	bear	brainpan-3SG

goanɪ,	xoto-nɪ	gɪrmaksa-nɪ	—	čaa=tanɪɪ
certainly	brainpan-3SG	bone-3SG		that.ACC=TOP

ǰoog-do-arɪ	nəučə-i-či	goanɪ,	piktə	balǰɪ-očɪa-nɪ.
house-DAT-REFL.PL	keep-PRS.P-3PL	certainly	child	be.born-COND-3SG

If a baby was born, they preserved the bear's skull in their house.

Gəə,	təi	goɪ	gurun,	goɪ	gurun	waa-xa-nɪ	mapa,
well	that	other	people	other	people	catch-PST.P-3SG	bear

təi	mapa	xoto-wa-nɪ	tul tul	bu-dii	puril
that	bear	brainpan-ACC-3SG	always	die-PRS.P	children

əninəə-ni	ɪŋsoo-rɪɪ-čɪ	əmun	ǰuər	ɪlaan	aɪŋanɪ-do=daa.
mothers-3SG	lend-PRS.P-3PL	one	two	three	year-DAT=ADD

They lend the skull of a bear for one, two, even three years that was caught by someone else to mothers whose children died.

Mənə	ǰoog-čɪ-arɪ	ǰapa-go-raa,	mənə
oneself	house-DIR-REFL.PL	bring-REV-ANT	oneself

ǰoog-do-ar	loo-čɪ-ɪ-čɪ	təi	mapa	gɪrmaksa-wa-nɪ.
house-DAT-REFL.PL	hang-FR-PRS.P-3PL	that	bear	bone-ACC-3SG

They brought the bear skull to their own house and hung it

somewhere in the house.

Piktə-ni	təi	ərin-du=ə	tul tul	uləən	balǰɪ-ɪ,	uləən
child-3SG	that	days-DAT=MIR	always	good	be.born-PRS.P	well

urə-i	osɪnɪ,	aja.
grow-PRS.P	if	good

If the child grew safe and sound at that time, it was good.

Ilaan	aɪŋanɪ-do=a	nəučə-pəəri,	təi	mapa
three	year-DAT=MIR	keep-COND.PL.IMPS	that	bear

xoto-wa-nɪ	buu-gu-i-či	əǰən-du-ə-ni.
brainpan-ACC-3SG	give-REV-PRS.P-3PL	owner-DAT-OCM-3SG

They returned the bear skull to the owner after borrowing it for three years.

Gəə.	xaɪ	un-dii-či	goanɪ,	banjaala-go-ɪ-čɪ	goan
well	what	say-PRS.P-3PL	certainly	thank-ITER-PRS.P-3PL	certainly

təi	ǰapa...	ɪŋsoo-čɪ-xan-barɪ	xaǰon-dola-nɪ,
that	take	lend-FR-PST.P-REFL.PL	stuff-LOC-3SG

puril-bəri	xorɪ-čɪ-ɪ-do-a-nɪ.
children-REFL.PL	protect-FR-PRS.P-DAT-OCM-3SG

They thank the owners, saying “what you had lent protected our children.”

Gəə,	puril-bəri,	xoonɪ=daa	xəm	tui	ərdələ-məəri,
well	children-REFL.PL	how=ADD	all	that.way	produce-SIM.PL

xorɪ-ɪ-čɪ	bi-či-či	goanɪ	urə-gu-ə-či,	ajaǰɪɪ
protect-PRS.P-3PL	be-PST.P-3PL	certainly	grow-PURP-OCM-3PL	well

bi-gu-ə-či,	mənə	oroondola-ɪ-arɪ	očogo-go-a-čɪ.
be-PURP-OCM-3PL	oneself	substitute-PRS.P-REFL.PL	remain-PURP-OCM-3PL

Their children were born, protected in that way, growing up, living safely, and staying instead of us.

2.3. Wedding rituals

Xəǰəni-səl	əǰi-gu-əri,	asɪ-go-arɪ	baa-rɪɪ-čɪ
Nanai-PL	husband-DSG-REFL.PL	wife-DSG-REFL.PL	take-PRS.P-3PL

tui	bi-či-ni	goanɪ.
so	be-PST.P-3SG	certainly

When taking a bride or a groom, Nanai people did as following:

Mədəsi-məəri,	baa-rɪɪ.
ask-SIM.PL	take-PRS.P

Taking a bride or a groom after request.

Totapɪ	ǰuəčin-ǰi	baa-rɪɪ.
then	exchange-INS	take-PRS.P

Taking a bride or a groom by exchange (between two families).

Saa-ɪča-mɪ	baa-rɪɪ.
seek-DES-SIM	take-PRS.P

Taking a bride or a groom after search.

Goɪ goɪ	xačɪn-ǰɪ	baa-rɪɪ	bi-či-či	goanɪ
various	kind-INS	take-PRS.P	be-PST.P-3PL	certainly

piktə-wə-əri	əǰi-gu-ə-ni,	piktə-wə-əri
child-ACC-REFL.PL	husband-DSG-OCM-3SG	child-ACC-REFL.PL

asɪ-go-a-nɪ=daa.
wife-DSG-OCM-3SG=ADD

There were many ways for the Nanai people to marry off their own children.

Tui=dəə.

so=ADD

It's like that.

Əgǰi	gurun,	baɪ	tui	mədəsi-məəri,	baa-rɪɪ
many	people	just	so	ask-SIM.PL	take-PRS.P

bi-či-či	goanɪ.
be-PST.P-3PL	certainly

Many people got married just by request.

Gəə,	əsi	mii	čaa	gusərə-gu-ji-ə.
OK	now	I	that.ACC	tell-COHOR-1SG-OCM

Now I'll tell the story.

Mədəsi-mi,	mədəsi-mi,	əǰi-gu-ji,	asɪ-go-jɪ
ask-SIM	ask-SIM	husband-DSG-REFL	wife-DSG-REFL

baa-orɪ=a.
take-PRS.IMPS.P=MIR

After repeated request, a husband or wife is taken.

Balana,	boa…	boatoačɪ-ɪ-do-arɪ,	xusə	gursəl,
long.ago	hunt	hunt-PRS.P-DAT-REFL.PL	male	people.PL

bota-orɪ	ərin-du,	dawa	waa-orɪ	ərin-du,
cast.a.net-PRS.IMPS.P	time-DAT	salmon	catch-PRS.IMPS.P	time-DAT

njəŋnjə	bota-orɪ-du	əgǰi	naɪ-sal	gəsə
spring	cast.a.net-PRS.IMPS.P-DAT	many	person-PL	together

osɪ-go-ɪ	bi-či-ni	goanɪ.
become-ITER-PRS.P	be-PST.P-3SG	certainly

In the past, when hunting, casting a net for salmons in the spring, many people gathered together.

Narɪ-ɪ-čɪ	goanɪ	gəsə=dəə.
cast.a.net-PRS.P-3PL	certainly	together=ADD

They cast nets together.

Jara-ɪ,	narɪ-ɪ	ta-ɪ-čɪ,	sogdata
navigate-PRS.P	cast.a.net-PRS.P	do-PRS.P-3PL	fish

waa-rɪɪ-čɪ	goanɪ.
catch-PRS.P-3PL	certainly

They navigate boats, cast nets for fishing.

Duilə=tənii	bəjun-səl-bə,	njəpultə-wə	waa-rɪɪ
in.the.taiga=TOP	animal-PL-ACC	fur-ACC	catch-PRS.P

bi-či-či.
be-PST.P-3PL

In the taiga, they got animals and furs.

Gəə,	təi	ərin-du,	ǰɪa	ǰɪa-ǰɪ-arɪ	gusə...
OK	that	time-DAT	friend	friend-INS-REFL.PL	talk

gusərəəndu-məəri,	saa-ɪča-ɪ-čɪ	goanɪ,	ui	asɪa
talk-SIM.PL	know-DES-PRS.P-3PL	certainly	who	female

piktə-ku,	ələə	əǰi-gu-ji	baa-mɪ	aja,	səə-ku.
child-PROP	soon	husband-DSG-REFL	take-SIM	good	age-PROP

At that time they talk to one another to find if anyone had a daughter of marriageable age.

Ui	xusə	piktə-ku,	asɪ-go-jɪ	baa-mɪ	aja.
who	male	child-PROP	wife-DSG-REFL	take-SIM	good

And they try to know who has a son good for marriage.

Waaɪča-mɪ	otolɪ-ɪ,	duisi
hunt-SIM	understand-PRS.P	to.the.taiga

amɪn-ǰɪ-jɪ	gəsə	pulsi-i.
father-INS-REFL	together	walk-PRS.P

When one can hunt, he goes to the taiga with his father.

Tui əlkəǰiəni, tui ǰɪa ǰɪa-ǰɪ-arɪ

so gradually so friend friend-INS-REFL.PL

gusərəəndu-məəri, tui saa-rɪɪ-čɪ goanɪ.

talk-SIM.PL so know-PRS.P-3PL certainly

Talking together, they gradually get to know these things in this way.

Əm ɪxon-do balǰɪ-ɪ gurun-səl ǰɪa

one village-DAT live-PRS.P people-PL friend

ǰɪa-warɪ saa-rɪɪ-čɪ goanɪ.

friend-REFL.PL know-PRS.P-3PL certainly

People living in a same village know one another.

Təi gurun aso gusərəəndu-ədəəsi=ə ǰɪa

that people so.much talk-NEG.PRS.P=MIR friend

ǰɪa-ǰɪ-arɪ, čawa xəm saa-maarɪ.

friend-INS-REFL.PL that.ACC all know-SIM.PL

Even though they don't talk to one another too much, they know everything.

Gəə, goɪ ɪxonkaan, təi gurun-səl

OK other village.dweller that people-PL

ərdəŋgə-si-i-či goanɪ.

interesting-VBZ-PRS.P-3PL certainly

They are interested in other village residents.

Poaldoanɪ, Nɪkan boa-čɪ-a-nɪ xoda-ǰɪ

sometimes China place-DIR-OCM-3SG price-INS

pulsi-məəri, čado goɪ boa-du… goɪ

go-SIM.PL then other place-DAT other

boa-du balǰɪ-ɪ gurun, ǰɪa ǰɪa-warɪ

place-DAT live-PRS.P people friend friend-REFL.PL

taako-raa,	taakoalı-raa,	čado	gusərəəndu-məəri,
be.familiar.with-ANT	meet-ANT	then	talk-SIM.PL

əlkəǰiən	mədəsi-i-či	goanı,	gəə,	ui-du	bi-ə=m
gradually	ask-PRS.P-3PL	certainly	OK	who-DAT	be-PRS=REPO

tui	bi-i	puril.
so	be-PRS.P	children

Sometimes when they go to trade in China, they get to know and meet people of other places, and they gradually talk to and ask who has such children.

Čaa	saa-paarı=tanıı,	təi	mədəsi-i	naı,
that.ACC	know-COND.PL.IMPS=TOP	that	ask-PRS.P	person

saa-xan-bı	naı-čı,	ajası-ı	naı-čı
know-PST.P-REFL	person-DIR	be.suitable-PRS.P	person-DIR

ənə-rəə,	gusə…	gusərəəndu-i-ni	goanı:
go-ANT	talk	talk-PRS.P-3SG	certainly

Knowing this, the inquiring man goes to the man he thinks suitable, and begins to talk.

— Gəə,	mindu	xusə	piktə-ji	daaı	ələ,
OK	I.DAT	male	child-1SG	big	enough

ası-go-jı	baa-rıı=daa	aja.
wife-DSG-REFL	take-PRS.P=ADD	good

“Well, I have a full grown son. It is a high time for him to get married.

Gəə,	mii	piktə-ji	ası-go-a-nı	gələ-məəči-mi,	tui
OK	I	child-1SG	wife-DSG-OCM-3SG	search-RECP-SIM	so

mədəsi-i,	sinǰi	gusərəəndu-i.
ask-PRS.P	you.INS	talk-PRS.P

Well, I am looking for a wife for my son, and I ask and talk to you.

Sindu (mii saa-xan-bɪ, un-dii) — asɪa piktə
you.DAT I know-PST.P-1SG say-PRS.P female child

bi-ə=m=dəə.
be-PRS=REPO=ADD

I have come to know by hearsay that you have a daughter.

Mii sinči ičəǰə-i: sii uləən naɪ; saɪnaa,
I you.DIR look-PRS.P you good person perhaps

piktə-si=dəə uləən, biǰərə.
child-2SG=ADD good likely

I see you are a good man and, in all likelihood, your daughter must be good also.

Totamɪ mii sii piktə-wə-si xusə piktə-ji asɪ-go-a-nɪ
therefore I you child-ACC-2SG male child-1SG wife-DSG-OCM-3SG

ǰapa-ɪča-an-bɪ=am.
take-DES-PRS-1SG=REPO

Therefore I wish to take your daughter as a wife for my son."

Təi=tənii un-gu-i-ni goanɪ:
that=TOP say-REV-PRS.P-3SG certainly

The reply to that is:

— Gəə, ajasɪ-ɪ osɪnɪ, ǰapa-ɪ=daa aja.
OK be.suitable-PRS.P if take-PRS.P=ADD good

"OK. If you find her suitable, you may take her.

Totamɪ=daa mii sii piktə-wə-si ičə-ičə-ən-bi=ə,
therefore=ADD I you child-ACC-2SG see-DES-PRS-1SG=MIR

saa-ɪča-an-bɪ=am=daa.
know-DES-PRS-1SG=REPO=ADD

Then I wish to see your son and know more about him."

— Gəə, murči-ǰəən-bi, ǰoog-čɪ-jɪ, ənu-pi.
OK think-FUT-1SG house-DIR-REFL go-COND.IMPS

"OK. After returning home, I will think about it.

Asɪ-ǰɪ-jɪ gusərəəndu-i, ǰɪa-sɪl-ǰɪ-jɪ gusərəəndu-i,
wife-INS-REFL talk-PRS.P friend-PL-INS-REFL talk-PRS.P

mənə gəsə balǰɪ-ɪ gurun-ǰi gusərəəndu-i
oneself together live-PRS.P people-INS talk-PRS.P

ta-pɪ=a, gəə, saa-waan-ǰaan-bɪ=maa.
do-COND.IMPS=MIR OK know-CAUS-FUT-1SG=CON

I'll let you know after talking with my wife, with my friends and with the people living with me."

Čɪxala-ɪ osɪnɪ, aja. Mənə ǰi-duu-su. Sunǰi
agree-PRS.P if good oneself come-IMP-2PL you.PL.INS

gəsə gusərəəndu-i=dəə aja.
together talk-PRS.P=ADD good

It is good if he agrees. He says, "OK. Please come yourself. It is good to talk with you."

Gəə, narɪ-maarɪ xoǰɪ-xa-nɪ, boatoŋgo-sal=daa
OK cast.a.net-SIM.PL finish-PST.P-3SG hunter-PL=ADD

dujə-ǰiə əu-gu-xə-ni.
taiga-side descend-REV-PST.P-3SG

Well, fishing was over and the hunters came down from the taiga.

Gəə, totaraa=tanɪɪ təi mədəsi-xən naɪ=tanɪɪ, gəə,
OK and.then=TOP that ask-PST.P person=TOP OK

təi gusərəəndu-xə-mi naɪ-čɪ ǰi-dii-ni goanɪ.
that talk-PST.P-1SG person-DIR come-PRS.P-3SG certainly

Afterwards, the man who has asked before about marriage goes to the man he has asked.

Əmuučən ǰi-dəsi-ni goanı.
alone come-NEG.PRS.P-3SG certainly
He does not go alone.

Guči məən papa-sal-bı, dada-sal-bı olbı-mı,
again oneself uncle-PL-REFL aunt-PL-REFL bring-SIM
ǰi-dii-ni.
come-PRS.P-3SG
Again, he takes his uncles and aunts.

Totaraa=tanıı tukuru-ku ǰi-dii-či goanı.
and.then=TOP bottle-PROP come-PRS.P-3PL certainly
And then they take a bottle.

Baı xaıgoarı... mədəsi-gu-əri.
only for.what ask-PURP-REFL.PL
For the purpose of request.

Gəə, naı-a ačan-kın gurun, čaa
OK person-ACC meet-PST.P people that.ACC
gusərəəndu-məəri, mədəsi-i-či goanı:
talk-SIM.PL ask-PRS.P-3PL certainly
People who met the man ask him in the following way:

— Xoon bi-i-su?
how be-PRS.P-2PL
"How do you do?"

Aja-so=nuu?

good-2PL=Q

"Are you doing well?"

Ui-ǰi uləən bi-i-su?
who-INS good be-PRS.P-2PL

"Whom are you on good terms with?"

Boatoačɪ-ɪ-so=nuu?
hunt-PRS.P-2PL=Q

"Do you hunt nowadays?"

Gəə, waa-rɪɪ-so=nuu?
OK catch-PRS.P-2PL=Q

"Do you fish nowadays?"

A... təi ǰi-dii-či ǰuliə-lə-ni=tənii,
R. but that come-PRS.P-3PL front-LOC-3SG=TOP

njoančɪ=daa, goɪ gurun-ǰi gusərəəndu-məəri,
they=ADD other people-INS talk-SIM.PL

saa-ɪča-ɪ-čɪ goanɪ, xoonɪ bi-i naɪ=am
know-DES-PRS.P-3PL certainly how be-PRS.P person=REPO

təi njoančɪačɪ pulsi-xən gurun.
that they.DIR walk-PST.P people

But before the son's family comes, the daughter's family also talk to other people. They want to know what the people who had approached them were like.

Ajasɪ-ɪ osɪnɪ, piktə-ji buu-wuri-ə
be.suitable-PRS.P if child-REFL give-PRS.IMPS.P-ACC

čɪxala-ɪ osɪnɪ, naɪ tukuru-wə-ni omɪ-ɪ-l.
agree-PRS.P if person bottle-ACC-3SG drink-PRS.P-3PL

If he is deemed suitable, and the daughter is allowed to get married, they drink the bottle.

Osɪsɪ-ɪ	osɪnɪ=tanɪɪ,	tukuru-ə	dəgbəli-wəən-dəsi.
refuse-PRS.P	if=TOP	bottle-ACC	open-CAUS-NEG.PRS.P

If they refuse the marriage, they don't let the bottle open.

— Osɪsɪ-a-pu, —	un-dii.	— Buu-rəsi-pu=m=dəə	piktə-ji.
refuse-PRS-1PL	say-PRS.P	give-NEG.PRS.P-1PL=REPO=ADD	child-REFL

They say, "We decline. We will not give you our child."

Gəə,	xoonɪ?
OK	how

Then what?

Naɪ	buu-rəsi-wə-ni,	xoonɪ	ta-orɪ?
person	give-NEG.PRS.P-ACC-3SG	how	do-PRS.IMPS.P

What can one do if someone doesn't give up his daughter for marriage?

Gəə,	tui	xaɪ=daa	anaa	tui	ənu-i-či	goanɪ	ǰoog-čɪ-arɪ.
OK	so	what=ADD	without	so	go-PRS.P-3PL	certainly	house-DIR-REFL.PL

They return home empty-handed.

Naɪ	čɪxala-ɪ-nɪ	osɪnɪ=tanɪɪ,	tukuru-ə	dəgbəli-rəə,	čadu	gəsə	təi	araki-kaan-ba	omɪ-ɪ.
person	agree-PRS.P-3SG	if=TOP	bottle-ACC	open-ANT	then	together	that	alcoholic.drink-DIM-ACC	drink-PRS.P

If the person accepts the marriage, then they open the bottle and drink the liquor together.

ǰoo	ǰi...	əǰən-səl-ni=tənii	sɪa-orɪ-a	aŋgo-ɪ
house	host	host-PL-3SG=TOP	eat-PRS.IMPS.P-ACC	make-PRS.P

čadu,	sɪa-rɪɪ	ta-maarɪ	bi-i.
then	eat-PRS.P	do-SIM.PL	be-PRS.P

Then the host makes food and they eat together.

— Gəə,	totapɪa,	mədəsi-ndə-məəri,	ǰi-duu-su, —	un-dii.
OK	a.bit.later	ask-INT-SIM.PL	come-IMP-2PL	say-PRS.P

OK, the daughter's family says, "Come to us a bit later to require."

Gəə,	gəə,	ənu-xə-l.
OK	OK	go-PST.IMPS.P-PL

And so, the son's family left.

Totapɪa,	əm	xadowa	bi-pi=ə=tənii,	tərək
a.bit.later	one	several	be-COND.IMPS=MIR=TOP	just

ǰiǰu-i-či	goanɪ,	mədəsi-ndə-məəri.
come.back-PRS.P-3PL	certainly	ask-INT-SIM.PL

A bit later, after some time has passed, they come back to propose.

Təi	amɪnɪ,	ənini,	aojan	— əm	xadowa	naɪ
that	father.3SG	mother.3SG	groom	one	several	person

ǰi-dii-či	goanɪ.
come-PRS.P-3PL	certainly

Several people come, including the groom, his father and mother, and so on.

Xas[6]	tukuru-ku,	sɪaptaŋgɪ-ku,	suglən-ku
again	bottle-PROP	food-PROP	gift-PROP

ǰi-dii-či	goanɪ	təi,	mədəsi-ndə-məəri	təi
come-PRS.P-3PL	certainly	that	ask-INT-SIM.PL	that

əktə-wə.
female-ACC

Again they come bearing a bottle, food and gifts to propose to her.

Gəə,	gəə,	naɪ	čɪxala-ɪ-nɪ	osɪnɪ,	xas
OK	OK	person	agree-PRS.P-3SG	if	again

ǰoog-čɪ-jɪ	ənu-i.
house-DIR-REFL	go-PRS.P

Well if this is accepted, they enter the house once again.

Čadu,	xaɪ-wa,	torɪ-wa	murči-i-či	goanɪ.
then	what-ACC	bridewealth-ACC	think-PRS.P-3PL	certainly

Then, they discuss the bridewealth:

Xaɪ-wa	xado-wa	olbɪn-borɪ=am=daa.
what-ACC	how much-ACC	bring PRS.IMPS.P-REPO=ADD

"What and how much shall we bring?"

Təi	mədəsi-i-du-ə-či=dəə,	təi	əktə	amɪnɪ
that	ask-PRS.P-DAT-OCM-3PL=ADD	that	female	father.3SG

un-dii-ni	goanɪ:
say-PRS.P-3SG	certainly

During this proposal, the father of the bride says the following:

— Gəə, murči-u-su suə=dəə=də.

6) A colloquial form of *xais*.

OK	think-IMP-2PL	you.PL=ADD=ADD

"OK. Please consider this.

Mii	tujəə,	saɪnaa,	gələ-ǰəən-bi=əm	sundulə
I	so.much	perhaps	request-FUT-1SG=REPO	you.PL.LOC

torɪ-wa:	njəpultə-wə,	səurə-wə.
bridewealth-ACC	fur-ACC	silk-ACC

Perhaps I shall ask you much for the bridewealth: fur and silk."

Gəə,	xaɪ	bi-i-ni	osɪnɪ,	xaɪ	aja	goanɪ=a.
OK	what	be-PRS.P-3SG	if	indeed	good	certainly=MIR

Whatever it is, it is good.

Sɪa-orɪ	ǰaka-sal-ba,	nəuči-uri	ǰaka-sal-ba.
eat-PRS.IMPS.P	thing-PL-ACC	keep-PRS.IMPS.P	thing-PL-ACC

It could be food or wardrobe also.

Xoonɪ=a	buu-rii...,	totapɪa	gusərəəndu-gu-əri=əm.
how=MIR	give-PRS.P	a.bit.later	talk-ITER-REFL.PL=REPO

How the bridewealth will be given, they will talk of it later.

Gəə,	totaraa	ənu-i-či	goanɪ.
OK	and.then	go-PRS.P-3PL	certainly

And then they return home.

Təi	gərbu-ni	«mədəliku»,	«mədəliku».
that	name-3SG	*mədəliku*	*mədəliku*

This is called *medeliku* (request).

Mədəsi-ndə-mi	ǰi-či-ni	goanɪ,	buu-rii=nuu=m=dəə
ask-INT-SIM	come-PST.P-3SG	certainly	give-PRS.P=Q=REPO=ADD

piktə-ji	xusə	piktə	asɪ-go-a-nɪ.
child-REFL	male	child	wife-DSG-OCM-3SG

The father comes to inquire whether they would give their daughter as a wife for his son.

Gəə,	čado=tol	təi	xusə	piktə	təi	əktə	piktə-ni
OK	then=EXCL	that	male	child	that	female	child-3SG

amɪnaa-nɪ,	əninəə-ni=tənii	uləən	ičəǰə-i-či	goanɪ,
fathers-3SG	mothers-3SG=TOP	good.INS	look-PRS.P-3PL	certainly

xoonɪ	bi-i	naɪ=nuu	təi:	mərgəən=nuu,
how	be-PRS.P	person=Q	that	clever=Q

uləən=nuu,	murun-ku=nuu.
good=Q	thought-PROP=Q

At that time, the bride's uncles and aunts look at the young man carefully to see how he is, to see whether he is clever, good-natured, and thoughtful.

Gəə,	naɪ-ǰɪ	gusərəəndu-mi,
OK	person-INS	talk-SIM

otolɪ-orɪ-nɪ	goanɪ	čawa	xəm=dəə.
understand-PRS.IMPS.P-3SG	certainly	that.ACC	all=ADD

While talking with him, they come to know all these things.

ǰoog-čɪ	ənu-pəəri=tənii,	murči-i-či	goanɪ:
house-DIR	go-COND.PL.IMPS=TOP	think-PRS.P-3PL	certainly

gəə,	xaɪ-wa	buu-mi	mutə-uri	buə.
OK	what-ACC	give-SIM	be.able.to-PRS.IMPS.P	we

While returning home, they think, "What can we give them?"

Gəə,	čaa…	čawa	bɪa-do=o,	ǰuə	bɪa-do=daa
OK	that	that.ACC	month-DAT=CONC	two	month-DAT=ADD

murči-i=dəə, saawaasɪ=a.

think-PRS.P=ADD maybe=MIR

They might think about this for one or two months.

Totapaarı=tanıı jəŋsilə-ndə-məəri ǰi-dii-či.
then=TOP match-INT-SIM.PL come-PRS.P-3PL

Then they go back to the bride's house to discuss the matter.

Gəə, təi jəŋsilə-i-du-əri...
OK that match-PRS.P-DAT-REFL.PL
jəŋsilə-i-du-əri=tənii, gəə, tərək toktoo-rıı-čı:
match-PRS.P-DAT-REFL.PL=TOP OK just agree-PRS.P-3PL

When discussing this, they deliberate without any ambiguity:

Xado səəpə-wə, xado solı-wa, xado bəjun-bə,
how.much sable-ACC how.much fox-ACC how.much elk-ACC
xado səurə-wə — gəə, goı goı ǰaka-sal-ba
how.much silk-ACC OK various thing-PL-ACC
torı-do olbın-go... olbın-go-arı.
bridewealth-DAT bring-PURP bring-PURP-REFL.PL

They discuss how many pieces of sable skin, fox skin, elk skin, silk, and various things they will bring as the bridewealth.

ǰıxa-ko osını, (ǰıxa agbın-bo-očıa-nı=a goanı=a),
money-PROP if money appear-TR-COND-3SG=MIR certainly=MIR
ǰıxa-ko osını, ǰıxa=daa aja.
money-PROP if money=ADD good

If they have money (after money had appeared to Nanai), money is good also.

Xaı=daa aısı-ma, məŋgu-mə xaǰon bi-i osını,
what=ADD made.with.gold made.with.silver stuff be-PRS.P if

gəə,	təi=dəə	uləəni	goanı:	xoda-nı	maŋga.
OK	that=ADD	good.3SG	certainly	price-3SG	expensive

Whatever it is, gold or silver, or an expensive property, it is good.

Gəə,	xoonı=a	olbın-borı=a.
OK	how=MIR	bring-PRS.IMPS.P=MIR

Now how will they bring it?

Naı	torı-wa	daaı-a	gələ-i-ni
person	bridewealth-ACC	large-ACC	request-PRS.P-3SG

osını,	ambaan	əgǰi	bıa-do=o,	poaldoanı
if	fairly	many	month-DAT=CONC	sometimes

aıŋanı-a	aıŋanı-sı-mı,	təi…	təi	torı-wa
year-ACC	year-VBZ-SIM	that	that	bridewealth-ACC

naı	omo-orı-nı	goanı,	naı	xaıgoanı
person	collect-PRS.IMPS.P-3SG	certainly	person	what.for

piktə-ji,	təi	xusə	piktə-ji	ası-go-a-nı
child-REFL	that	male	child-REFL	wife-DSG-OCM-3SG

buu-gu-ə-ni.
give-PURP-OCM-3SG

If they ask for a large bridewealth, it takes several months or even a year to gather for it, that his son can get married.

Poaldoanı,	təi	torı-a	xətə-mi
sometimes	that	bridewealth-ACC	obtain-SIM

mutə-əsi	osıpı=tanıı,	gəə,	xoonı	ta-orı?
be.able.to-NEG.PRS.P	if=TOP	OK	how	do-PRS.IMPS.P

If one cannot gather the bridewealth, what is one to do?

— Mutə-əsin-bi=ə, —	un-dii-či	goanı.
be.able.to-NEG.PRS.P-REFL=MIR	say-PRS.P-3PL	certainly

They say, “I cannot do this.”

Gəə, čado=tanıı, gəə, təi əktə=dəə
OK then=TOP OK that female=ADD

əǰi-gu-ji təi naı-čı, əǰi-lə-ndə-mi təi
husband-DSG-REFL that person-DIR husband-VBZ-INT-SIM that

naı-čı ənə-əsi.
person-DIR go-NEG.PRS.P

Then the lady who was going to get married does not marry the man.

Təi naı=daa təi əktə-ǰi ası-go-jı baa-rası.
that person=ADD that female-INS wife-DSG-REFL take-NEG.PRS.P

The man also cannot marry her.

Goı əktə ǰapa-ı-nı goanı.
other female take-PRS.P-3SG certainly

He must marry another lady.

Tui=dəə.
so=ADD

That’s the way it goes.

Mutə-i osını=tanıı, guči ǰiǰu-i-či
be.able.to-PRS.P if=TOP again come.back-PRS.P-3PL

goanı.
certainly

If they can prepare for the bridewealth, they return to the bride’s home again.

Təi ılıačıa, ılıačıa modan ǰiǰu-i-či=tənii
that third third time come.back-PRS.P-3PL=TOP

gərbu-ni «dəgbəliku», «dəgbəliku».
name-3SG *dəgbəliku* *dəgbəliku*

The name of the third visit is *degbeliku.*

Gəə, čado=tanɪɪ torɪ-a xəm xətə-xə-ni
OK then=TOP bridewealth-ACC all obtain-PST.P-3SG

gurun xəm olbɪn-dɪɪ.
people all bring-PRS.P

Then, if someone gathered up all of the things for the bridewealth, he brings them.

Təi=tənii daaɪ sarɪn, daaɪ anjaa
that=TOP large banquet large feast

osɪ-ɪ-nɪ goanɪ čadu.
become-PRS.P-3SG certainly then

At that time, they throw a grand banquet.

Čaa xəm əm modan olbɪ-mɪ mutə-əsi
that.ACC all one time bring-SIM be.able.to-NEG.PRS.P

gurun=tənii pasɪ-a olbɪn-dɪɪ-čɪ goanɪ.
people=TOP part-ACC bring-PRS.P-3PL certainly

If they cannot bring all of the bridewealth, they bring part of it.

Tokon-ba-nɪ, dolɪn-ba-nɪ. Dolɪn-do-a-nɪ əgǰi-ləə
center-ACC-3SG half-ACC-3SG half-DAT-OCM-3SG many-SUFF

bi-i-wə.
be-PRS.P-ACC

They take half or more than half of it.

Təi puləə-wə-ni=təni totapɪa buu-gu-əri
that residue-ACC-3SG=TOP a.bit.later give-PURP-REFL.PL

ta-ɪ-čɪ goanɪ.

do-PRS.P-3PL certainly

The remaining things will be given later.

Tui=dəə.
so=ADD

That's the way it goes.

Gəə, čadu daaı anjaa, arakı-a omı-ı,
OK then large feast alcoholic.drink-ACC drink-PRS.P

əgǰi saolın-ba aŋgo-ı.
many banquet-ACC make-PRS.P

Then they held a grand banquet, where they drink and treat the guests well.

Məən məən xaı-sal-bı, ǰıa-sıl-barı, mənə
each.separately what-PL-REFL friend-PL-REFL.PL oneself

balǰı-xam sagǰı-l-barı — xəm gələ-rəə čadu.
live-PST.P.REFL elder-PL-REFL.PL all invite-ANT then

Then they invite each other's friends and elder relatives who live alone.

Gəə, təi ərin-du təi aojan-ǰı, puǰin-ǰi (ası-ǰı-a-nı,
OK that time-DAT that groom-INS heroine-INS wife-INS-OCM-3SG

təi patalaan-ǰı=daa) gəsə akpan-dıı=daa aja.
that lady-INS=ADD together lie.down-PRS.P=ADD good

At that time the groom and the bride may sleep together.

Naı tukuru-ə nixəli-xə-ni. Tui ta-mı
person bottle-ACC open-PST.P-3SG so do-SIM

ajası-ı-čı goanı tui ta-mı.
be.suitable-PRS.P-3PL certainly so do-SIM

When people opened the bottle cap, this was allowed.

Gəə,	totapaarı=maat	toktoo-rıı-čı	goanı.
OK,	then=CON	agree-PRS.P-3PL	certainly

After that, they make an agreement.

Təi	əktə-wə	xaalı	ŋaanı-go-orı=am=daa
that	female-ACC	when	go.to.take-REV-PRS.IMPS.P=REPO=ADD

təi	piktə...	xusə	piktə	ası-go-a-nı.
that	child	male	child	wife-DSG-OCM-3SG

When will they take the bride, the wife of their son?

Naanaı	ası-go-jı	baa-rıı-nı	ərin	tul tul
Nanai	wife-DSG-REFL	take-PRS.P-3SG	time	always

ǰoa	bi-či-ni.
summer	be-PST.P-3SG

Marriage for the Nanai people always took place in the summer.

Əmdə əmdə	tuə.	Tuə=kəs	xaı?
rarely	winter	winter=EMP	what

It is rare for it to take place in the winter. Why not in the winter?

Xusə	gurun	xəm	duəntə-du	bi-i,	boatoačı-ı.
male	people	all	taiga-DAT	be-PRS.P	hunt-PRS.P

ǰoa=kas	aja.
summer=EMP	good

All of the men are hunting in the taiga. That is why the summer is good.

Xaı,	sogǰama-sı-mı	xoǰı...	xoǰı-xan,	təi	ərin-du
indeed	fish-DUR-SIM	finish...	finish-PST.P	that	time-DAT

kaokaa	bi-i	gurun	goanı.
quietly	be-PRS.P	people	certainly

When men finish fishing, they are free of work.

Totamaarı	təi	əkəsəl-bə,	patalaan-sal-ba,	xaı,
therefore	that	woman.PL-ACC	lady-PL-ACC	indeed

ǰoa	ŋaso-ı-čı	bi-či-ni	goanı.
summer	carry-PRS.P-3PL	be-PST.P-3SG	certainly

Therefore they took their bride in summer.

ǰoa	guči	xoonı	ta-maarı	gıamata-la-ı-čı
summer	again	how	do-SIM.PL	wedding-VBZ-PRS.P-3PL

bi-či-ni?
be-PST.P-3SG

How was the wedding ceremony performed in the summer?

Gıamata-wa	daaı	gıla-ǰı,	daaı	ogda-ǰı
bride-ACC	large	wedding.boat-INS	large	boat-INS

ıra-ı	bi-či-či	goanı=a.
carry-PRS.P	be-PST.P-3PL	certainly=MIR

They brought the bride by *gila*, a big wedding boat.

Təi	gıla-wa=tanıı	təi	gıamata-du	aŋgo-ı,
that	wedding.boat-ACC=TOP	that	wedding-DAT	make-PRS.P

sikuun	gıla-wa,	daaı-wa.
new	wedding.boat-ACC	large-ACC

They make this new big boat for wedding ceremony.

Gıamata	bəun-gu-ə-ni,	gıamata	miruə-ni
bride	place-DSG-OCM-3SG	bride	dowry-3SG

bəun-gu-ə-ni,	daxala-mǰı-sal	bəun-gu-ə-či
place-DSG-OCM-3SG	follow-AGT-PL	place-DSG-OCM-3PL

ogda-sal-ba	aŋgo-kta-ı-čı	goanı.
boat-PL-ACC	make-DISTR-PRS.P-3PL	certainly

The boats, on which the bride sits, the dowry (*mirue* in Nanai) is loaded, and bridesmaids ride, were made.

Gəə,	təi…	təi=dəə	ambaan	əgǰi	ərin-bə
OK	that	that=ADD	fairly	many	time-ACC

gələ-i-ni	goanı.
need-PRS.P-3SG	certainly

It takes a fairly long time.

Xaı,	əmun	ǰuər	ini-du	xaalı=daa	aŋgo-mı
indeed	one	two	day-DAT	when=ADD	make-SIM

korpı-wası.
finish-NEG.PRS.IMPS.P

It is not possible to finish it in one or two days.

Totamı	bıa-wa	bıaŋsa-mı	tui.
therefore	month-ACC	spend.time-SIM	so

Therefore several months pass.

Gəə,	tui	əǰi-gu-ji,	ası-go-jı
OK	so	husband-DSG-REFL	wife-DSG-REFL

baa-rıı-čı=kas	goro-nı	goanı.
take-PRS.P-3PL=EMP	long.time-3SG	certainly

Like this it takes a long time to take a bride or a groom.

Təi	aıŋanı=daa	sii-rii.
that	year=ADD	take.time-PRS.P

It can take even one year.

Poaldoanı	ǰuər,	ılaan	aıŋanı=daa	sii-rii.
sometimes	two	three	year=ADD	take.time-PRS.P

Tui=dəə.
so=ADD

Sometimes it takes two or three years. That's the way it goes.

Čaa xaɪ-rɪɪ-do-a-čɪ, mədəsi-i, jəŋsilə-i,
that.ACC do.what-PRS.P-DAT-OCM-3PL ask-PRS.P match-PRS.P

totapɪ=tanɪɪ dəgbəli-i, ɪra-ɪ, totapɪ=maat, xaɪ-wa,
then=TOP open-PRS.P carry-PRS.P then=CON what-ACC

təi patalaan-ba, gɪamata-wa, ŋaanɪ... ŋaanɪ-ɪ-čɪ.
that lady-ACC bride-ACC go.to.take go.to.take-PRS.P-3PL

After request (*medesi*), match-making (*yengsi*) and uncorking (*degbeliku*), they come to take the bride.

Gəə, čaa xəm ta-paarɪ=maat, gɪamata-wa
OK that.ACC all do-COND.PL.IMPS=CON bride-ACC

ŋaanɪ-maarɪ, ǰi-dii-či.
go.to.take-SIM.PL come-PRS.P-3PL

After doing all of these, they come to take the bride.

Aojanɪ, aojanɪ amɪnɪ, ənini ǰi-dəsi.
groom.3SG groom.3SG father.3SG mother.3SG come-NEG.PRS.P

The groom, the father and mother of him do not come.

Baɪ njoančɪ xaɪ-čɪ=daa: gusin-či, əksən-či
only they what-3PL=ADD uncle-3PL uncle-3PL

čado, dada-sal-čɪ — ǰi-dii-či təi gɪamata
then aunt-PL-3PL come-PRS.P-3PL that bride

ŋaanɪ-maarɪ.
go.to.take-SIM.PL

The younger brothers of his mother, the younger brothers of his father, and/or the elder sisters of his mother come to take the bride.

Aojan,	aojan	amını,	ənini=tənii	ǰoog-do
groom	groom	father.3SG	mother.3SG=TOP	house-DAT

xalačı-ı-čı	čado	ǰi-dii-wə-či.
wait-PRS.P-3PL	then	come-PRS.P-ACC-3PL

The groom and the father and mother of him wait their arrival at home.

Gəə,	tui=dəə	goanı.
OK	so=ADD	certainly

That's how it happened.

A...	xaı...	ənini,	xaı...	patalaan	ənini,
R. and	indeed	mother.3SG	indeed	lady	mother.3SG

amını=tanıı	təi	patalaan	miruə-wə-ni
father.3SG=TOP	that	lady	dowry-ACC-3SG

bargı-ı-čı	goanı.
prepare-PRS.P-3PL	certainly

And the mother and father of the bride prepare the bride's dowry.

Əktə	piktɔ	naı	mɔdə...	mədəsi-i-ni	ǰuliə-lə-ni
female	child	person	ask	ask-PRS.P-3SG	front-LOC-3SG

xaǰon-go-jı	bargı-ı	bi-či-ni	goanı,	əgǰi-wə.
thing-DSG-REFL	prepare-PRS.P	be-PST.P-3SG	certainly	many-ACC

The girl prepared a lot before an request (*medesi*).

ǰoan,	ǰoan	ǰuər	səə	arčokaan	xaı-wa=daa
ten	ten	two	age	girl	what-ACC=ADD

xəm	ulpi-mi,	ılga-la-mı	otolı-ı
all	sew-SIM	pattern-VBZ-SIM	understand-PRS.P

bi-či-ni.
be-PST.P-3SG

Every girl at the age of ten to twelve years old could do needle work and embroidery.

Totamı	ənin-ǰi-ji,	əikə…	əikə-səl-ǰi-ji
therefore	mother-INS-REFL	elder.sister	elder.sister-PL-INS-REFL

mənə	gəsə=dəə	tətuə-gu-əri	aŋgo-ı
oneself	together=ADD	clothes-DSG-REFL.PL	make-PRS.P

bi-či-či	goanı,	goı goı	tətuə-wə.
be-PST.P-3PL	certainly	various	clothes-ACC

Therefore they made their own and various clothes with their mother and sisters.

Əgǰi-ə	gələ-i	bi-či-či	goanı	tətuə-wə.
many-ACC	need-PRS.P	be-PST.P-3PL	certainly	clothes-ACC

Many kinds of clothes were needed.

Naı	mədəsi-i-du-ə-ni,	xaıgoarı	tui	əgǰi-ə
person	ask-PRS.P-DAT-OCM-3SG	what.for	so	many-ACC

tətuə-wə	aŋgo-ı-so=am,	sagǰı	gurun
clothes-ACC	make-PRS.P-2PL=REPO	old	people

tui	un-dii	bi-či-ni	goanı:
so	say-PRS.P	be-PST.P-3SG	certainly

When people ask "why do you make so many clothes?", the elders answered as follows:

— Əktə,	əǰi-gu-ji	baa-pı,	ǰobo-nı	ǰoog-do
female	husband-DSG-REFL	take-COND.IMPS	work-3SG	house-DAT

əgǰi.
many

"Once a woman gets married, there is a lot of work to do at home.

Piktə-gu-ji=dəə baa-rıı, puril-bə

child-DSG-REFL=ADD take-PRS.P children-ACC

dəŋsi-i, ǰoo… ǰoo dəŋsi-i, boa-la=daa
serve-PRS.P house house serve-PRS.P outside-LOC=ADD

ɪnda-sal, moo-wa moo-lsɪ-ɪ, muə-wə
dog-PL tree-ACC gather.firewood-HAB-PRS.P water-ACC

muə-lsi-i.
fetch.water-HAB-PRS.P

They have to give birth to babies, take care of the children, do housework, and outside, they have to take care of the dogs, gather firewood, and also fetch water outside.

Xaɪ, tətuə-səl-bə ulpi-mi xaalɪ korpɪ-ɪ-nɪ?
indeed clothes-PL-ACC sew-SIM when finish-PRS.P-3SG

And so, when can they finish making clothes?

Əmbə əmbə xaɪ-du… ərin-du xaɪ-wa=daa ta-mɪ
each what-DAT time-DAT what-ACC=ADD do-SIM

mutə-i osɪnɪ, əgǰi-ə ta-mɪ korpɪ-asɪ.
be.able.to-PRS.P if many-ACC do-SIM finish-NEG.PRS.P

Everything takes time to do, so one cannot finish many things.

Xaɪ, ǰobo-nɪ əgǰi-ni goanɪ.
indeed work-3SG many-3SG certainly

There is that much work to do.

Tui ta-mɪ əǰi-gu-ji baa-rɪɪ ǰuliə-lə-ni
so do-SIM husband-DSG-REFL take-PRS.P front-LOC-3SG

xəm aŋgo-orɪ.
all make-PRS.IMPS.P

Therefore they should make everything before getting married.

Tui tamaarɪ tui aŋgo-ɪ bi-či-či goanɪ

therefore so make-PRS.P be-PST.P-3PL certainly

xaǰon-ba, əgǰi-ə.
stuff-ACC many-ACC

Therefore they made many things."

Gəə, təi əktə miruə-gu-ə-ni, xusə gurun
OK that female dowry-DSG-OCM-3SG male people

ogda-wa, jaotaan-go-a-nɪ, xaɪ-wa=daa xəm
boat-ACC awning-DSG-OCM-3SG what-ACC=ADD all

ta-ɪ-do-a-čɪ, əkəsəl bargɪ-ɪ bi-či-či
do-PRS.P-DAT-OCM-3PL woman.PL prepare-PRS.P be-PST.P-3PL

goanɪ.
certainly

While men made the boat and the awning on it, women prepared the bride's dowry.

Əktə miruə-du-ə-ni tətuə manjaa=daa
female dowry-DAT-OCM-3SG clothes only=ADD

bi-əči-ni goanɪ.
be-NEG.PST.P-3SG certainly

In the dowry, there were not only clothes.

Kagba-sal, xaɪ=daa xəm ləlu-səl, kurkə-səl,
crock-PL what=ADD all apron-PL reel.of.thread-PL

ulpi-uri xaǰon-sal, xaɪ=daa xəm kotaan-sal
sew-PRS.IMPS.P thing-PL what=ADD all cup-PL

— gələ-uri ǰaka, ǰoog-do bi-i-du-ji,
need-PRS.IMPS.P thing house-DAT live-PRS.P-DAT-REFL

gələ-uri ǰaka xəm bargɪ-ɪ bi-či-či
need-PRS.IMPS.P thing all prepare-PRS.P be-PST.P-3PL

goanɪ.
certainly

They prepared everything needed in everyday life, such as dishes, aprons, reel of thread, sewing kits, cups and so on.

Mənə	xaǰon-ko,	xaɪ,	patalaan	(təi	əǰi-gu-ji
oneself	thing-PROP	indeed	lady	that	husband-DSG-REFL

baa-rɪɪ	əktə,	«gɪamata=m»,	naɪ	gərbiə-si-i)
take-PRS.P	female	bride=REPO	person	call-DUR-PRS.P

mənə	xaǰon-ko	əǰi-či-ji	ənə-i-wə-ni
oneself	thing-PROP	husband-DIR-REFL	go-PRS.P-ACC-3SG

gələ-i.
need-PRS.P

A bride (*giamata* in Nanai) has to bring her own things to the home of the groom.

Təəm	njoanɪ	xaǰonɪ=ragda	njoaŋgɪ-nɪ	osɪ-ɪ
only	she	thing.3SG=LIM	hers-3SG	become-PRS.P

əǰi-du-ə-ni.
husband-DAT-OCM-3SG

At groom's home only the things she brings are her own.

Əǰi-ji	ǰoog-čɪ-a-nɪ	ii-pi,	təi	čadu
husband-REFL	house-DIR-OCM-3SG	enter-COND.IMPS	that	there

bi-i	xaǰon	xəm	əǰi-ni,	əǰi-ni	əkəsəl-ni,
be-PRS.P	thing	all	husband-3SG	husband-3SG	woman.PL-3SG

aag-sal-nɪ,	ənini,	amɪnɪ	xaǰonɪ.
elder.brother-PL-3SG	mother.3SG	father.3SG	thing.3SG

When she enters the groom's home, everything there belongs to the sisters, brothers, mother and father of the groom.

Njoanɪ	xaǰonɪ=tanɪɪ	təəm	njoanɪ	miruə-du-ə-ni
she	thing.3SG=TOP	only	she	dowry-DAT-OCM-3SG

bi-či-ni xaǰon=ragda.

be-PST.P-3SG thing=LIM

Only the things she has brought as the dowry are her own.

Goɪ xaǰon aba.
other thing not

Other things are not hers.

Tui ta-mɪ, mənə xaǰon-go-jɪ tui bargɪ-ɪ
so do-SIM oneself thing-DSG-REFL so prepare-PRS.P
bi-či-ni goanɪ, əǰi-gu-ji baa-rɪɪ
be-PST.P-3SG certainly husband-DSG-REFL take-PRS.P
ǰuliə-lə-ni.
front-LOC-3SG

Therefore she prepared her own things before getting married.

Təi miruə, naɪ təi miruə-wə bargɪ-mɪ,
that dowry person that dowry-ACC prepare-SIM
əmutuu unəəči-i=maa ta-ɪ bi-či-či goanɪ.
as.if compare-PRS.P=SML do-PRS.P be-PST.P-3PL certainly

While preparing the dowry, it was as if it was being compared to bridewealth.

Torɪ daaɪ-nɪ osɪnɪ, miruə=dəə əgǰi.
bridewealth large-3SG if dowry=ADD many

The bigger the bridewealth, the bigger the dowry.

Torɪ nuuči-ni osɪnɪ, miruə=dəə oɪ.
bridewealth small-3SG if dowry=ADD few

The smaller the bridewealth, the smaller the dowry.

Poanɪ aojan-sal sinəǰii bi-či-ni goanɪ.
some groom-PL poor be-PST.P-3SG certainly

Some grooms were poor.

Xaɪ=daa	anaa.
what=ADD	without

They do not have anything.

Totamaarɪ=tanɪɪ	torɪ-a	buu-mi=dəə
therefore=TOP	bridewealth-ACC	give-SIM=ADD

mutə-əsi.	Torɪ-a	buu-mi=dəə
be.able.to-NEG.PRS.P	bridewealth-ACC	give-SIM=ADD

mutə-əsi.
be.able.to-NEG.PRS.P

Therefore, they cannot even give a bridewealth. They cannot give a bridewealth.

Totamɪ	təi	əktə-kəən	amɪnɪ,	təi
therefore	that	female-DIM	father.3SG	that

naonǰokaan-čɪ	ičəǰə-mi,	ajapo-ɪ-nɪ	osɪnɪ,
boy-DIR	look-SIM	love-PRS.P-3SG	if

təi	naonǰoan,	tui	bi-əsi=dəə,	uləən	naɪ,
that	young	so	be-NEG.PRS.P=ADD	good	person

murun=dəə	uləən,	naɪ-wa=daa	kidu-i,
mind=ADD	good	person-ACC=ADD	respect-PRS.P

uləəni,	ǰoboso,	gəə,	čaa	ičə-i	osɪnɪ=tanɪɪ,
good.INS	hardworking	OK	that.ACC	see-PRS.P	if=TOP

təi	əktə	amɪnɪ	un-dii-ni	goanɪ:
that	female	father.3SG	say-PRS.P-3SG	certainly

Therefore, if the father of the girl recognizes that the young man, is endearing, and though poor, is good natured, respects his elders, and works well, then the father says the following:

— Gəə, aja. Bunči ii-rəə, bi-ruu. Bunči

OK good we.DIR enter-ANT live-2SG.IMP we.DIR

ii-rəə, bi-ruu, — un-dii.
enter-ANT live-2SG.IMP say-PRS.P

"OK. Come into my home. Stay and lead a life in my home."

Gəə, təi naonǰoan ənini, amɪnɪ=daa,
OK that young mother.3SG father.3SG=ADD

gəə, čɪxala-ɪ: sinəǰii.
OK agree-PRS.P poor

As they are poor, mother and father of the young man agree.

Torɪ-a bargɪ-go-jɪ xaɪ-wa=daa baa-rasɪ.
bridewealth-ACC prepare-PURP-REFL what-ACC=ADD take-NEG.PRS.P

They don't take the prepared bridewealth at all.

Torɪ-a buu-gu-i.
bridewealth-ACC give-REV-PRS.P

They return the bridewealth.

Gəə, totamaarɪ mənə piktə-wə-əri
OK therefore oneself child-ACC-REFL.PL

təi əktə amɪnɪ, amɪnaa-nɪ,
that female father.3SG fathers-3SG

əninəə-ni ǰoog-čɪ-a-nɪ ii-wəən-dii-či goanɪ.
mothers-3SG house-DIR-OCM-3SG enter-CAUS-PRS.P-3PL certainly

That is why they allow their son to enter the home of the father, uncles and aunts of the bride.

Gəə, čaa gərbiə-si-i bi-či-či goanɪ:
OK that.ACC call-DUR-PRS.P be-PST.P-3PL certainly

ii-xən, ii-xən naɪ, ii-xən
enter-PST.P enter-PST.P person enter-PST.P

aojan,	ii-xən	əǰi...	ii-xən	əǰi.
groom	enter-PST.P	husband	enter-PST.P	husband

They called him “man who entered, groom who has taken, husband who entered, that is, son-in-law who lives with wife’s family.”

Gəə,	təi	əǰi=tənii,	təi	əktə-kəən-ǰi	asɪ-la-raa,
OK	that	husband=TOP	that	female-DIM-INS	wife-VBZ-ANT

təŋ	kičə-mi	ǰobo-ɪ-wa-nɪ	gələ-i.
very	make.efforts-SIM	work-PRS.P-ACC-3SG	need-PRS.P

Well, after marriage, the groom must work hard in wife’s home.

Təi	əktə-kəən	xoda-wa-nɪ	taoda-ɪ=maa=daa,
that	female-DIM	price-ACC-3SG	respond-PRS.P=SML=ADD

ǰobo-ɪ-nɪ	goanɪ	čadu.
work-PRS.P-3SG	certainly	then

He works there as if it pays for the bridewealth.

Gəə,	tui=dəə,	təi=dəə	tui	bi-či-ni	goanɪ.
OK	so=ADD	that=ADD	so	be-PST.P-3SG	certainly

That was the way it was.

Gəə,	gɪamata	əǰi-či-ji	ənə-i-ni,
OK	bride	husband-DIR-REFL	go-PRS.P-3SG

aojan-čɪ-jɪ	ənə-i-ni	ərin	ɪsɪ-očɪa-nɪ,	ogda
groom-DIR-REFL	go-PRS.P-3SG	time	arrive-COND-3SG	boat

tooɪ-čɪ	xaa-rɪɪ-čɪ	goanɪ,	əgǰi	ogda.
riverside-DIR	go.ashore-PRS.P-3PL	certainly	many	boat

When it is the time for the bride to go to the groom, many boats are at the riverside.

Təi gɪamata ənə-i-ni ogda=tanɪɪ — gɪla.

that bride go-PRS.P-3SG boat=TOP wedding.boat

The boat the bride is aboard on is called *gila*.

Čadu gıamata bəun-gu-ə-ni aŋgo-ı-čı
then bride place-DSG-OCM-3SG make-PRS.P-3PL

jaotaan-ba, xaı-do, təi gıla tokon-do-a-nı.
awning-ACC what-DAT that wedding.boat center-DAT-OCM-3SG

In the center of the boat, where there is a seat for the bride, there is an arch-shaped awning.

Ta… talo-ǰı, ılga-la-maarı, aŋgo-ı-čı.
birch.bark birch.bark-INS pattern-VBZ-SIM.PL make-PRS.P-3PL

It is embroidered with birch bark.

Təi gıla=daa xəm xooŋko-nı,
that wedding.boat=ADD all bow.of.the.boat-3SG

kətəni — xaı-nı=daa xəm xəm ılga-ko,
stern.of.the.boat.3SG what-3SG=ADD all all pattern-PROP

xəm gučkuli; gıamata naı olbın-dıı-nı gıla.
all beautiful bride person bring-PRS.P-3SG wedding.boat

The front and back of the boat, *gila*, which is decorated with embroidery, is very beautiful. It is the *gila* which people will use to take the bride there.

Guči=tənii, miruə əgǰi-ni osını, guči əm
again=TOP dowry many-3SG if again one

xadowa xaı-wa, ogda aŋgo-ı-čı goanı təi
several what-ACC boat make-PRS.P-3PL certainly that

miruə… miruə-wə ıra-go-arı.
dowry dowry-ACC carry-PURP-REFL.PL

If dowry is too big, they make one more boat for carrying the dowry.

Guči=tənii	daxala-mǰɪ	(təi	gɪamata	ɪra-ɪ
again=TOP	follow-AGT	that	bride	carry-PRS.P

gurun)	oo-go-a-čɪ,	ənə-gu-ə-či,	čado=daa
people	board-PURP-OCM-3PL	go-PURP-OCM-3PL	then=ADD

ogda	aŋgo-ɪ-čɪ	goanɪ.
boat	make-PRS.P-3PL	certainly

For carrying bridesmaids (who accompany the bride), they also make boats.

Gəə,	tui=dəə.
OK	so=ADD

That's the way it goes.

Xaɪ,	gɪamata	ǰoog-ǰɪaǰɪ-jɪ	niə-gu-ə-ni,
indeed	bride	house-ABL-REFL	exit-PURP-OCM-3SG

njoambanɪ	gɪamata	tətuə-wə-ni	tətu-wəən-dii-či,
she.ACC	bride	clothes-ACC-3SG	dress-CAUS-PRS.P-3PL

gɪamata	tətuə-wə-ni.
bride	clothes-ACC-3SG

When the bride leaves her home, she is made to wear the bridal gown (See Fig. 8 on page x above).

Čuu	doo-la,	xərəktə-du-ə-ni,	tətu-wəən-dii-či=tənii,
most	inside-LOC	skin-DAT-OCM-3SG	dress-CAUS-PRS.P-3PL=TOP

xaɪ,	təi	doo-la	təčičə-uri	tətuə-wə.
indeed	that	inside-LOC	wear-PRS.IMPS.P	clothes-ACC

She has to wear underwear on the buff.

«Əŋgərəgdə=m»,	gərbiə-si-i	bi-či-či.
underwear=REPO	call-DUR-PRS.P	be-PST.P-3PL

It was called *enggeregde.*

Təi əŋgərəgdə tətu-wəən-dii.
that underwear dress-CAUS-PRS.P

She is made to wear that *enggeregde*.

Əŋgərə... əŋgərəgdə ojaa-la-nɪ=tanɪɪ pokto-a
underwear underwear surface-LOC-3SG=TOP light.gown-ACC
tətu-wəən-dii, nəmi-kuukəən tətuə-kəəm
dress-CAUS-PRS.P thin-EXTR clothes-DIM.ACC
tətu-wəən-dii.
dress-CAUS-PRS.P

Over the *enggeregde*, she is made to wear a light gown called *pokto*.

Təi pokto ojaa-la-nɪ=tanɪɪ guči ləluə-wə
that light.gown surface-LOC-3SG=TOP again bib-ACC
tətu-wəən-dii.
dress-CAUS-PRS.P

Over that, she is made to wear a bib-like piece of clothing.

Təi ləluə-du=tənii, xaɪ, sələ-mə xaɪ-sal
that bib-DAT=TOP indeed made.with.iron what-PL
bi-i-ni goanɪ, tolɪ=maa bi-i
be-PRS.P-3SG certainly breastplate=SML be-PRS.P
ǰaka-sal-ba ulpi-uxən.
thing-PL-ACC sew-PST.IMPS.P

There are metal fittings on that bib. A metal fitting much like the one that shamans put on their chest was sewed on.

Xaɪgojɪ tui tətu-wəən-dii-či?
for.what so dress-CAUS-PRS.P-3PL

Why do they dress her like that?

Təi gɪamata duərə-i-du-ə-ni, təi
that bride step-PRS.P-DAT-OCM-3SG that

tolɪ-sal=maa bi-i sələ-səl=tənii, ǰɪa
breastplate-PL=SML be-PRS.P iron-PL=TOP friend

ǰɪa-warɪ tui toŋgala... toŋga-sɪ-maarɪ
friend-REFL.PL so touch touch-DUR-SIM.PL

xaɪ-rɪɪ-čɪ goanɪ, koŋgɪrɪ-ɪ-čɪ, koŋgɪrɪ-ɪ-čɪ.
do.what-PRS.P-3PL certainly ring-PRS.P-3PL ring-PRS.P-3PL

Koŋgɪrɪ-ɪ-čɪ.
ring-PRS.P-3PL

When the bride walks, what happens is the metal fittings clang by bumping into one another.

Təi koŋgɪrɪ-ɪ-nɪ=tanɪɪ təi ambaan-sal-ba
that ring-PRS.P-3SG=TOP that evil.spirit-PL-ACC

əusi taosɪ čoča-go-waan-dɪɪ.
to.here.and.there run-REV-CAUS-PRS.P

When the sounds clang, evil spirits are chased off here and there.

Təi ambaan-sal ŋəələ-i-či təi koŋgɪrɪ-ɪ-ǰɪ-a-nɪ.
that evil.spirit-PL be.frightened-PRS.P-3PL that ring-PRS.P-INS-OCM-3SG

As soon as these make sounds, the evil spirits are frightened.

Gɪamata-wa=tanɪɪ, gɪamata-wa=tanɪɪ təi=tənii
bride-ACC=TOP bride-ACC=TOP that=TOP

xaɪ-rɪɪ-nɪ goanɪ, əmutuu ətuu-rii=məə
do.what-PRS.P-3SG certainly as.if protect-PRS.P=SML

bi-i-či goanɪ čadu.
be-PST.P-3PL certainly then

It's like the sounds protect her from evil spirits at that time.

Təi ləluə ojaa-la-nɪ=tanɪɪ gɪamata tətuə...
that bib surface-LOC-3SG=TOP bride clothes

gɪamata tətuə-wə-ni tətu-wəən-dii-či.
bride clothes-ACC-3SG dress-CAUS-PRS.P-3PL

Over that bib, the bridal gown is put on.

Təi gɪamata tətuə-ni=tənii xaɪnɪ=daa xəm
that bride clothes-3SG=TOP what-3SG=ADD all

xəm ɪlga-ko.
all pattern-PROP

The bridal gown is wholly covered with embroideries.

Əm ulpi-uxən xaɪ=daa ɪlga anaa
one sew-PST.IMPS.P indeed=ADD embroidery without

bi-əsi. Xaɪ=daa, muirə-du-ə-ni,
be-NEG.PRS.P indeed=ADD shoulder-DAT-OCM-3SG

əi xuəksə-ni ulpi-čə-du-ə-ni, xaɪ,
this sleeve-3SG sew-PASS-DAT-OCM-3SG indeed,

darama-nɪ, darama-do-a-nɪ=tanɪɪ.
back-3SG back-DAT-OCM-3SG=TOP

There is no place where there is sewing where there is no embroidery. There is embroidery in the shoulders, in the sleeves, and in the back as well.

Xaɪ, təən-du-ə-ni omolgɪča-čɪ-a-nɪ jək ǰuə moo,
indeed hem-DAT-OCM-3SG waist-DIR-OCM-3SG to.end two tree

ǰuə moo.
two tree

From the hem to the waist, two trees are embroidered (See Fig. 4 on page viii above).

Njoanɪ balǰɪ-xa-nɪ, xaɪ, sagǰɪ-l-sal-nɪ bi-či-ni

she	live-PST.P-3SG	indeed	elder.PL-PL-3SG	live-PST.P-3SG	
boa-wa	naɪ	čaa	aŋgo-oxan	təi	moo-do.
place-ACC	person	that.ACC	make-PST.IMPS.P	that	tree-DAT

The place where she had lived, and where her elders had lived was depicted through these trees.

Təi	moo	təxə-du-ə-ni,	xaɪ-boa-do-a-nɪ	njoanɪ
that	tree	base-DAT-OCM-3SG	what-place-DAT-OCM-3SG	she

bi-či-ni	osɪnɪ,	xurəən-səl-ku	boa-do-a-nɪ
live-PST.P-3SG	if	hill-PL-PROP	place-DAT-OCM-3SG

bi-či-ni	osɪ-ɪ-nɪ=tanɪɪ,	xurəən-səl-bə
live-PST.P-3SG	become-PRS.P-3SG=TOP	hill-PL-ACC

aŋgo-mɪ,	ulpi-uxən.
make-SIM	sew-PST.IMPS.P

If she lived in a mountainous area, mountains were embroidered under the trees.

Təi	xurəən-səl	ojaa-la-nɪ=tanɪɪ,	xaɪ,	xərə,	xaɪ,
that	hill-PL	surface-LOC-3SG=TOP	what	frog	what

goɪ	nuuči	kolaan-sal-ba	ulpi-məəri,	aŋgo-ɪ
other	small	insect-PL-ACC	sew-SIM.PL	make-PRS.P

bi-či-či	goanɪ.
be-PST.P-3PL	certainly

Above the mountains small animals like frogs and other small insects were embroidered.

Xaɪ,	moo	ojaa-la-nɪ,	moo	xorakta-nɪ=maa=tanɪɪ,
indeed	tree	surface-LOC-3SG	tree	bark-3SG=SML=TOP

xaɪ-wa,	muiki-səl-bə	ulpi-i	bi-či-či.
what-ACC	snake-PL-ACC	sew-PRS.P	be-PST.P-3PL

Snakes were embroidered on the tree like bark.

Xaɪ-do-a-nɪ=tanɪɪ, uilə=tənii, suuktu-ni ojaa-la-nɪ=tanɪɪ

what-DAT-OCM-3SG=TOP above=TOP branch-3SG surface-LOC-3SG=TOP

gormaxon-sal, nəktəkəən-səl, goɪ goɪ bəjun-səl.

rabbit-PL boar-PL various beast-PL

On the branch of the tree, there are a hare, a boar or other animals.

Čuu uwui suuktu-du-ə-ni=tənii nuučiku

most upper branch-DAT-OCM-3SG=TOP little

niəčəə-kəən-səl ulpiu... ulpi-uri bi-či-ni.

bird-DIM-PL sew sew-PRS.IMPS.P be-PST.P-3SG

Little birds had to be embroidered on the top of the branches.

Təi niəčəə-kəən-səl=tənii, təi pik... xaɪ, gɪamata,

that bird-DIM-PL=TOP that child indeed bride

əǰi-gu-ji baa-pɪ, totapɪ piktə-gu-ji

husband-DSG-REFL take-COND.IMPS then child-DSG-REFL

baa-go-a-nɪ.

get-PURP-OCM-3SG

Those birds were embroidered, that the bride may have a baby if she got married.

Gəə, təi piktə-səl-bə, əmutuu niəčəə-kəən=məə, tui

well that child-PL-ACC as.if bird-DIM=SML so

aŋgo-ɪ bi-či-či goanɪ, ulpi-i

make-PRS.P be-PST.P-3PL certainly sew-PRS.P

bi-či-či goanɪ čadu, təi moo ojaa-la-nɪ.

be-PST.P-3PL certainly there that tree surface-LOC-3SG

They saw children as birds. So they embroidered them on the branch.

Gəə, təi moo=tanɪɪ əmutuu təi əktə-kəən balǰɪ-xa-nɪ,

well that tree=TOP as.if that female-DIM live-PST.P-3SG

bi-či-ni, ǰuləsi bi-gi… bi-gilə-i-ni ǰuulgəəni
be-PST.P-3SG forward live… live-OBLG-PRS.P-3SG fate.3SG

— xəm čawa gusərə-i. Xəm čawa gusərə-i.
all that.ACC tell-PRS.P all that.ACC tell-PRS.P

The trees tell people all about the bride, things like the way of past and future life of the bride, the destiny that would unfold for her, and so on.

Təi moo ujələ-ni=tənii, darama-nɪ bado-do-a-nɪ,
that tree over-3SG=TOP back-3SG opposite.side-DAT-OCM-3SG

xaɪ, ɪlaan iduǰi aŋgo-oxan uwui boa.
indeed three in.turn make-PST.IMPS.P upper place

On the back side, over the trees, the three Worlds were embroidered in order.

Čadu əndur-səl balǰɪ-ɪ-nɪ boa. Dolɪn boa:
there god-PL live-PRS.P-3SG place middle place

naɪ-sal, bəjun-səl bi-i-či, xaɪ, xurəən-səl,
person-PL beast-PL live-PRS.P-3PL what hill-PL

naa-sal bi-i-či. Guči=tənii pəgui boa.
land-PL be-PRS.P-3PL again=TOP lower place

Pəgui boa.
lower place

The gods live in the Upper World. In the Middle World, there are people and animals, as well as mountains, and the ground. And there is also the Lower World.

Na… Naa pəgiə-lə-ni, xaɪ, namo-sal, maŋbo-sal,
land land bottom-LOC-3SG what sea-PL river-PL

xəwəən-səl pəgiə-ni.
lake-PL under-3SG

Under the ground, there are seas, rivers, lakes and so on.

Guči=tənii təi pəgiə-lə-ni, təi
again=TOP that bottom-LOC-3SG that

ǰakpa-do-a-nɪ=tanɪɪ — buni, buni.
around-DAT-OCM-3SG=TOP underworld underworld

And beneath that, there is the Lower World.

Bui-kin gurun čadu xəm bi-i-či goanɪ, čadu.
die-PST.P people there all be-PRS.P-3PL certainly there

All the dead people are there.

Gəə, čawa aŋgo-maarɪ, ulpi-i bi-či-či goanɪ.
well that.ACC make-SIM.PL sew-PRS.P be-PST.P-3PL certainly

Well, they embroidered those things in.

Təi gɪamata tətuə-ni təŋ uləən-ǰi ɪlga-ko,
that bride clothes-3SG very good-INS pattern-PROP

uləən-ǰi ɪlga-la-oxan, ulpi-čə-ni=dəə təŋ gučkuli.
good-INS pattern-VBZ-PST.IMPS.P sew-PASS-3SG=ADD very beautiful

The wedding robe is well-patterned, well-embroidered, and sewn up beautifully.

Gɪamata tətuə-wə-ni tətu-wəən-dii.
bride clothes-ACC-3SG dress-CAUS-PRS.P

The bride is dressed in this wedding gown.

Təi gɪamata tətuə-ni ojaa-la-nɪ=tanɪɪ poaldoanɪ
that bride clothes-3SG surface-LOC-3SG=TOP sometimes

naɪ amɪrɪ-a tətu-wəən-dii bi-či-ni.
person fish.skin.robe-ACC dress-CAUS-PRS.P be-PST.P-3SG

And at times, they put a fish skin dress on her, over the wedding gown.

Tui tamaarı	təi	amırı-wa=daa	poanı	gərbiə-si-i
therefore	that	robe-ACC=ADD	some	call-DUR-PRS.P

bi-či-ni,	gıamata	tətuə-ni=əm=dəə.
be-PST.P-3SG	bride	clothes-3SG=REPO=ADD

Some people called that fish skin dress the wedding gown.

Təi	amırı-wa	sogbo-ǰı	aŋgo-orı.
that	robe-ACC	fish.skin-INS	make-PRS.IMPS.P

Those clothes are made with fish skin.

Nəə	sogbo-ǰı	aŋgo-orı	bi-či-ni.
certainly	fish.skin-INS	make-PRS.IMPS.P	be-PST.P-3SG

They were definitely made with fish skin.

Təi=dəə,	əmutuu	gıamata	tətuə-ni=maa,	uwui
that=ADD	as.if	bride	clothes-3SG=SML	upper

boa-wa,	dolın	boa-wa,	pəgui	boa-wa,
place-ACC	half	place-ACC	lower	place-ACC

ılga-la-maarı,	naı	ičuən-dii	bi-či-či	goanı.
pattern-VBZ-SIM.PL	person	show-PRS.P	be-PST.P-3PL	certainly

Those were also embroidered on the upper, middle, and lower parts to be shown to other people.

Xa,[7]	darama-do-a-nı	xəm	ılga-ko.
indeed	back-DAT-OCM-3SG	all	pattern-PROP

There were patterns all over the back as well.

Xaı-ǰı,	ulpi-čə-ni=dəə	xəm	ılga-ǰı
what-INS	sew-PASS-3SG=ADD	all	embroidery-INS

dası-oxan.

---

7) A colloquial form of *xaı*.

cover.up-PST.IMPS.P

The sewn areas were also all covered with embroidery.

Təi amırı təŋ maŋga aŋgo-orı sogbo-ǰı.
that robe very hard make-PRS.IMPS.P fish.skin-INS

The *amiri* (fish skin gown) is made very elaborately.

Sogbo-a goıda-mı uji-uri, uləən-ǰi
fish.skin-ACC last.long-SIM process-PRS.IMPS.P good-INS
uji-uri, nəmi-kuukəən osı-ı goanı.
process-PRS.IMPS.P thin-EXTR become-PRS.P certainly

They process fish skin extremely thinly for a long time.

Totapı=maa tətuə-wə aŋgo-orı.
then=CON clothes-ACC make-PRS.IMPS.P

After that, they make the clothes.

Təi boso-ǰı, səurə-ǰi aŋgo-oxan, kupən-ǰi
that cloth-INS silk-INS make-PST.IMPS.P thread-INS
ulpi-uxən gıamata tətuə-wə-ni=tənii, tui
sew-PST.IMPS.P bride clothes-ACC-3SG=TOP so
gıamata-la-raa, tui nəəku-i-ni goanı čado,
wedding-VBZ-ANT so put-PRS.P-3SG certainly there
guisə-du, təi tətuə-wə.
box-DAT that clothes-ACC

After the wedding, the wedding gown that was made with fabric and silk and sewn with thread is kept in wardrobe.

Amırı-jı=tanıı tul tul təčičə-i.
robe-REFL=TOP always wear-PRS.P

They always put on an *amiri*, a fish skin gown.

Moo-lsɪ-ɪ-do-jɪ	tətu-i,
gather.firewood-HAB-PRS.P-DAT-REFL	wear-PRS.P

tuə	xədun-du	tətu-i.
winter	wind-DAT	wear-PRS.P

They put on *amiri* when gathering firewood and on a windy day as well.

Xaɪ,	xədun	xədun-dii=dəə,	xas,	čaa	luktu
indeed	wind	blow-PRS.P=ADD	again	that.ACC	totally

xədun-dəsi-ni	goanɪ.	Njama.
blow-NEG.PRS.P-3SG	certainly	warm

Even when the wind blows, it blocks the wind completely. It's warm.

Totamɪ	təi	amɪrɪ-wa	əktə,	xoonɪ=a	bi-i	osɪnɪ,
therefore	that	robe-ACC	female	how=MIR	be-PRS.P	if

aɪŋanɪ	taon-do-a-nɪ	tuə	taon-do-a-nɪ	təčičə-i.
year	every-DAT-OCM-3SG	winter	every-DAT-OCM-3SG	wear-PRS.P

Therefore what women did was put on an *amiri* every winter.

ǰoa=tanɪɪ	aso	əgǰi	modan
summer=TOP	so.much	many	time

tətu-wəsi-ni	goanɪ:	pəku.
wear-NEG.PRS.IMPS.P-3SG	certainly	hot

In the summer, they rarely put it on because it is hot.

Totapɪ=tanɪɪ,	tugdə-i	osɪnɪ=tanɪɪ,	sogbo
then=TOP	rain-PRS.P	if=TOP	fish.skin

čakpa-ɪ-nɪ	goanɪ.
soak-PRS.P-3SG	certainly

When it rains, the fish skin get wet.

Čakpa…	čakpa-pɪ=tanɪɪ,	xəm	tui	tata-go-ɪ.
soak	soak-COND.IMPS=TOP	all	so	pull-REV-PRS.P

Guči	uju-gu-uri-ə	gələ-i.
again	process-REV-PRS.IMPS.P-ACC	need-PRS.P

When got wet, it shrinks. And it has to be processed again.

Ilga	xəm	bojaa-rɪɪ.	Totamaarɪ	tugdə-du
embroidery	all	break-PRS.P	therefore	rain-DAT

təčičə-əsi	bi-či-ni	goanɪ.	Tui=dəə.
wear-NEG.PRS.P	be-PST.P-3SG	certainly	so=ADD

All the embroidery also became twisted. That was why they didn't put on *amiri* when it rained. That's how it is.

Gəə,	čaa	xəm	tətu-pi,	guči=tənii	xoɪpon,
well	that.ACC	all	wear-COND.IMPS	again=TOP	earring

sidəri,	xonjakaan-sal	— xəm	ək…	əktə	təi,
bracelet	ring-PL	all	female	female	that

xaɪ-do,	gɪamata-du	tətu-gu-wəən-dii.
what-DAT	bride-DAT	wear-ITER-CAUS-PRS.P

After she is all dressed, she puts on her earrings, bracelets, and rings. The bride is dressed up in all of these.

Nuktə-wə-ni=dəə	sili-gu-i.
hair-ACC-3SG=ADD	braid-ITER-PRS.P

Her hair is braided.

ǰuə	xaɪ-do…	sili-čə-ǰi	sili…	sili-gu-rəə,
two	what-DAT	braid-PASS-INS	braid	braid-ITER-ANT

ǰɪlɪ-wa-nɪ	kəəndəli	nəə-rəə,	uiptəŋgi-wə-ni=tənii
head-ACC-3SG	around	set-ANT	upwards-ACC-3SG=TOP

əusi,	sɪanɪ	čɪa-la-nɪ	tui	nuktə-ǰi-ə-ni	gəsə
this.way	ear.3SG	behind-LOC-3SG	so	hair-INS-OCM-3SG	together

tugbugu-i.
put.down-PRS.P

Her hair is braided into two parts, and this hair is wrapped around and raised. Then it is made to fall behind the ears.

Čaa	gərbiə-si-i	bi-či-či	goanı,	təi	tui
that.ACC	call-DUR-PRS.P	be-PST.P-3PL	certainly	that	so

sili-či-uri-ə,	gıamata	sili-čə-wə-ni,
braid-FR-PRS.IMPS.P-ACC	bride	braid-PASS-ACC-3SG

«tugbugu-uri...	tugbugu-uri	sili-čə=m=dəə»,
put.down-PRS.IMPS.P	put.down-PRS.IMPS.P	braid-PASS=REPO=ADD

«gıamata	sili-čə-ni».
bride	braid-PASS-3SG

The type of braid that the bride wears is called “drop braiding”, or “bridal braiding”.

Vot.	Tui	bi-či-ni	goanı.	Guči	aapon-ko.
R. well	so	be-PST.P-3SG	certainly	again	hat-PROP

OK. It was done like that. And she wears a hat.

Guči=tənii	gıamata...	gıamata,	ǰoog-ǰıaǰı-jı
again=TOP	bride	bride	house-ABL-REFL

niə-rii-du-ji,	ǰuulin-či=dəə	kəčəri-əsi=ə,
exit-PRS.P-DAT-REFL	*Juulin*-DIR=ADD	turn-NEG.PRS.P=MIR

ǰuulin-či=dəə	un-dəsi=ə,	mimbiə
Juulin-DIR=ADD	say-NEG.PRS.P=MIR	I.ACC

bələči-ruu=əm=dəə.
help-2SG.IMP=REPO=ADD

And when the bride leaves home, she does not turn herself to *Juulin*,[8] nor does she say “help me” either (See Fig. 11 on page xii above).

---

8) A human figured God who keeps house and family safe.

Un-dəsi.	Njoanı	mənə	xala-ǰıaǰı-jı	goı
say-NEG.PRS.P	she	oneself	tribe-ABL-REFL	other

xala-čı	ii-rii-ni.
tribe-DIR	enter-PRS.P-3SG

She does not say anything. She is leaving her clan and joining another clan.

Goı	xala-čı	ənə-i-ni.	Totamı	ǰuulin
other	tribe-DIR	go-PRS.P-3SG	therefore	*Juulin*

njoaŋgı-nı	osı-ası-nı.
hers-3SG	become-NEG.PRS.P-3SG

She goes to the other clan. Therefore the *Juulin* does not belong to her anymore.

Njoambanı=daa	bələči-əsi=ə	təi	ǰuulin.
she.ACC=ADD	help-NEG.PRS.P=MIR	that	*Juulin*

The *Juulin* does not help her.

Totamı	njoanı	təi	ǰuulin-či=dəə	xaı-wa=daa
therefore	she	that	*Juulin*-DIR=ADD	what-ACC=ADD

un-dədəəsi=ə.
say-NEG.PRS.P=MIR

Therefore she does not say anything to the *Juulin*.

Totapı=tanıı,	xaı,	niə-rii-du-ji,	niə-rii…
Then=TOP	indeed	exit-PRS.P-DAT-REFL	exit-PRS.P

niə-rii	ǰuliə-lə-ni,	ǰuə	ənjuə-wə	nəə-rii-či	goanı
exit-PRS.P	front-LOC-3SG	two	pot-ACC	put-PRS.P-3PL	certainly

kəndərxiən	dookıa-la-nı,	kəndərxiən	boakıa-la-nı.
threshold	inner-LOC-3SG	threshold	outdoor-LOC-3SG

And before leaving, two pots are placed, one inside of the threshold and another outside of the threshold.

Əm…	Təi	dookɪa-la-nɪ	bi-i	ənini	ənjuə-ni.
one	that	inner-LOC-3SG	be-PRS.P	mother.3SG	pot-3SG

The one inside is the mother's.

Kəndərxiən	boakɪa-la-nɪ	bi-i=tənii	aojan
threshold	outdoor-LOC-3SG	be-PRS.P=TOP	groom
əninəə-ni	ənjuə-ni.		
mothers-3SG	pot-3SG		

The pot placed outside the threshold is the groom's mother's.

Təi	njoančɪ	torɪ-do	olbɪn-kɪ-čɪ	əi-du
that	they	bridewealth-DAT	bring-PST.P-3PL	this-DAT
buu-gu-əri.				
give-REV-REFL.PL				

That is what was brought over as a "bridewealth".

Gəə,	təi	ənjuə-či	gɪraan-borɪ.
OK	that	pot-DIR	tread-PRS.IMPS.P

And she is made to tread on the pot.

Ənjuə-či	ʊʊ-worɪ=am,	un-dii	bi-či-či
pot-DIR	board-PRS.IMPS.P=REPO	say-PRS.P	be-PST.P-3PL
goanɪ	balana.		
certainly	long.ago		

In the past, this was called "Climbing on the pot".

Xaɪgoarɪ	čaa	nəə-rii-či?
why	that.ACC	put-PRS.P-3PL

Why do they placed it there?

Kəndərxiən-du…	xaɪ-du…	xuəl
threshold-DAT	what-DAT	across

taktoola-ɪ-do-jɪ=tanɪɪ,	ǰulə	doo-la	bi-i
step.on-PRS.P-DAT-REFL=TOP	front	inside-LOC	be-PRS.P

ənjuə-či	taktoola-ɪ	əm	bəgǰi-ǰi-ji.
pot-DIR	step.on-PRS.P	one	leg-INS-REFL

When stepping over the threshold, the bride steps into the pot inside the threshold with one foot.

Totapɪ=tanɪɪ	goɪ	bəgǰi-ǰi-ji=tənii	kəndərxiən-bə
then=TOP	other	leg-INS-REFL=TOP	threshold-ACC

xuəl.
across

With the other foot, she crosses the threshold.

Tui	ta-raa,	boakɪa-la	bi-i	ənjuə-či	taktoola-ɪ.
so	do-ANT	outdoor-LOC	be-PRS.P	pot-DIR	step.on-PRS.P

Totapɪ=maat	naa-čɪ	taktoola-go-ɪ.
then=CON	land-DIR	step.on-REV-PRS.P

Then she steps into the pot outside. After that, she steps on the ground.

Gəə,	tui	taktoola-ɪ-do-a-nɪ	ənjuə
well	so	step.on-PRS.P-DAT-OCM-3SG	pot

xaɪ-rasɪ...	tuiŋku-əsi	osɪnɪ,	təi
do.what-NEG.PRS.P	quake-NEG.PRS.P	if	that

gɪamata	ǰul...	ǰuulgəən-ji	uləən	osɪ-ɪ.
bride	fate	fate-REFL	good.INS	become-PRS.P

If she steps into the pot, and it does not shake, the bride will have good fate.

Kəsi-ku	balǰɪ-ɪ	təi	əktə.
happiness-PROP	live-PRS.P	that	female

The bride will live a happy life.

Təi əŋjuə njaŋgaa tuiŋku-xə-ni osını,
that pot a.little quake-PST.P-3SG if

bi-gilə-i-ni, təi əktə bi-gilə-i-ni aso
live-OBLG-PRS.P-3SG that female live-OBLG-PRS.P-3SG so.much

uləən osi-asi.
good.INS become-NEG.PRS.P

If the pot shook a little, the fate of the bride will not be good.

Masι-ǰι tuiŋku-i-ni osını, bi-gilə-i-ni təŋ
strong-INS quake-PRS.P-3SG if live-OBLG-PRS.P-3SG very

čukin.
bad

If it shakes a lot, the life she should live will be very bad.

Gəə, ǰuulgəən-bə-ni saa-go-arı, təi čaa
well fate-ACC-3SG know-PURP-REFL.PL that that.ACC

tui ta-ı-čı goanı.
so do-PRS.P-3PL certainly

This is done in this way to foresee the fate of the bride.

Gučı=tənii mii=tənii oŋbo-xan-bı gusərə-gu-i.
again=TOP I=TOP forget-PST.P-1SG tell-ITER-PRS.P

One more thing, I'll tell the story that I forgot to tell.

Təi ənə-i ǰuliə-lə-ni xaı-du... dəgbəliku-du
that go-PRS.P front-LOC-3SG what-DAT opening-DAT

xaı... ənin-či-ji... ənin-či-ji mıxoraan-dıı,
what mother-DIR-REFL mother-DIR-REFL bow-PRS.P

amın-čı-jı mıxoraan-dıı.
father-DIR-REFL bow-PRS.P

Before leaving, during *degbeliku* (uncorking), the bride bows to her mother and father.

Xaɪ-wa...	koči-kaan-do	arakɪ-a	nəə-rəə=tənii,
what-ACC	wineglass-DIM-DAT	alcoholic.drink-ACC	put-ANT=TOP

xaɪ-rɪɪ	xaɪ-wa...	ǰoo	doo-wa-nɪ	čəktəri-i.
do.what-PRS.P	what-ACC	house	inside-ACC-3SG	scatter-PRS.P

After pouring vodka into a glass, she sprinkles here and there inside the home.

Totapɪ=tanɪɪ	gərəən	gurun-bə	xəri-i.
then=TOP	people	people-ACC	treat-PRS.P

After that, she entertains several guests.

Gəə,	təi	niə-rii	ǰuliə-lə-ni=dəə	tui	xəm
OK,	that	exit-PRS.P	front-LOC-3SG=ADD	so	all

ta-ɪ-nɪ	goanɪ	təi	əktə.
do-PRS.P-3SG	certainly	that	female

Before leaving, the bride carries all of that out.

Čado=tanɪɪ,	ənin-či-ji,	amɪn-čɪ-jɪ
then=TOP	mother-DIR-REFL	father-DIR-REFL

mɪxoraan-dɪɪ-do-jɪ=tanɪɪ,	kəsi-ə	gələ-i-ni	goanɪ:
bow-PRS.P-DAT-REFL=TOP	luck-ACC	need-PRS.P-3SG	certainly

When she bows to her parents, she asks for their blessings.

— Bələči-usu,	mii,	xaŋgɪsɪ	ənə-i=dəə,	mii
help-2PL.IMP	I	away	go-PRS.P=ADD	I

xaɪs	suə	piktə-su,	suə	piktə-su.
again	you.PL	child-2PL	you.PL	child-2PL

“Help me please. Though I am going far away, I am still your daughter.

Mimbiwə	bələči-usu,	bələči-usu.	Əǰi	oŋbo-a-so.
I.ACC	help-2PL.IMP	help-2PL.IMP	not	forget-INF-2PL

Tui	un-dii-ni.
so	say-PRS.P-3SG

Help me please. Don't forget me." She says things like this.

Ənini	soŋgo-ɪ-nɪ	goanɪ=a	piktə-ji
mother.3SG	cry-PRS.P-3SG	certainly=MIR	child-REFL

ənu-i-du-ə-ni.	Tui=dəə.
go-PRS.P-DAT-OCM-3SG	so=ADD

The mother of the bride cries when the bride leaves. That's the way it goes.

Totamɪ=tanɪɪ,	təi	gɪamata	susuuči-i-du-əri,
therefore=TOP	that	bride	see.off-PRS.P-DAT-REFL.PL

əgǰi=ə	soŋgo-wasi=a,	un-dii	bi-či-ni	goanɪ.
many=MIR	cry-NEG.PRS.IMPS.P=MIR	say-PRS.P	be-PST.P-3SG	certainly

But it was said the mother should not cry so much when sending off the bride.

Xaɪ,	piktə,	təi	gɪamata=daa	ǰuulgəəni	orkɪn
indeed	child	that	bride=ADD	fate.3SG	bad

osɪ-ɪ=jam	soŋgo-orɪ-do.
become-PRS.P=REPO	cry-PRS.IMPS.P-DAT

It is said that if she cries, the fate of the bride will become bad.

Totamɪ	aso	əgǰi-ǰi	soŋgo-asɪ	bi-či-ni.
therefore	so.much	many-INS	cry-NEG.PRS.P	be-PST.P-3SG

Thus she did not cry much.

Gəə,	təi	gɪamata-wa=tanɪɪ,	susuuči-məəri,	xamɪala...
ok,	that	bride-ACC=TOP	see.off-SIM.PL	later

gɪamata=daa	aaŋgɪa	ŋaala-do-a-nɪ	tunjəpu-m
bride=ADD	right	hand-DAT-OCM-3SG	walk.with.stick-NMLZ.ACC

buu-rii	bi-či-či	goanı.	Tunjəpu-m.
give-PRS.P	be-PST.P-3PL	certainly	walk.with.stick-NMLZ.ACC

After that, when they sent off the daughter, a staff was put in her right hand.

Tunjəpu-m	buu-rii,	pokto-do-a-nı=tanıı,	waısı
walk.with.stick-NMLZ.ACC	give-PRS.P	way-DAT-OCM-3SG=TOP	to.the.shore

əu-rii-du-ə-ni=tənii,	ılgamo-ı	bi-či-či	goanı
descend-PRS.P-DAT-OCM-3SG=TOP	put-PRS.P	be-PST.P-3PL	certainly

əjə,	taja-la-nı	ılaan	ılaan	moo-wa.
here	there-LOC-3SG	three	three	bar-ACC

When she goes down the road to the riverside holding her staff, three sticks were made to stand here and there.

Təi	moo-sal	ujə	duə	duə-ni=tənii	saorı-a
that	bar-PL	top	end	end-3SG=TOP	wood.chip-ACC

xaı-rıı	bi-či-či	goanı.
do.what-PRS.P	be-PST.P-3PL	certainly

The top of those poles were decorated with wood chips (*saoris*).

Təi	daaı-ookaan-ǰı	saorı-oxan.
that	big-EXTR-INS	whittle-PST.IMPS.P

Those were whittled very thickly.

Təi=tənii	təi	moo	duə-ǰiəǰi-ə-ni	pəisi
that=TOP	that	bar	end-ABL-OCM-3SG	down

tuu-gu-i-ni.	Tui=dəə.
fall-REV-PRS.P-3SG	so=ADD

The wood chips at the end of those poles are draped down. This is how it was made.

Təi	ǰuə	mudən-či	paačɪ-la-oxan
that	two	riverbank-DIR	mallet-VBZ-PST.IMPS.P

tora-sal	tokon-do-a-nɪ=tanɪɪ	pokto	osɪ-ɪ-nɪ	goanɪ.
pillar-PL	middle-DAT-OCM-3SG=TOP	way	become-PRS.P-3SG	certainly

The way between the hammered sticks on both sides toward riverbank becomes the path.

Gəə,	təi	pokto-la	gɪamata,	tunjəpu-či-mi,
OK	that	way-LOC	bride	walk.with.stick-FR-SIM

waɪsɪ	ogda-čɪ	əu-rii-ni,	gɪla
to.the.shore	boat-DIR	descend-PRS.P-3SG	wedding.boat

baaroa-nɪ.
direction-3SG

The bride goes following the road while holding a staff, and goes down to the *gila*, the wedding boat.

Vot.	Xamɪa-la-nɪ=tanɪɪ	ɪlaan	əktə	njoambanɪ
R. well	back-LOC-3SG=TOP	three	female	she.ACC

daxala-ɪ-čɪ.	Tui=dəə.
follow-PRS.P-3PL	so=ADD

Behind the bride, three women follow her. That's the way it goes.

Totaraa	xəm	waɪsɪ	əu-xən.	Totapɪ-maarɪ
and.then	all	to.the.shore	descend-PST.P	therefore

təi	xaɪ-wa...	čuu	boŋgo-do	gɪamata-wa	njoanɪ
that	what-ACC	most	first-DAT	bride-ACC	she

gɪla-do-a-nɪ	jaotaan-do	təə-wəən-dii.
wedding.boat-DAT-OCM-3SG	awning-DAT	sit-CAUS-PRS.P

Finally everyone came down. Then after, the bride is seated under the awning of the *gila*.

Čawa	təə-wəən-p…	təə-wəən-pəəri=məət,	goɪ
that.ACC	sit-CAUS-	sit-CAUS-COND.PL.IMPS=CON	other

gurun	goɪ	ogda-do	təə-rii.
people	other	boat-DAT	sit-PRS.P

Only the bride is seated on the *gila*. After that, others get on the other boats.

Daxala-ɪ	gurun,	njoambanɪ	susuuči-gu-əri,	goɪ
follow-PRS.P	people	she.ACC	see.off-PURP-REFL.PL	other

ogda-do	təə-rii.
boat-DAT	sit-PRS.P

The bridesmaids who are seeing off the bride get on the other boats.

Miruə-wə-ni=tənii	goɪ	ogda-do	təuči-i.	Tui=dəə.
dowry-ACC-3SG=TOP	other	boat-DAT	load-PRS.P	so=ADD

The dowry is loaded on the other boat. This is how it is done.

Təi	gɪamata	ogda-wa-nɪ	taɪsɪ
that	bride	boat-ACC-3SG	from.shore

ana-go-ɪ-do-a[9]	(gəə-gə-gə,	təi	xaɪ)
push-REV-PRS.P-DAT-REFL.PL	OK-OK-OK,	that	what

gɪamata	ogda-do-a-nɪ	ǰakpon,	ǰoan ǰuər	gɪala…
bride	boat-DAT-OCM-3SG	eight	twelve	row

gɪolɪ-mǰɪ-sal	təə-rii	bi-či-ni.	Daaɪ	ogda.
row-AGT-PL	sit-PRS.P	be-PST.P-3SG	big	boat

When pushing away the *gila* from the riverside, eight to twelve rowers sat in the boat. It was a large boat.

Totamɪ	baɪ	tui	bi-i	ogda-do=tanɪɪ,	əmuni
therefore	ordinary	so	be-PRS.P	boat-DAT=TOP	one.person

9) A colloquial form of *ana-go-ɪ-do-arɪ*.

təə-si-mi,	tuɪ	gɪolɪ-ɪ-nɪ	goanɪ	ǰuər	gɪol-ǰɪ.
sit-DUR-SIM	so	row-PRS.P-3SG	certainly	two	oar-INS

In an ordinary boat, there is only one rower with a pair of oars.

Čado=tanɪɪ	ǰɪa	ǰɪa-arɪ	ǰakpa-do-arɪ
then=TOP	friend	friend-REFL.PL	next-DAT-REFL.PL

təəŋku-du	ǰuərni	təə-si-i.
saddle-DAT	two.persons	sit-DUR-PRS.P

In the *gila*, two men sit on the seat side by side.

Naɪ	taonɪ	əmun	əmun	gɪol.[10)]
person	every.3SG	one	one	oar

Each man with one oar.

Əm-ǰimə	əmǰiə	gɪol-ǰɪ,	əm-ǰimə...	goɪ-ǰɪma	goɪ
one-SEL	one	oar-INS	one-SEL	other-SEL	other

gɪol-ǰɪ	gɪolɪ-maarɪ,	gəə,	tui	daaɪ	gɪla-ǰɪ.
oar-INS	row-SIM.PL	OK,	so	big	wedding.boat-INS

The boat is so big that each rower sits on either side of it to row.

Gəə,	təi	gɪla-wa	ana-go-ɪ-do-arɪ,	kətən
OK	that	wedding.boat-ACC	push-REV-PRS.P-DAT-REFL.PL	stern

ǰakpa-do-a-nɪ	bi-i	səlxəən-du	topto-a	uju-i
next-DAT-OCM-3SG	be-PRS.P	crossbar-DAT	rope-ACC	tie-PRS.P

bi-či-či	goanɪ.
be-PST.P-3PL	certainly

When pushing the *gila*, they tied a rope to the crossbar near the stern of the boat.

---

10) A colloquial form of *gɪolko* 'one oared'.

Topto-a uju-rəə=tənii, tooɪ-do dərəǰi-i xusə
rope-ACC tie-ANT=TOP riverside-DAT stay-PRS.P male

gursəl təi gɪamata (əm xala gurun, xusə
people.PL that bride one tribe people male

gurun manja, mas... masɪ gursəl) təi topto
people only strong strong people.PL that rope

duə-wə-ni=tənii, tooɪ-do ɪlɪ-sɪ-maarɪ,
end-ACC-3SG=TOP riverside-DAT stand-DUR-SIM.PL

ǰapača-ɪ-čɪ goanɪ.
grab-PRS.P-3PL certainly

After binding it, the men on the riverside, all of whom are from the same clan as the bride, strong men, grab the end of the rope.

Gəə, təi gɪamata ənə-i-du-ə-ni=tənii, təi
OK that bride go-PRS.P-DAT-OCM-3SG=TOP that

gɪla tooɪ-ǰɪa muə baaroa-nɪ ana-go-ɪ.
wedding.boat riverside-side water direction-3SG push-REV-PRS.P

When the bride leaves, the people toward the riverside push the *gila* into the river.

Təi xusə, tooɪ-do bi-i xusə gursəl=tənii,
that male riverside-DAT be-PRS.P male people.PL=TOP

təi topto duə duə-ni ǰapača-maarɪ=tanɪɪ, təi
that rope end end-3SG hold-SIM.PL=TOP that

gɪamata-wa tui məənčiəri tui tata-go-ɪ-čɪ goanɪ.
bride-ACC so oneself.DIR.PL so pull-REV-PRS.P-3PL certainly

Tui tata-go-ɪ-čɪ.
so pull-REV-PRS.P-3PL

But the men on the riverside who are grasping the end of the rope pull the bride toward themselves.

Xaɪgoarɪ	tui	ta-ɪ-čɪ?
what.for	so	do-PRS.P-3PL

Why do they do that?

Baɪ,	ičuən-dii-či	goanɪ	naɪ-sal-ba	xəm=dəə:
only	show-PRS.P-3PL	certainly	person-PL-ACC	all=ADD
təi	buu-rii-či	əktə,	gɪamata-la-ɪ-čɪ	
that	give-PRS.P-3PL	female	wedding-VBZ-PRS.P-3PL	
əktə,	mɪawan-čɪ,	mɪawan	əktə,	njoančɪ
female	favorite-3PL	favorite	female	they
uləəsi-i-ni	əktə,	njoančɪ	aso	buu-ičə-əsi-či,
love-PRS.P-3SG	female	they	so.much	give-DES-NEG.PRS.P-3PL
kaɪran-dɪɪ-čɪ.				
pity-PRS.P-3PL				

This is just to show everyone that they do not really want to give her away, that they are torn about the girl being given away, getting married, the girl they like in their hearts, the girl they love.

Ənə-i-wə-ni,	gəə,	xoonɪ	ta-orɪ?
go-PRS.P-ACC-3SG	OK	how	do-PRS.IMPS.P

But what can they do when she leaves.

Gəə,	tui tamaarɪ	təi	ǰakpon,	ǰoan ǰuər	gɪolɪ-mǰɪ
OK	therefore	that	eight	twelve	tworow-AGT
masɪ-ǰɪ	gɪolɪ-ɪ-čɪ	osɪnɪ=tanɪɪ,	təi	topto-a	
strong-INS	row-PRS.P-3PL	if=TOP	that	rope-ACC	
ŋaala-la-čɪ	lopto,	tui	xaɪ-maarɪ,	tui	
hand-LOC-3PL	right.away	so	do.what-SIM.PL	so	
ana-ɪ-čɪ	goanɪ.				
push-PRS.P-3PL	certainly				

When the eight or twelve rowers row the boat with all their

might, only then do they release the rope in their hands.

Təi, xaɪ, ogda muə-du...
that indeed boat water-DAT

muə-du gɪolɪ-maarɪ ənə-i-či goanɪ.
water-DAT row-SIM.PL go-PRS.P-3PL certainly

Sitting on the boat, they go by rowing on the water.

Tokon-čɪ ənə-i təi, maŋbo tokon-čɪ-a-nɪ.
middle-DIR go-PRS.P that river middle-DIR-OCM-3SG

They go to the middle of the river.

Gəə, təi, xaɪ, gɪla xamɪa-la-nɪ=tanɪɪ goɪ
OK that indeed wedding.boat back-LOC-3SG=TOP other

ogda-sal xəm, tui gɪolɪ-maarɪ, ənə-i-či goanɪ.
boat-PL all so row-SIM.PL go-PRS.P-3PL certainly

Behind the *gila*, the other boats follow by rowing.

Gəə, tui ərdəŋgə-ǰi tui xaɪ-rɪɪ-čɪ,
OK so interesting-INS so do.what-PRS.P-3PL

gɪamata-la-ɪ-čɪ.
wedding-VBZ-PRS.P-3PL

The wedding is conducted in such an interesting way.

Gɪamata ɪra-ɪ-čɪ. Ira-ɪ-čɪ.
bride carry-PRS.P-3PL carry-PRS.P-3PL

The bride is taken away.

Gɪamata ɪra-ɪ-do-a-čɪ, aojan=daa ǰi-dəsi.
bride carry-PRS.P-DAT-OCM-3PL groom=ADD come-NEG.PRS.P

When they take bride, the groom himself does not come.

Mii	un-ki-mi	čaa.
I	say-PST.P-1SG	that.ACC

I said that a little while ago.

Aojan	amını,	ənini=dəə	ǰi-dəsi.
groom	father.3SG	mother.3SG=ADD	come-NEG.PRS.P

The father and mother of the groom do not come either.

Təəm	njoanı	xaı-nı,	əksəni,	gusini,
only	he	what-3SG	uncle.3SG	maternal.uncle.3SG

əukən-səl-ni,	dada-sal-nı,	gıamata	ŋaanı-maarı,
sister.in.law-PL-3SG	aunt-PL-3SG	bride	go.to.take-SIM.PL

ǰi-dii-či	goanı.
come-PRS.P-3PL	certainly

Uncles, maternal uncles, sisters-in-law, and maternal aunts of the groom come to take the bride.

Gəə-gə-gə.	Guči=tənii,	gıamata	ǰoog-ǰıaǰı-jı
OK-OK-OK	again=TOP	bride	house-ABL-REFL

niə-rii-du-ə-ni,	ənini	gıamata-du	buu-rii-ni
exit-PRS.P DAT OCM 3SG	mother.3SG	bride-DAT	give-PRS.P-3SG

čiun-bə,	borakta-wa,	silčuksə-wə	buu-rii-ni.
flint-ACC	firestone-ACC	phosphorus-ACC	give-PRS.P-3SG

Also, when the bride leaves home, the mother of the bride gives her flint, firestone, and phosphorus.

Gıamata,	naı	ǰoog-čı-a-nı	ənə-pi,	goı	gurun
bride	person	house-DIR-OCM-3SG	go-COND.IMPS	other	people

ǰoog-čı-a-nı	ənə-pi,	məən	tawa-ku
house-DIR-OCM-3SG	go-COND.IMPS	oneself	fire-PROP

osı-go-a-nı.	Məən	tawa-ku	osı-go-a-nı.
become-PURP-OCM-3SG	oneself	fire-PROP	become-PURP-OCM-3SG

The reason is that when the bride goes to the other's home, she can be someone with her own fire.

Gəə, njoanı məən xaǰon-ko, məən tawa-ku.
OK she oneself stuff-PROP oneself fire-PROP

Her own possession, her own fire.

Tawa — təŋ uləən ǰaka. Tawa anaa ui=dəə
fire very good thing fire without who=ADD

balǰı-asɪ.
live-NEG.PRS.P

Fire is very important. Without fire one cannot make a living.

Tui ta-mɪ nəə tawa goanɪ buu-rii. Čawa
so do-SIM certainly fire certainly give-PRS.P that.ACC

xəm=dəə.
all=ADD

That is why she makes sure to give her daughter all those things for making fires.

Gəə, tui ɪra-ɪ-čɪ goanɪ. Goro-čɪ ənə-i
OK so carry-PRS.P-3PL certainly distant.place-DIR go-PRS.P

osɪnɪ, goɪ… goɪ ɪxon-do, goro-laa bi-i
if other other village-DAT far-SUFF be-PRS.P

ɪxon-do ənə-i osɪnɪ, aoŋga-maarɪ ənə-i.
village-DAT go-PRS.P if spend.night-SIM.PL go-PRS.P

Əm aon, ǰuə aon.
one day two day

Like that, she is taken away. If they must go to somewhat far place, to a faraway village, they stay at the other villages on the way, one or two nights.

Gəə,	Naɪxɪn-ǰɪaǰɪ	Kondon-čɪ	ɪra-ɪ	osɪnɪ,	xaɪ,
OK	Naikhin-ABL	Kondon-DIR	carry-PRS.P	if	indeed

ǰuər	ɪlaan	modan	aoŋga-čɪ-maarɪ,	ənə-i.
two	three	time	spend.night-FR-SIM.PL	go-PRS.P

If they go from Naikhin to Kondon, they stay two or three nights.

Vot.	Xaɪ,	poaldoanɪ=tanɪɪ	əm	ɪxon-do=maa,	əm
R. well	indeed	sometimes=TOP	one	village-DAT=SML	one

ɪxon-do	bi-i,	balǰɪ-ɪ	gurun,	əi-du	gɪamata,
village-DAT	be-PRS.P	live-PRS.P	people	this-DAT	bride

əi-du=tənii	aojan	bi-i.
this-DAT=TOP	groom	be-PRS.P

Sometimes there are cases in which the bride and the groom live in the same village.

Xas	maŋbo-čɪ	tui	čɪsa-ɪ.	Tui	čɪsa-raa=tanɪɪ,
again	river-DIR	so	sail-PRS.P	so	sail-ANT=TOP

aojan	toorɪ-la-nɪ	xaa-rɪɪ.
groom	riverside-LOC-3SG	go.ashore-PRS.P

Even in this case the bride goes by boat. She goes to the groom's riverside by boat.

Tui tamaarɪ	ənə-i.	ǰɪǰa	bi-mi=u,	goro	bi-mi=u
therefore	go-PRS.P	near	be-SIM=CONC	distant	be-SIM=CONC

ənə-i-či.
go-PRS.P-3PL

She goes like that regardless of the distance.

Ələə	ɪsɪ-ɪ-do-arɪ,	toorɪ-čɪ	xaa-rɪɪ,
soon	arrive-PRS.P-DAT-REFL.PL	riverside-DIR	go.ashore-PRS.P

toorɪ-čɪ.

riverside-DIR

They will arrive at the riverside shortly.

Tooɪ-čɪ xaa-raa=tanɪɪ, tawa ɪwan-dɪɪ-čɪ goanɪ.
riverside-DIR go.ashore-ANT=TOP fire kindle-PRS.P-3PL certainly

After landing at the riverside near to groom's, they start a fire.

Gəə, tawa ɪwan-daa=tanɪɪ, tajaǰɪ=tanɪɪ mučuun-bə,
OK, fire kindle-ANT=TOP opposite.side=TOP charcoal-ACC

ǰəgdə-i mučuun-bə ǰapa-raa (gɪamata
burn-PRS.P charcoal-ACC take-ANT bride

gɪla-do-a-nɪ sələ-mə xaɪ… sɪlɪa=maa
wedding.boat-DAT-OCM-3SG made.with.iron what plate=SML

bi-i alɪo bi-i-ni goanɪ), gəə, təi altama…
be-PRS.P tableware be-PRS.P-3SG certainly OK, that basin

xaɪ… sələ-mə altama-čɪ təi mučuun-bə nəə-rəə,
what made.with.iron basin-DIR that charcoal-ACC put-ANT

totapɪ guči ana-go-ɪ ogda-warɪ.
then again push-REV-PRS.P boat-REFL.PL

Taking the firebrand left-over from the burning, they bring it to the bride's boat and put it in the metal bowl (There is a plate-like metal bowl in the bride's boat.), and afterwards they push the boat out again.

Totapɪ… tota… totapɪ=maat aojan-barɪ tooɪ-la-nɪ
then do.so then=CON groom-REFL.PL riverside-LOC-3SG

xaa-rɪɪ.
go.ashore-PRS.P

Only after doing that do they land on the groom's riverside.

Gəə, xaɪgoarɪ təi mučuun-bə olbɪn-dɪɪ-čɪ?
OK what.for that charcoal-ACC bring-PRS.P-3PL

Təi=dəə əmutuu.
that=ADD as.if

Well, why do they bring the firebrand like that?

Gıamata məən tawa-jı aojan-bı ǰoog-do-a-nı
bride oneself fire-REFL groom-REFL house-DAT-OCM-3SG

bi-i tawa-čı, ısı-raa, nəə-rii-ni, xaı... golǰon-do
be-PRS.P fire-DIR arrive-ANT put-PRS.P-3SG what stove-DAT

nəə-rii-ni.
put-PRS.P-3SG

She brings her fire to the fire in the groom's home and puts it into the furnace.

Njoanı əsi təi tawa-ǰı gəsə njoančı aojanı
she now that fire-INS together they groom.3SG

xala-čı-a-nı ii-rii-ni. Tui=dəə.
tribe-DIR-OCM-3SG enter-PRS.P-3SG so=ADD

With that fire, the bride joins the groom's clan. That's the way it goes.

Guči=tənii, təi gıamata ıra ı do-arı-tanıı,
again=TOP that bride carry-PRS.P-DAT-REFL.PL=TOP

balana ləkəə-či-i bi-či-či goanı. Əsi=tənii,
long.ago arrow-VBZ-PRS.P be-PST.P-3PL certainly now=TOP

əsi=ə undəə, əi səəgǰən gıanı
now=MIR regarding this red rule.3SG

osı-očıa-nı=a=tanıı, xaı-ǰı... mıočaačı-ı
become-COND-3SG=MIR=TOP what-INS gun.VBZ-PRS.P

bi-či-či goanı.
be-PST.P-3PL certainly

And when they brought the bride, in the past, they shot arrows. Now, after the Soviet Era, they shot guns.

Kətən-ǰiəǰi xamasɪ. Kətən-ǰiəǰi xamasɪ mɪočaačɪ-ɪ
stern-ABL backward stern-ABL backward gun.VBZ-PRS.P

bi-či-či goanɪ.
be-PST.P-3PL certainly

From the back of the boat, out the back. From the stern of the boat, they shot guns out the back.

Daaɪ gurun-səl tui un-dii bi-či-či goanɪ:
large people-PL so say-PRS.P be-PST.P-3PL certainly

The elders said as follows:

— Gɪamata ənə-i-wə-ni ambaan-sal xəm
bride go-PRS.P-ACC-3SG ghost-PL all

doolǰɪ-ɪ=jam, xəm saa-rɪɪ=jam=daa.
hear-PRS.P=REPO all know-PRS.P=REPO=ADD

"Evil spirits hear and know the fact that the bride is leaving home.

Njoambačɪ xasɪsɪ-ɪ təi ambaan-sal.
they.ACC chase-PRS.P that ghost-PL

Evil spirits chase them.

Gəə, tui ənə-i-du-ə-či=ə, ɪsɪ-očɪa-čɪ=a=daa,
OK so go-PRS.P-DAT-OCM-3PL=MIR arrive-COND-3PL=MIR=ADD

təi əktə bi-i-wə-ni orkin osɪ-waan-dɪɪ=daa,
that female live-PRS.P-ACC-3SG bad become-CAUS-PRS.P=ADD

saawaasɪ, ənusi-wəən-dii=dəə, saawaasɪ.
maybe illness.VBZ-CAUS-PRS.P=ADD maybe

If the evil spirits reach them, the evil spirits may make the bride's life bad, or make her sick."

Totamaarɪ təi xaɪ-wa… ambaan-sal-ba… ambaan-sal-ba

therefore that what-ACC ghost-PL-ACC ghost-PL-ACC

ŋəəluu-či-məəri,	ləkəə-či-i,	mɪočaačɪ-ɪ	ta-xa-čɪ
frighten-FR-SIM.PL	arrow-VBZ-PRS.P	gun.VBZ-PRS.P	do-PST.P-3PL

goanɪ.
certainly

Therefore they shot arrows and guns to scare the evil spirits.

Gəə,	təi=dəə	tul tul	tui	bi-či-ni	goanɪ,	gəə.
OK,	that=ADD	always	so	be-PST.P-3SG	certainly	OK.

This was always so.

Xaɪ-wa…	aojan-bɪ	tooɪ-wa-nɪ	ɪsɪ-paarɪ,
what-ACC	groom-REFL	riverside-ACC-3SG	arrive-COND.PL.IMPS

xaa-rɪɪ.
go.ashore-PRS.P

Arriving at the groom's riverside, they land.

Xaa-rɪɪ-do-a-čɪ=tanɪɪ,	aojan,	njoanɪ	ənini,
go.ashore-PRS.P-DAT-OCM-3PL=TOP	groom	he	mother.3SG

amɪnɪ,	əkəsəl-ni,	aag-sal-nɪ	njoambačɪ	ača…
father.3SG	woman.PL-3SG	elder.brother-PL-3SG	they.ACC	meet

ačan-dɪɪ-čɪ	goanɪ.
meet-PRS.P-3PL	certainly

When they land, the groom, his mother, father, aunts, and uncles welcome them.

Xaɪ,	gɪamata-wa	ačan-dɪɪ,	ǰoog-čɪ-arɪ	too-bo-ɪ.
indeed	bride-ACC	meet-PRS.P	house-DIR-REFL.PL	carry-TR-PRS.P

After greeting the bride, they bring her to their home.

Daxala-mǰɪ-sal-ba=daa	xəm	too-bo-ɪ.	Təwə-wə=dəə
follow-AGT-PL-ACC=ADD	all	carry-TR-PRS.P	cargo-ACC=ADD

xəm too-bo-ɪ. Təi miruə-wə.
all carry-TR-PRS.P that dowry-ACC

They bring all of the bridesmaids. And all of the load, that is, the dowry.

Ogda-sal-ba xəm naa-čɪ tata-ɪ. Tui tamaarɪ.
boat-PL-ACC all land-DIR pull-PRS.P therefore

While doing so, they drag all boats onto the ground.

Gəə, təi gɪamata ɪsɪ-očɪa-nɪ, ǰoog-do naɪ
OK that bride arrive-COND-3SG house-DAT person

saolɪn-ba aŋgo-ɪ-čɪ goanɪ.
banquet-ACC make-PRS.P-3PL certainly

When the bride and her company arrive, the people at home give a warm reception.

Gɪamata, aojan-bɪ ǰoog-čɪ-a-nɪ
bride groom-REFL house-DIR-OCM-3SG

ii-rii-du-ji=dəə, guči ənjuə-wə taktoola-ɪ
enter-PRS.P-DAT-REFL=ADD again pot-ACC step.on-PRS.P

bi-či-ni.
be-PST.P-3SG

When entering the bride's home, she again stepped on the pots.

Ənjuə-či oo-rɪɪ bi-či-ni goanɪ.
pot-DIR board-PRS.P be-PST.P-3SG certainly

She stepped on the pots.

Ənim buu-xə-ni... xaɪ... aojan-bɪ... xaɪ-wa...
mother.REFL give-PST.P-3SG what groom-REFL what-ACC

ənim buu-xə-ni ənjuə-wə boakɪa-ǰɪaǰɪ,
mother.REFL give-PST.P-3SG pot-ACC outside-ABL

ənim... aojanɪ ənini ənjuə-ni=tənii dookɪa-ǰɪ,
mother groom.3SG mother.3SG pot-3SG=TOP inner.side-INS

do... ǰoo dookɪa-ǰɪaǰɪ-a-nɪ.
inner house inner.side-ABL-OCM-3SG

The pot her mother gave is laid outside of home and the pot of the groom's mother is laid inside of home.

Guči təi kəndərxin-bə gɪraan-dɪɪ-do-jɪ, əm
again that threshold-ACC tread-PRS.P-DAT-REFL one

ənjuə-ǰiəǰi ǰoog-čɪ ii-rii, əm ənjuə-ǰiəǰi
pot-ABL house-DIR enter-PRS.P one pot-ABL

goɪ ənjuə-či taktoola-ɪ.
other pot-DIR step.on-PRS.P

Again she treads on the pot then passes over the threshold. When she enters the home, she steps on the other pot.

Gəə, təi=dəə tui.
OK that=ADD so

It is done like that.

Gəə, xoonɪ əi... əi ǰoo-wa osɪ-pɪ, əi ǰoog-do
OK how this this house-ACC become-COND.IMPS this house-DAT

osɪ-pɪ, xoonɪ njoanɪ bi-gilə-i-wə-ni
become-COND.IMPS how she live-OBLG-PRS.P-ACC-3SG

— gəə, čaa ičə-gu-əri, taktoola-waan-dɪɪ-čɪ goanɪ.
OK that.ACC see-PURP-REFL.PL step.on-CAUS-PRS.P-3PL certainly

To foretell what life she should live after entering the home, she is made to step on the pots.

Gɪamata, ǰoog-čɪ ii-pi, gəə, njaŋgaa čadu
bride house-DIR enter-COND.IMPS OK a.little there

bi-i gursəl-ǰi gəsə sɪa-rɪɪ.

be-PRS.P	people.PL-INS	together	eat-PRS.P

When the bride enters the home, she briefly eats a meal with the people there.

Totaraa=tanɪɪ	guči	ǰobo-lo-go-ɪ.
and.then=TOP	again	work-INCH-ITER-PRS.P

Afterwards, she begins to work.

Nəə,	təi	ini=ə	ɪsɪ-ɪ,	ɪsɪ-xam	ǰoog…
certainly	that	day=MIR	reach-PRS.P	reach-PST.P	house

ini-du=tul	ǰobo-lo-go-ɪ.
day-DAT=EXCL	work-INCH-ITER-PRS.P

She certainly begins to work on the very day she arrives.

Muə-wə	muə-lsi-i,	ǰoo…	xaɪ-wa…	moo-wa
water-ACC	fetch.water-HAB-PRS.P	house	what-ACC	wood-ACC

xaɪ-rɪɪ…	ii-wu-i	ǰoog-čɪ,	tawa	ɪwa-čɪ-ɪ,
do.what-PRS.P	enter-TR-PRS.P	house-DIR	fire	kindle-FR-PRS.P

sɪa-orɪ-a	pujuu-či-i	ta-ɪ.
eat-PRS.IMPS.P-ACC	cook-FR-PRS.P	do-PRS.P

She carries water, gathers firewood, makes a fire in the furnace, and prepares food.

Čado=tol	ǰi-čin	gurun,	təi	aojan	əninəə-ni
then=EXCL	come-PST.P	people	that	groom	mothers-3SG

ičə-i-či	goanɪ:	xoonɪ	bi-i	əktə=əm=dəə:
see-PRS.P-3PL	certainly	how	be-PRS.P	female=REPO=ADD

səčən=nuu.	ǰoboso=noo,	uləən=nuu.
nimble=Q	industrious=Q	good=Q

Then the women of the groom's side along with the people observe her, to see how the bride is, whether she works well or not, whether she works hard or not, and whether she is good or not.

Gəə, čaa ičuən-gu-ji=tənii təi əktə čawa
OK that.ACC show-PURP-REFL=TOP that female that.ACC

xəm ta-ɪ.
all do-PRS.P

The bride does all of the work to show them.

Gəə, təi ǰului ini=ə aja, aso əgǰi-ə
OK, that first day=MIR good so.much many-ACC

ǰobo-asi=daa aja.
work-NEG.PRS.P=ADD good

It is okay not to do so much work on the first day.

Totapɪ, čaa njaŋgaa njaŋgaa ta-raa, naɪ-ǰɪ gəsə
then that.ACC a.little a.little do-ANT person-INS together

təə-si-i, anjaara-ɪ ta-ɪ.
sit-DUR-PRS.P celebrate-PRS.P do-PRS.P

After doing a little bit of the work, she sits and enjoys the banquet with the people.

Gəə, naɪ goɪ gurun-či ǰi-či-ni=kəs, xaɪ
OK person other people-DIR come-PST.P-3SG=EMP what

əmutuu mənə ǰoog-do-jɪ bi-i=məə bi-gilə-i.
as.if oneself house-DAT-REFL live-PRS.P=SML live-OBLG-PRS.P

When one goes to another's home, how can one live as if one were at one's own home?

Doolaa doolaa bi-i-ni goanɪ.
quietly live-PRS.P-3SG certainly

She must behave modestly.

Saa-rasɪ, naɪa-sal-ba=daa aso
know-NEG.PRS.P person-PL-ACC=ADD so.much

taako-asɪ.
be.familiar.with-NEG.PRS.P

She does not know. She is not familiar with the people.

ǰuəjəčiə ini-du=tənii njoanɪ naɪ ǰuliə-lə-ni,
second day-DAT=TOP she person front-LOC-3SG

gərəən naɪ ǰuliə-lə-ni təə-rii.
people person front-LOC-3SG sit-PRS.P

On the second day, the bride gets up in front of many people.

Moo-wa ii-wu-gu-rəə, golǰom ɪwan-go-ɪ,
wood-ACC enter-TR-REV-ANT stove.ACC kindle-ITER-PRS.P

waɪsɪ muə-wə muə-lsi-i.
to.the.shore water-ACC fetch.water-HAB-PRS.P

She carries firewood, makes a fire in the furnace, and goes to the shore to draw water.

Ənjuə-du tɪas muə-wə muə-lsi-rəə, saola-du
pot-DAT full water-ACC fetch.water-HAB-ANT water.container-DAT

muə-wə muə-lsi-rəə, sɪa-orɪ-a pujuu-rii.
water-ACC fetch.water-HAB-ANT eat-PRS.IMPS.P-ACC cook-PRS.P

After filling the pot completely with water and filling the water pail, she prepares food.

Totapɪ=tanɪɪ miruə-ji xəm agbɪn-bo-ɪ, boa-la
then=TOP dowry-REFL all appear-TR-PRS.P outside-LOC

tətuə-səl-bə, polta-sal-ba, səktəpun-səl-bə, təi
clothes-PL-ACC blanket-PL-ACC mat.of.cloth-PL-ACC that

xaɪ-wa=daa xəm olbɪn-kɪm ǰaka-wa — xəm
what-ACC=ADD all bring-PST.P.REFL thing-ACC all

loo-rɪɪ.
hang-PRS.P

Then she unpacks her dowry and hangs all her clothes, bedding, and blankets she brought.

Naɪ	ičə-gu-ə-ni.	Xoonja	məən	miruə-ji
person	see-PURP-OCM-3SG	to.what.extent	oneself	dowry-REFL

olbɪn-kɪn-bɪ.
bring-PST.P-REFL

She lets the other people look at all of the dowry she brought.

Kurkə-səl-bə,	təi	xaɪ-ǰɪ=daa	xəm	aŋgo-xa-nɪ;
reel.of.thread-PL-ACC	that	what-INS=ADD	all	make-PST.P-3SG

talo-ǰɪ,	moo-ǰɪ,	sələ-ǰi	aŋgo-xa-nɪ
birch.bark-INS	wood-INS	iron-INS	make-PST.P-3SG

ǰaka-sal-ba	xəm,	tui	dəri-mi,	nəə-rii-ni	goanɪ.
thing-PL-ACC	all	so	spread-SIM	put-PRS.P-3SG	certainly

She brings out and spread everything she made and brought: baskets and other things made with thread, birch bark, wood, and iron (See Fig. 10 on page xi above).

Gərəəni,	naɪ	ɪxon-do-a-nɪ	balǰɪ-ɪ	gurun,	xəm
people	person	village-DAT-OCM-3SG	live-PRS.P	people	all

ičə-gu-ə-ni,	xoonɪ	bi-i	əktəə
see-PURP-OCM-3SG	how	be-PRS.P	woman.ACC

baa-xa-čɪ=am	təi	piktə-əri	asɪ...	piktə-wə-əri
find-PST.P-3PL=REPO	that	child-REFL.PL	wife	child-ACC-REFL.PL

asɪ-go-a-nɪ:	bajan=nuu,	sinəǰii=nuu,	ulpisu=nuu,
wife-DSG-OCM-3SG	rich=Q	poor=Q	artfully.embroider=Q

paksɪ=nuu,	mogo=noo	— xoonɪ	bi-i	əktə
master=Q	unskillful=Q	how	be-PRS.P	female

baa-xa...,	xoonɪ	bi-i	əktə	ǰi-či-ni	əi	ɪxon-čɪ.
find-PST.P	how	be-PRS.P	female	come-PST.P-3SG	this	village-DIR

Many people of the village want to see what kind of bride the groom got married to, whether she is rich or poor, good at needlework, and whether or not she is skillful and what the bride came this village is like.

Gərəəni	iča-gu-ə-ni	təi	mənə	xaǰon-bɪ
people	see-PURP-OCM-3SG	that	oneself	stuff-REFL

ičuən-dii-ni	goanɪ	təi	əktə.
show-PRS.P-3SG	certainly	that	female

The bride shows many people that this is all her property.

Tui	ta-mɪ	balana	gərbiə-si-i-či	bi-či-či	goanɪ
so	do-SIM	long.ago	call-DUR-PRS.P-3PL	be-PST.P-3PL	certainly

təi	ǰuəjə	ǰi-či-ni	ini	— təi	gɪamata
that	second	come-PST.P-3SG	day	that	bride

ini-ni=əm=dəə.
day-3SG=REPO=ADD

Therefore, from the past, there has been a name for it. They called the second day the bride's day.

Njoambanɪ	xəm	tui	ičuən-dii-či	bi-či-ni	goanɪ.
she.ACC	all	so	show-PRS.P-3PL	be-PST.P-3SG	certainly

In this way, everyone was to see her things.

Gəə,	totapɪ=tanɪɪ,	gəə,	naɪ	anjaara-ɪ,	ǰɪaja
OK	then=TOP	OK	person	celebrate-PRS.P	next

ini-ə=dəə	anjaara-ɪ.
day-ACC=ADD	celebrate-PRS.P

And then they celebrate the next day.

Totapɪ	naɪ	əǰi	asɪ	osɪ-ɪ.
then	person	husband	wife	become-PRS.P

Then strangers become a husband and a wife.

Tui	əlkəǰiəni	tui	balǰɪ-ɪ-čɪ	goanɪ.
so	gradually	so	live-PRS.P-3PL	certainly

And just like that, gradually they come to live together.

Totapɪ=tanɪɪ	mii	njaŋgaa	gusərə-gu-i	ta-ɪ	goanɪ.
then=TOP	I	a.little	tell-ITER-PRS.P	do-PRS.P	certainly

I have more story.

Xaɪ,	gɪamata	taonɪ	ǰuulgəəni	uləən
indeed	bride	every.3SG	fate.3SG	good

bi-əči-ni	goanɪ	balana.
be-NEG.PST.P-3SG	certainly	long.ago

Long ago, not all brides were so lucky.

Čawa=daa	otolɪ-orɪ-nɪ	goanɪ.
that.ACC=ADD	understand-PRS.IMPS.P-3SG	certainly

That should be also understood.

Əǰi-gu-ji	baa-rɪɪ	naɪ-a=daa	əktə
husband-DSG-REFL	get-PRS.P	person-ACC=ADD	female

saa-rasɪ.
know-NEG.PRS.P

The bride does not know what her husband will be like.

Poaldoanɪ	ǰi-pi=məə	ičə-i,	naɪ
sometimes	come-COND.IMPS=CON	see-PRS.P	person

ǰoog-čɪ-a-nɪ	ǰi-pi=məə,	ičə-i	mənə
house-DIR-OCM-3SG	come-COND.IMPS=CON	see-PRS.P	oneself

əǰi-ji.
husband-REFL

Sometimes she sees him only after getting married. Only after she arrives at his house does she look at her husband for the first time.

Naonǰoan naɪ=daa poaldoanɪ bi-əsi.
young person=ADD sometimes be-NEG.PRS.P
Sometimes he is not so young.

Poaldoanɪ təŋ naonǰoan arčokaan, əktə-kəən sagǰɪ
sometimes very young girl female-DIM old
mapa-ǰɪ əǰi... əǰi-ku osɪ-ɪ-nɪ goanɪ.
old.man-INS husband husband-PROP become-3SG certainly
Sometimes a very young lady gets married to old man.

Gəə, poanɪ əǰi-ni asɪ-čɪ-jɪ uləən
OK some husband-3SG wife-DIR-REFL good.INS
xaɪ-rɪɪ bi-či-ni... asɪ-jɪ uləəsi-i, kidu-i,
do.what-PRS.P be-PST.P-3SG wife-REFL love-PRS.P respect-PRS.P
asɪ-jɪ bodo-ɪ.
wife-REFL consider-PRS.P
Some husbands treat their wives well. They love their wives, respect them, and think of them.

Poaldoanɪ=tanɪɪ təi əktə əgǰi əǰi-ǰi-ji,
sometimes=TOP that female many husband-INS-REFL
əŋpə-ǰi-ji, aŋpa... aŋpa-ǰɪ-jɪ
mother.in.law-INS-REFL father.in.law father.in.law-INS-REFL
aso uləən=dəə balǰɪ-ɪ bi-əči=ə.
so.much good=ADD live-PRS.P be-NEG.PST.P=MIR
But sometimes the wife was on bad terms with her husband, mother-in-law, and father-in-law.

Tui bi-či-ni goanɪ.
so be-PST.P-3SG certainly

It was possible.

Siŋgərə-i	bi-či-či	təi	əktə.
insult-PRS.P	be-PST.P-3PL	that	female

They would offend her.

Əgǰi=ə	ǰobo-waan-dɪɪ,	guči=tənii	poaldoanɪ
many=MIR	work-CAUS-PRS.P	again=TOP	sometimes

əǰi-ni	xaɪ…	goɪ	əkəsəl-ǰi	xoan-dɪɪ.
husband-3SG	indeed	other	woman.PL-INS	be.capricious-PRS.P

The husband would make her work hard, and sometimes would around with other women.

Tui.
so

That's how it was.

Asɪ-jɪ	njoančɪan	xaɪ=daa	un-dii	osɪnɪ=tanɪɪ
wife-REFL	he.DIR	what=ADD	say-PRS.P	if=TOP

asɪ-jɪ	toɪkaan-dɪɪ.
wife-REFL	beat PRS.P

If his wife complains to him, he would beat her.

Tui	bi-či-ni	goanɪ.
so	be-PST.P-3SG	certainly

Things were like that.

Vot.
R. well

Well.

Gəə, totaraa=tanɪɪ poaldoanɪ=tanɪɪ əktə=tənii
well and.then=TOP sometimes=TOP female=TOP

bim… bi-mi — balǰɪ-mɪ mutə-əsi osɪ-raa=tanɪɪ,
be-SIM be-SIM live-SIM be.able.to-NEG.PRS.P become-ANT=TOP

gusinəə-či-ji xaɪ-rɪɪ bi-či-ni goanɪ…
uncles-DIR-REFL do.what-PRS.P be-PST.P-3SG certainly

guǰiən-bə gələ-i bi-či-ni goanɪ.
mercy-ACC ask.for-PRS.P be-PST.P-3SG certainly

Sometimes if the wife felt her husband was impossible to be with, or to live with, then she asked her maternal uncles for help.

Əmdə əmdə tui bi-či-ni goanɪ: xaɪ=daa
rarely so be-PST.P-3SG certainly what=ADD

ǰoǰa-n=daa anaa gusinəə-ni=tənii, ǰi-dəə, təi
judge-NMLZ=ADD without uncles-3SG=TOP come-ANT that

piktərəən-bəri=tənii ǰapa-go-ɪ bi-či-či goanɪ.
niece-REFL.PL=TOP take-REV-PRS.P be-PST.P-3PL certainly

Sometimes there was the following case: her uncles came and took their niece without a custom trial.

ǰapa-go-ɪ bi-či-či.
take-REV-PRS.P be-PST.P-3PL

They took her.

Təi əǰi-ni=tənii gələ-ndə-gu-i bi-či-ni goanɪ.
That husband-3SG=TOP ask.for-INT-REV-PRS.P be-PST.P-3SG certainly

Her husband came in order to take her back.

Njoanɪ gələ-ndə-gu-učiə-ni, baɪ tui
he ask.for-INT-REV-COND-3SG just so

buu-gu-əsi asɪ-wa-nɪ.

give-REV-NEG.PRS.P wife-ACC-3SG

Though he asks for her, they don't simply give her back.

Xəsə ǰapa-ɪ təi aojan-dola-nɪ, əǰi-lə-ni
word take-PRS.P that groom-LOC-3SG husband-LOC-3SG

xəsə ǰapa-ɪ.
word take-PRS.P

They ask the groom, the husband for convincing words.

Gəə, xoonɪ balǰɪ-ǰaa-čɪ ǰuləsi: tui=məə əədən…
well how live-FUT-2SG forward so=SML fool

əədən-ǰi, orkɪn-ǰɪ, asɪ-jɪ siŋgərə-mi, toɪkaa-mɪ
fool-INS bad-INS wife-REFL insult-SIM beat-SIM

— tui balǰɪ… balǰɪ-ɪ-sɪ osɪnɪ, buu-gu-əsi-ni
so live live-PRS.P-2SG if give-REV-NEG.PRS.P-3SG

goanɪ sindu.
certainly you.DAT

"Well, how will you live in the future? We will not give your wife back if you live foolishly and shamefully, and if you make her angry, or beat her."

Gəə, xaɪ un-dii? Uləən ta-ǰaan-bɪ,
well what say-PRS.P well.INS do-FUT-1SG

uləəsi-ǰəən-bi, siŋgərə-əsin-bi.
love-FUT-1SG insult-NEG.PRS.P-1SG

Then what he says is, "I will be well. I'll love her, and I'll not make her angry."

Gəə, totaraa buu-gu-i-či goanɪ xamasɪ
well and.then give-REV-PRS.P-3PL certainly backward

təi əktə-wə.
that female-ACC

Well, then they give her back.

Poaldoanı=tanıı buu-gu-əsi. Buu-gu-əsi.
sometimes=TOP give-REV-NEG.PRS.P give-REV-NEG.PRS.P

Sometimes they don't give her back.

Gəə, tui naı buu-gu-əsi-ni osını, təi
well so person give-REV-NEG.PRS.P-3SG if that

əǰi-ni amınaa-nı təi asɪ-nı amınaa-la-nı
husband-3SG fathers-3SG that wife-3SG fathers-LOC-3SG

paaǰɪ... xaɪ... torɪ pasɪ-wa-nı gələ-gu-i.
separate indeed bridewealth part-ACC-3SG ask.for-REV-PRS.P

If they don't give her back, then the fathers of the husband demand to the fathers of the wife a part of the bridewealth.

Torɪ pasɪ-wa-nı gələ-gu-i. Tui
bridewealth part-ACC-3SG ask.for-REV-PRS.P so

ta-mɪ əktə-wə təŋ oɪ modan ǰapa-go-ɪ
do-SIM female-ACC very few time take-REV-PRS.P

bi-či-či goanı.
be-PST.P-3PL certainly

They demand the bridewealth back. Then they rarely, if ever, took the woman.

Baa-xam ǰaka buu-gu-uri maŋga.
get-PST.P.REFL thing give-REV-PRS.IMPS.P difficult

It is difficult to give back what was received.

Tui ta-mɪ.... Gəə, tui tamaarı siŋgərə-i
so do-SIM well therefore insult-PRS.P

bi-či-či goanı.
be-PST.P-3PL certainly

That is why they were angry with each other.

Tui	ta-raa	poaldoanɪ=tanɪɪ	tui	əǰi	asɪ
so	do-ANT	sometimes=TOP	so	husband	wife

paaǰɪla-go-ɪ	goanɪ,	ǰoǰa-n…	ǰoǰa-m
separate-REV-PRS.P	certainly	judge-NMLZ	judge-NMLZ.ACC

gələ-i	bi-či-či	goanɪ.
ask.for-PRS.P	be-PST.P-3PL	certainly

Then sometimes, the husband and wife demanded a custom trial for divorce.

ǰoǰa-n=tanɪɪ	əjə,	əǰi-ni	kaltaaǰɪa-la-nɪ	bi-i
judge-NMLZ=TOP	here	husband-3SG	region-LOC-3SG	be-PRS.P

sagǰɪ	gurun	— naɪ	kidu-i-ni	gurun,	asɪ-nɪ
old	people	person	respect-PRS.P-3SG	people	wife-3SG

kaltaaǰɪa-la-nɪ	bi-i	sagǰɪ	gurun,	gəsə
region-LOC-3SG	be-PRS.P	old	people	together

osɪo…	osɪ…	osɪ-go-raa,	ǰoǰa-go-ɪ-čɪ	goanɪ.
become	become	become-ITER-ANT	judge-ITER-PRS.P-3PL	certainly

For the custom trial, the elders, the respected elders of the husband's village and of the wife's village gathered to arbitrate.

Gəə,	xoonɪ	ta-orɪ	təi?	Gəsə	bi-wəən-buri=nuu,
well	how	do-PRS.IMPS.P	that	together	live-CAUS-PRS.IMPS.P=Q

asɪ-wa-nɪ	ǰapa-go-orɪ=nuu?
wife-ACC-3SG	take-REV-PRS.IMPS.P=Q

"Well, what should we do? Shall we make them live together? Shall we permit him to take his wife back?

Xoonɪ	ta-orɪ?	Əǰi-wə-ni	papola-orɪ=nuu,
how	do-PRS.IMPS.P	husband-ACC-3SG	forbid-PRS.IMPS.P=Q

papola-wasɪ=nuu?

forbid-NEG.PRS.IMPS.P=Q

What should we do? Shall we forbid the husband or not?"

Gəə,	təi	ǰoǰa-n	xoonɪ	osɪ-waan-dɪɪ-nɪ
well	that	judge-NMLZ	how	become-CAUS-PRS.P-3SG

osɪnɪ,	gəə,	tui	osɪ-go-ɪ-nɪ	goanɪ.
if	well	so	become-ITER-PRS.P-3SG	certainly

Whatever the decision is at the custom trial, it must be obeyed.

Gəə,	ui=dəə	xaŋgɪsɪ	ta-mɪ	mutə-əsi
well	who=ADD	away	do-SIM	be.able.to-NEG.PRS.P

ǰoǰa-n	toktoo-xan-ba-nɪ.	Təŋ	tui=rəgdə.
judge-NMLZ	agree-TR-PST.P-ACC-3SG	very	so=LIM

Nobody can go against that decision. One must obey it.

Gəə,	poaldoanɪ=tanɪɪ	(əsi	tui	bi-i-ni	goanɪ…	tui
well	sometimes=TOP	now	so	be-PRS.P-3SG	certainly	so

əsi	aba-nɪ	goanɪ,	balan	tui	bi-či-ni	goanɪ),
now	not-3SG	certainly	long.ago	so	be-PST.P-3SG	certainly

poaldoanɪ=tanɪɪ	əktə,	bi-mi	—	balǰɪ-mɪ	mutə-əsi
sometimes=TOP	female	be-SIM		live-SIM	be.able.to-NEG.PRS.P

osɪ-pɪ,
become-COND.IMPS

Sometimes (she does not do this now, but in the past, she did), if the bride felt her husband was impossible to live with,

moolo-pɪ	xaosɪ=daa	təi	boačaan-čɪ,	goro-ǰɪaǰɪ…
walk-COND.IMPS	whereto=ADD	that	island-DIR	distant.place-ABL

ɪxon-ǰɪaǰɪ	goro-laa	ənə-pi,	xaosɪ=daa
village-ABL	far-SUFF	go-COND.IMPS	whereto=ADD

ənə-pi=dəə,	gusin-bi,	əikəi…	xaɪ…	—	ənin-bi
go-COND.IMPS=ADD	uncle-REFL	elder.sister	what		mother-REFL

nəu-wə-ni, xusə nəu-wə-ni, ogda-wa-nɪ=daa... xaɪ...,
brother-ACC-3SG male brother-ACC-3SG boat-ACC-3SG=ADD what

utuŋgi-wə-ni=dəə ičə-i osɪnɪ=tanɪɪ, xəəsi-i
canoe-ACC-3SG=ADD see-PRS.P if=TOP call-PRS.P

bi-či-ni goanɪ.
be-PST.P-3SG certainly

She went to the island, or to the place somewhat far from the village. Then she called her maternal uncle, or younger brother of her mother if she saw a passing boat.

— Gučəkə, gučəkə, ičə-ruu=əm mimbiwə.
uncle uncle see-2SG.IMP=REPO I.ACC

“Uncle, please, come see me.

İčə-ruu=əm, dooljɪ-roo=am mimbiwə,
see-2SG.IMP=REPO hear-IMP=REPO I.ACC

bələči-ndə-gu-ruu=əm.
help-INT-REV-IMP=REPO

Come to see me. Listen to me. Come to help me.”

Tui xəəsi-i bi-či-ni goanɪ gujiəm gɔlɔ-mi.
so call-PRS.P be-PST.P-3SG certainly mercy.ACC ask.for-SIM

She called her uncle for help.

Xaɪ... njoanɪ gujiəsi-gu-wəən-i.
indeed she mercy.VBZ-ITER-CAUS-PRS.P

She is pitied.

Poaldoanɪ təi gusini njoambanɪ xorɪ-ɪ,
sometimes that maternal.uncle.3SG she.ACC help-PRS.P

japa-go-ɪ.
take-REV-PRS.P

Sometimes the uncle helps her and takes her.

Poaldoanɪ=tanɪɪ	ǰoǰa-m…	ǰoǰa-n-ba	gələ-i.
sometimes=TOP	judge-NMLZ.ACC	judge-NMLZ-ACC	request-PRS.P

Sometimes he demands a custom trial.

ǰoǰa-n-ba	gələ-i.
judge-NMLZ-ACC	request-PRS.P

He demands a custom trial.

Təi…	xaɪ…	xoan-dɪɪ	gursəl=dəə	tui
that	what	be.capricious-PRS.P	people.PL=ADD	so

bi-či-či	goanɪ.
be-PST.P-3PL	certainly

It was the same for people who were unfaithful.

Əǰi-ni	tul tul	xoan-dɪɪ,	goɪ	əkəsəl-či
husband-3SG	always	be.capricious-PRS.P	other	woman.PL-DIR

pulsi-i	ta-ɪ-nɪ	osɪnɪ,	*vot…*	gəə,	čado=daa
go-PRS.P	do-PRS.P-3SG	if	R. well	well	then=ADD

təi	əktə	ənu-ičə-i-ni	goanɪ	mənə	boa-čɪ-jɪ,
that	female	go-DES-PRS.P-3SG	certainly	oneself	place-DIR-REFL

mənə	ǰoog-čɪ-jɪ.
oneself	house-DIR-REFL

If the husband is unfaithful and always goes to another woman, the wife would want to return to her hometown, to her home.

Əktəni	təəm	modan	goɪ	naɪ-ǰɪ,	goɪ
female	once	time	other	person-INS	other

xusə	naɪ-ǰɪ	ao-xa-nɪ	osɪnɪ,	gəə,	əǰi-ni
male	person-INS	sleep-PST.P-3SG	if	OK,	husband-3SG

nəə puŋnə-gu-i təi əktə. Nəə puŋnə-gu-i.

certainly expel-REV-PRS.P that female certainly expel-REV-PRS.P

But when a wife sleeps with another man, then her husband throws her out without fail. This is always so.

Puŋnə-gu-pi=tənii	xaɪ-wa…	mənə	buu-xən-bi
expel-REV-COND.IMPS=TOP	what-ACC	oneself	give-PST.P-1SG

torɪ-jɪ	gələ-gu-i	xamasɪ.
bridewealth-REFL	ask.for-REV-PRS.P	backward

When he throws her out, he also demands the bridewealth back.

Xamasɪ	gələ-gu-i.
backward	ask.for-REV-PRS.P

He demands that back.

Tui tamaarɪ	əkəsəl	əmdə əmdə	tui	ta-ɪ
therefore	woman.PL	rarely	so	do-PRS.P

bi-či-či	goanɪ.
be-PST.P-3PL	certainly

Therefore women rarely did so.

Naɪ	buu-xə-ni	torɪ	əninəə-du-ə-ni,
person	give-PST.P-3SG	bridewealth	mothers-DAT-OCM-3SG

amɪnaa-do-a-nɪ	bi-i.
fathers-DAT-OCM-3SG	be-PRS.P

The bridewealth the husband brought is at her mothers and fathers' home.

Gəə,	təi	əninəə-ni,	amɪnaa-nɪ	orkɪn	osɪ-ɪ-nɪ
OK	that	mothers-3SG	fathers-3SG	bad	become-PRS.P-3SG

goanɪ.
certainly

Then her mothers and fathers become bad.

Tui ta-maarı tui xaı-rıı bi-či-či goanı:
so do-SIM.PL so do.what-PRS.P be-PST.P-3PL certainly

gəə, orkı-laa bi-i=dəə, xoonı ta-orı? Tui
OK bad-SUFF be-PRS.P=ADD how do-PRS.IMPS.P so

balǰı-ı bi-či-či goanı.
live-PRS.P be-PST.P-3PL certainly

Then what happened? There is no way but to live together, even if it's somewhat bad.

Totapı=tanıı paaǰıla-go-ı əkəsəl, paaǰı…
then=TOP separate-REV-PRS.P woman.PL separate

əǰi-ǰi-ji — ası-ǰı-jı paaǰıla-go-ı osını,
husband-INS-REFL wife-INS-REFL separate-REV-PRS.P if

əǰi-ni puril-bi xəm məənduji
husband-3SG children-REFL all oneself.DAT

osı-go-waan-dıı, ası-do-jı buu-gu-əsi.
become-ITER-CAUS-PRS.P wife-DAT-REFL give-REV-NEG.PRS.P

And when a husband and a wife divorce, the husband takes all of his children. The wife cannot take her children.

Gəə, tui ta-mı ası-nı ənu-əsi bi-či-ni goanı.
OK so do-SIM wife-3SG go-NEG.PRS.P be-PST.P-3SG certainly

For that reason, his wife did not go.

Gəə, naı məəpi orkı-la-ı=daa, xaıs
OK person oneself.ACC bad-VBZ-PRS.P=ADD again

əǰi-ǰi-ji bi-i, əǰi-ǰi-ji balǰı-ı
husband-INS-REFL be-PRS.P husband-INS-REFL live-PRS.P

bi-či-ni goanı. Tui bi-či-ni.
be-PST.P-3SG certainly so be-PST.P-3SG

Well, while she is cursing herself, she is made to be with her husband. She was made to live with him. That was the way it was.

Gəə, tui=dəə.
OK so=ADD

Well, that was done like that.

Tui=dəə.
so=ADD

That's the way it was.

2.4. Funeral rituals

Burpuun-bə guči xərgən-bə ta-orı naanaı
mourning-ACC again funeral.repast-ACC do-PRS.IMPS.P Nanai

kolı-sal-nı
custom-PL-3SG

Nanai people's customs of mourning and funeral repasts

Naı, ənusi-m bu-dii=dəə, bu-dii.
person illness.VBZ-SIM die-PRS.P=ADD die-PRS.P

People die of sickness.

Goı turgun-du-ə-ni bu-dii=dəə, bu-dii.
other reason-DAT-OCM-3SG die-PRS.P=ADD die-PRS.P

Muələn-dii, koorxıǰı-ı.
drown-PRS.P be.injured-PRS.P

They also die of other reasons, such as drowning or getting injured.

Poaldoanı=tanıı, naı bur-bučiə-ni, daaı gursəl tui
sometimes=TOP person die-COND-3SG big people.PL that.way

un-dii bi-či-či goanı:
say-PRS.P be-PST.P-3PL certainly

If a person died, seniors sometimes said as follows:

— Gəə, Boa ǰapa-go-xa-nı njoambanı.
well god take.away-REV-PST.P-3SG he.ACC

"God took him."

Njoambanı Boa ǰapa-go-xa-nı, un-dii.

he.ACC god take.away-REV-PST.P-3SG say-PRS.P

Bu-dii=dəə, naɪ bu-dəsi=ə, un-dii.
die-PRS.P=ADD person die-NEG.PRS.P=MIR say-PRS.P

It is said that even God had taken him, and he, in fact, does not die.

Tui=dəə.
that.way=ADD

That is the way it goes.

Əsi baɪ njoanɪ xaɪ-nɪ, ərgəni əsi əm ərsi-əsi
now just he what-3SG soul.3SG now not breathe-NEG.PRS.P

osɪ-xa-nɪ. ərgəni... ərgəni=tənii ujuun.
become-PST.P-3SG soul.3SG soul.3SG=TOP living

Now, though he has become unable to breathe, his spirit is alive.

Njoanɪ bui-ki-ni=dəə, ərgəni xaɪs ujuun, un-dii.
he die-PST.P-3SG=ADD soul.3SG still living say-PRS.P

Vot.
R. well

It is said that his spirit was still alive though he had died.

Tui tamaarɪ bui-kin naɪ-wa, əmutuu, ujuun
therefore die-PST.P person-ACC as.if living

naɪ=maa, bodo-ɪ bi-či-či goan.
person=SML consider-PRS.P be-PST.P-3PL certainly

Therefore, they thought of the deceased as if they were alive.

Naɪ bur-bučiə-ni, xoonɪ ta-ɪ bi-či-či?
person die-COND-3SG how do-PRS.P be-PST.P-3PL

What did they do if a person died?

ǰuə undəxən-bə, ǰuə undəxən-bə (əmun=dəə aja,
two board-ACC two board-ACC one=ADD good

daramɪ undəxən osɪnɪ, əi=məə daramɪ-nɪ undəxən osɪnɪ)
wide board if this=SML wide-3SG board if

palan-do nəə-rii, nakan-do nəə-rii-či
floor-DAT put-PRS.P heated.floor-DAT put-PRS.P-3PL

bi-či-ni goanɪ.
be-PST.P-3SG certainly

They laid two planks (one plank was laid if it was wide as this) on the heated floor.

Nakan-do tui nəə-rəə, ojaa-la-nɪ=tanɪɪ
heated.floor-DAT that.way put-ANT surface-LOC-3SG=TOP

xaɪ-wa=daa səkč... səkčiə-rii-či.
what-ACC=ADD lay lay-PRS.P-3PL

Čiptun-gu-ə-ni nəə-rii, təi ojaa-la-nɪ=tanɪɪ
pillow-DSG-OCM-3SG put-PRS.P that surface-LOC-3SG=TOP

naɪ-a ǰirkəgu-i.
person-ACC lay.in.state-PRS.P

Bui-kin naɪ-a ǰirkəgu-i. ǰirkəgu-i.
die-PST.P person-ACC lay.in.state-PRS.P lay.in.state-PRS.P

They spread a cushion on the plank and lay the deceased in state on it.

ŋaala-wa-nɪ=tanɪɪ xoldon-do-a-nɪ suŋg... suŋgurə
arm-ACC-3SG=TOP side-DAT-OCM-3SG at.full.length at.full.length

tui nəəku-i. Xaɪ-wa-nɪ... bəǰi-ə-ni=dəə
that.way put-PRS.P what-ACC-3SG leg-ACC-3SG=ADD

tui... xaɪ... suŋgurə nəəku-i.
that.way indeed at.full.length put-PRS.P

The arms of the deceased are spread widthways and straightened, and so are the legs.

Xaɪ… bəgǰi-ni duə-wə-ni čaagǰan boso-kaan-ǰɪ uju-i,
indeed leg-3SG end-ACC-3SG white cloth-DIM-INS bind-PRS.P

ǰɪa ǰɪa-ǰɪ-a-nɪ kirim osɪ-go-a-nɪ.
friend friend-INS-OCM-3SG stationary become-PURP-OCM-3SG

The end of the legs is fastened and bound together with a white cloth to be stationary.

Tui.
that.way

That is the way it is.

Balana, naɪ bur-bučiə-ni, dərəg-bə-ni dasɪ-ɪ bi-či-či.
long.ago person die-COND-3SG face-ACC-3SG cover-PRS.P be-PST.P-3PL

In the old days, they covered the face of the deceased.

Totapɪa=tanɪɪ dasɪ-ča anaa nəučə-i bi-čin. Tui.
later=TOP cover-PASS no keep-PRS.P be-PST.P that.way

In the later, covering it in that way was not kept.

Əniənəə un-dii bi-čin goan: Dərəg-bə-ni
mothers say-PRS.P be-PST.P certainly face-ACC-3SG

dasɪ-pɪ aja goanɪ=a, un-dii.
cover-COND.IMPS good certainly=MIR say-PRS.P

Mothers said, “The face is should be covered.

Iičəǰə-m maŋga=am. Soŋgomo.
watch-SIM difficult=REPO feel.like.crying

If it is not covered, it is hard to look at the body because we would feel like crying.”

Dasɪ-ča anaa osɪ-očɪa-čɪ=tanɪɪ, tənii təpčiu-učiə-či,
cover-PASS no become-COND-3PL=TOP just begin-COND-3PL

tui un-dii bi-či-či: əi orkı…
that.way say-PRS.P be-PST.P-3PL this uncomfortable

orkıkta-laa-nı un-dii. ičəǰə-mi.
uncomfortable-NMLZ-3SG say-PRS.P watch-SIM

Məən naı-jı ičəǰə-m, əmutuu ujuun=məə bi-i.
oneself person-REFL watch-SIM as.if living=SML be-PRS.P

After it began not to be covered, they said, “This is uncomfortable. The deceased himself sees his own men, as if he were alive.”

Totamı un-mi=dəə ačaası, xaı-m=daa ačaası.
therefore say-SIM=ADD inappropriate what-SIM=ADD inappropriate

In doing so, it became inappropriate to say so.

Tui bi-i=dəə, əs… əsi=dəə dası… dərəg-bə-ni
that.way be-PRS.P=ADD now now=ADD cover face-ACC-3SG

dası-ası-čı goan.
close-NEG.PRS.P-3PL certainly

In that way, they do not cover the face of the deceased now.

Tui=dəə.
that.way=ADD

That is the way it goes.

Tui ǰirkəgu-rəə, baı təə-si-ičə-i-ni
that.way lay.in.state-ANT just lie-DUR-DES-PRS.P-3SG

tətuə-ǰi-ə-ni tətuə-ku. Tui ǰirkəgu-rəə.
clothes-INS-OCM-3SG clothes-PROP that.way lay.in.state-ANT

After the deceased is laid in state on a table in that way, they lie down, dressed with shrouds.

Totaraa=tanıı xəm mənə saa-rıı gurun-bə, məən

and.then=TOP all oneself know-PRS.P people-ACC oneself

naɪ-sal-bɪ, məən xala-jɪ naɪ-wa
person-PL-REFL oneself family-REFL person-ACC

saa-waan-dɪɪ-nɪ goanɪ: tui bi-i naɪ
know-CAUS-PRS.P-3SG certainly that.way be-PRS.P person

o-čɪ=am=daa, o-čɪn.
pass.away-PST.P=REPO=ADD pass.away-PST.P

Then, all of his acquaintances and relatives are told that the man passed away.

Naanaɪ xəsə-ǰi-ə-ni təi «bur-buri, bur-buri»
Nanai language-INS-OCM-3SG that die-PRS.IMPS.P die-PRS.IMPS.P

— *poluchaetsja umeret* «bui-ki-ni» *umer.*
R. turned R. die die-PST.P-3SG R. died

That is called *burburi* ‘to die’ in the Nanai language.

Totapɪ=tanɪɪ un-dii: «o-čɪ-nɪ» — *skonchalsja,*
after.that=TOP say-PRS.P pass.away-PST.P-3SG R. passed.away

prestavilsja. Ili «abolɪ-xa-nɪ»,
R. reposed R. or depart.this.life-PST.P-3SG

«abolɪ xa nɪ» *nc dozhil, nc dotjanul.*
depart.this.life-PST.P-3SG R. not.survived R. not.prolonged.a.life

Vot takije vyrazhenija. Vot.
R. well R. such R. expression R. well

For the deceased, that was also called *očini* ‘to have passed away’, *abolixani* ‘to have departed this life’.

Naanaɪ xəsə-ǰi-ə-ni tui un-dii
Nanai language-INS-OCM-3SG that.way say-PRS.P

bi-či-ni goan bui-kin naɪ-wa.
be-PST.P-3SG certainly die-PST.P person-ACC

For the deceased, it was called so in Nanai.

Tui=dəə.
that.way=ADD

That is the way it goes.

Təi	naɪ	ǰirkəgu-uxə-ni	ujə-lə-ni	goaom
that	person	lay.in.state-PST.IMPS.P-3SG	top-LOC-3SG	quant.ACC

loo-rɪɪ-čɪ	goan.
hang-PRS.P-3PL	certainly

Above the deceased that laid in state on a table, a pole was hung.

Tui=dəə.	Tui=dəə.
that.way=ADD	that.way=ADD

That is the way it goes.

Uilə	tui	goaom	loo-rɪɪ-čɪ.
above	that.way	quant.ACC	hang-PRS.P-3PL

Above it a pole was hung in that way.

Təi	goaon-do=tanɪɪ	təi	bui-k...	bui-kin	naɪ-wa
that	quant-DAT=TOP	that	die-PST.P	die-PST.P	person-ACC

baarooli-orɪ	xaǰon-ba	loo-rɪɪ-čɪ	xəm=dəə.
put.on-PRS.IMPS.P	goods-ACC	hang-PRS.P-3PL	all=ADD

On the pole all the items that are to be put on the deceased are hung.

Totapɪ=tanɪɪ	naɪ,	ii-rii	gurun	olbɪn-kɪ-nɪ
after.that=TOP	person	enter-PRS.P	people	bring-PST.P-3SG

xaɪ-wa=daa:	boso	pasɪ-nɪ,	əktəni	osɪnɪ
what-ACC=ADD	cloth	piece-3SG	female	if

— puŋku,	xusəni	osɪnɪ —	guči	xaɪ=daa	ǰaka-nɪ,
shawl	male	if	again	what=ADD	goods-3SG

xaǰon-ba	buikini-du	olbɪn-dɪɪ-čɪ	goanɪ.
goods-ACC	the.deceased-DAT	bring-PRS.P-3PL	certainly

Then, people participating in the ritual bring to the deceased and hung on the pole stuff, such as pieces of clothing, and shawls for a woman, equipment for a man.

Čawa=daa	xəm	təi	ujə-lə-ni	təi	goaon-do	uilə
that.ACC=ADD	all	that	top-LOC-3SG	that	quant-DAT	above

loo-rɪɪ.
hang-PRS.P

On the pole all of them are hung.

Təi	əgǰi-ni	ǰipərə-i,	əgǰi-ni	xaɪ-wa=daa
that	many-3SG	patch-PRS.P	many-3SG	what-ACC=ADD

olbɪn-bo-očɪa-nɪ,	əgǰi	osɪnɪ	goanɪ	tado.
bring-TR-COND-3SG	many	if	certainly	then

At that time, if people bring much things, they are piled one on another.

Təi	goaon-ba	guči	masɪlto-ɪ,	čado=tol	uilə	xəm
that	quant-ACC	again	strengthen-PRS.P	then=EXCL	above	all

loo-rɪɪ	təi	buikini	xaǰon-go-a-nɪ	naɪ
hang-PRS.P	that	the.deceased	goods-DSG-OCM-3SG	person

olbɪn-dɪɪ-wa-nɪ.
bring-PRS.P-ACC-3SG

At that time, they hang all the things that participants bring to the deceased, after the pole is strengthened again.

Asɪ-nɪ=tanɪɪ	pəəjə-du-ji	čaagǰan	puŋku-kəən-bə	uju-i,
wife-3SG=TOP	forehead-DAT-REFL	white	shawl-DIM-ACC	bind-PRS.P

ŋaala-do-jɪ=daa	čaagǰan	puŋku-kəən-bə	uju...	uju-i.
arm-DAT-REFL=ADD	white	shawl-DIM-ACC	bind	bind-PRS.P

The wife of the deceased ties white handkerchiefs around her head and arms.

Njoanı	ǰooŋkan-do-a-nı	bi-i	gurun=dəə	xəm	čaagǰan
he	family-DAT-OCM-3SG	be-PRS.P	people=ADD	all	white

xaı-ka...	boso-kaan-ba	uju-i:	ŋaala-do-arı,
what-DIM	cloth-DIM-ACC	bind-PRS.P	arm-DAT-REFL.PL

ǰılı-do-arı	tui	uju-i-či.
head-DAT-REFL.PL	that.way	bind-PRS.P-3PL

The rest of the family also ties white a piece of cloth around their heads and arms.

Naı,	ičə-mi,	otolı-ı-nı	goanı:	əi	ǰoog-do
person	see-SIM	be.able.to-PRS.P-3SG	certainly	this	house-DAT

ui=dəə	o-čı-nı,	ui=dəə	o-čı-nı.
who=ADD	pass.away-PST.P-3SG	who=ADD	pass.away-PST.P-3SG

People can see that someone passed away in the family.

Balana,	xusəni	bur-bučiə-ni,	waaıča-ı-nı,
long.ago	male	die-COND-3SG	hunt-PRS.P-3SG

bota-ı-nı	xaǰon-ba	xəm	takto-do	manjaa
catch.a.fish-PRS.P-3SG	goods-ACC	all	warehouse-DAT	only

nəə-rii	bi-čin.
put-PRS.P	be-PST.P

In the old days, if a man died, all the equipment for hunting and fishing were placed in storage.

Təi	takto-čı,	naı	niə-wə...	bui-kin
that	warehouse-DIR	person	go.out-NEG.PRS.IMPS.P	die-PST.P

naı-a	niə-wəsi-lə-ni=ə,	ui=dəə	ii-m
person-ACC	go.out-NEG.PRS.IMPS.P-LOC-3SG=MIR	who=ADD	enter-SIM

mutə-əsi.

be.able.to-NEG.PRS.P

Before the deceased is let go, no one can get into the storage place.

Ui=dəə	ii-m	mutə-əsi,	xaɪ=daa	xaǰon-ba=daa
who=ADD	enter-SIM	be.able.to-NEG.PRS.P	what=ADD	goods-ACC=ADD

ǰapa-mɪ=daa	mutə-əsi.
take-SIM=ADD	be.able.to-NEG.PRS.P

No one can enter it and take out the items.

Totapɪa,	takto	aba	osɪ-očɪa-nɪ=tanɪɪ,	taja-či
later	warehouse	not	become-COND-3SG=TOP	that.place-DIR

bi-i	xaǰon-sal-ba=tanɪɪ	əm	boa-du	nəə-rii-či
be-PRS.P	goods-PL-ACC=TOP	one	place-DAT	put-PRS.P-3PL

goan.	Əm	boa-du.
certainly	one	place-DAT

After the temporary storage disappear, they put the items in one place.

Taosɪ	ui-wə=dəə	toŋgala-waan-dasɪ.	Ui=dəə
to.that.place	who-ACC=ADD	touch-CAUS-NEG.PRS.P	who=ADD

toŋgala-waan-dasɪ.	Ačaasɪ.
touch-CAUS-NEG.PRS.P	not.appropriate

No one is allowed to enter the place to touch the items.

Tui	bi-čin.	Tui=dəə.	Balana.
that.way	be-PST.P	that.way=ADD	long.ago

That was the way it went in the old days.

Xusəni,	ǰoog-do	bi-i	čuu	daaɪ	xusəni	bu...
man	house-DAT	be-PRS.P	most	big	male	die

bu-dii-ni osɪnɪ, goɪ naɪ, əm xala bi-əsi,

die-PRS.P-3SG if other person same family be-NEG.PRS.P

«anda-jɪ naɪ», naɪ un-dii, — «anda-jɪ naɪ»,
friend-REFL person person say-PRS.P friend-REFL person

goɪ naɪ, təi=tənii... xaɪ-wa... topto-a ǰapa-raa,
other person that=TOP what-ACC rope-ACC take-ANT

ǰoo-wa kəəndəli-i guičə pəgiə-lə-ni tui
house-ACC go.around-PRS.P roof bottom-LOC-3SG that.way

xərkə-i bi-čin, ǰoo-wa.
wind.round-PRS.P be-PST.P house-ACC

If the oldest member of the family died, his friend who was not a member of the family, and called *andai nai* (a person who is his friend) grabbed rope and went around the house, winding round the bottom of the roof.

Balana tui un-dii bi-či-či goanɪ: — ǰoo
long.ago that.way say-PRS.P be-PST.P-3PL certainly house

əǰəni bu-dii-ni osɪnɪ, ǰoo ǰool-ǰɪɪ-arɪ=jam,
owner.3SG die-PRS.P-3SG if house swell-PRS.P-REFL.PL=REPO

ǰoo boja-rɪɪ=jam.
house break-PRS.P=REPO

In the old days, they said, "If the owner of the house died, the house will swell and break."

Tui ta-m, təi ǰoo ǰool-ǰɪɪ-rasi
that.way do-SIM that house swell-PRS.P-NEG.PRS.P

osɪ-go-a-nɪ, ǰoog-do balǰɪ-ɪ gurun ajaǰɪɪ
become-PURP-OCM-3SG house-DAT live-PRS.P people safely

bi-gu-ə-či, təi ǰoo-wa masɪlto-ɪ bi-či-či
be-PURP-OCM-3PL that house-ACC fasten-PRS.P be-PST.P-3PL

goan, təi topto-ǰɪ uji-rəə.
certainly that rope-INS tie-ANT

Therefore, the rope was tied to the house and fastened, so that the house might not swell and those who had lived in the house might be safe.

Xaɪ... uji-čə-ni=tənii uikə ǰakpa-do-a-nɪ uji-gu-i
indeed tie-PASS-3SG=TOP door next-DAT-OCM-3SG tie-ITER-PRS.P
bi-či-či čawa.
be-PST.P-3PL that.ACC

They bound the tied rope to next to door.

Bui-kin axo... ǰoog-do ɪlaačɪa aɪŋanɪ... ɪlaačɪa
die-PST.P house house-DAT third year third
ini-du=məə xumu-m baa-rɪɪ.
day-DAT=CON bury-NMLZ.ACC take-PRS.P

The deceased is in the house and carried to the grave on the third day.

Təi bui-ki-ni ini, ǰɪaja ini, ɪlaačɪa ini ǰoog-do
that die-PST.P-3SG day next day third day house-DAT
bi-i-ni goan.
be-PRS.P-3SG certainly

The deceased is in the house on the first, second, and third day.

Čado=tanɪɪ təi bui-ki-ni ini-du=tul=dəə
then=TOP that die-PST.P-3SG day-DAT=EXCL=ADD
ǰirkəgu-xəm ǰakpa-do-a-nɪ dərə-kəəm,
lay.in.state-PST.P.REFL next-DAT-OCM-3SG table-DIM.ACC
nuuči-kəən dərə-kəəm nəə-rii-či.
small-DIM table-DIM.ACC put-PRS.P-3PL

On the day the person died, they put a small table next to the place where the deceased was laid in state.

Təi dərə-kəən ojaa-la-nɪ=tanɪɪ dooboča nəə-rii-či.
that table-DIM surface-LOC-3SG=TOP *doobocha* put-PRS.P-3PL

They put a *doobocha* (food offered to the deceased) on it.

Xaɪ-wa ǰooŋkan sɪa-rɪɪ-čɪ osɪnɪ, čado=daa təi
what-ACC family eat-PRS.P-3PL if then=ADD that

sɪaptaŋgɪ-a nəə-rii-či goan.
food-ACC put-PRS.P-3PL certainly

If the family eat any food, they put it on the table.

Bui-ki... buikini sɪa-rɪɪ=jam, təǰə-gu-ə-či=tənii,
die-PST.P the.deceased eat-PRS.P=REPO believe-PURP-OCM-3PL=TOP

ləluə aŋgo-ɪ-čɪ goan buikini-du.
apron make-PRS.P-3PL certainly the.deceased-DAT

They make a bib for the deceased, for they believe that he eats the food.

Ləluə-wə aŋgo-raa=tanɪɪ, təi ləluə-či, xaɪ... ləluə
apron-ACC make-ANT=TOP that apron-DIR indeed apron

ojaa-la-nɪ, baɪ kupən-ǰi ɪlga-la-maarɪ, ulpi-i-či
surface-LOC-3SG just thread-INS embroidery-VBZ-SIM.PL sew-PRS.P-3PL

əmutuu naɪ xəmdə-du-ə-ni bi-i puxin=məə=dəə,
as.if person abdomen-DAT-OCM-3SG be-PRS.P intestine=SML=ADD

kota, puxin bi-i-ni=məə=dəə.
esophagus intestine be-PRS.P-3SG=SML=ADD

They make a bib, and embroider and sew an esophagus and intestine on it, patterned after those in the body.

Totapɪ=tanɪɪ təi pəgiə-lə-ni=tənii təi ulpi-čə-či=tənii
after.that=TOP that bottom-LOC-3SG=TOP that sew-PASS-DIR=TOP

sɪan-ba ulpi-i-či; təi xoɪpon-do təčičə-uri
ear-ACC sew-PRS.P-3PL that earring-DAT keep-PRS.IMPS.P

sɪan-ba ulpi-i-či.
ear-ACC sew-PRS.P-3PL

And, at the bottom of the bib, they sew a ring, like an ear, which was connected with disks, like earrings.

Təi sɪan-ǰɪ=tanɪɪ... sɪan-čɪ=tanɪɪ... xaɪ-wa... kupən-bə

that ear-INS=TOP ear-DIR=TOP what-ACC thread-ACC

sii-rəə, onɪmɪ-ookaan, təŋ onɪmɪ-ookaan

string-ANT long-EXTR very long-EXTR

xaɪ-rɪɪ-čɪ..., təi duə-du-ə-ni=tənii soɪrakta

do.what-PRS.P-3PL that end-DAT-OCM-3SG=TOP bead

uji-i-či goan. Soɪrakta uji-i-či.

tie-PRS.P-3PL certainly bead tie-PRS.P-3PL

They thread a very long thread through the ear, and tie a bead in the end of the thread.

Əsi=tənii kupən-bə, əsi balǰɪ-orɪ-du kupən-bə

now=TOP thread-ACC now live-PRS.IMPS.P-DAT thread-ACC

tui onɪmɪ-a uji-əsi-l.

that.way long-ACC tie-NEG.PRS.P-3PL

Those who live now may tie a thread that is not so long.

Kupən tui... xaɪ... tujəə bi-i, biǰərə, omlaan.

thread that.way indeed so.much be-PRS.P likely length

It may be as long as this.

Xaɪgoarɪ čaa ta-ɪ-čɪ?

for.what that.ACC do-PRS.P-3PL

Why do they do so?

Təi bui-kin naɪ-wa mənə ǰooŋkan xado

that die-PST.P person-ACC oneself family how.many

modan sɪa-rɪɪ osɪnɪ, tui modan təi

time (turn) eat-PRS.P if that.way time that

o-čɪn	naɪ-a	sɪa-waan-dɪɪ.
pass.away-PST.P	person-ACC	eat-CAUS-PRS.P

It is because they feed the deceased as often as the family eat.

Təi	«əəriptun»,	«əəriptun»	—	təi	soɪrakta,	sɪan.
that	*eeriptun*	*eeriptun*		that	bead	ear

That is an *eeriptun* (funeral bib), a bead and an ear.

Buikini	təi	əəriptun-dulə	ərsi-i,	təi
the.deceased	that	*əəriptun*-LOC	breathe-PRS.P	that

əəriptun-dulə	muə-wə	omɪ-ɪ,	təi	əəriptun-dulə	sɪa-rɪɪ.
əəriptun-LOC	water-ACC	drink-PRS.P	that	*əəriptun*-LOC	eat-PRS.P

The deceased breathes, drinks water, and eats food through it.

Sɪa-rɪɪ	taon-do-a-nɪ	təi	dərə-kəən	ojaa-la-nɪ
eat-PRS.P	every-DAT-OCM-3SG	that	table-DIM	surface-LOC-3SG

sɪa-orɪ-wa	nəə-uri.
eat-PRS.IMPS.P-ACC	put-PRS.IMPS.P

Whenever they eat food, they should also put food on the table.

Təi	gərbu-ni	«dooboča»,	doobo-orɪ
that	name-3SG	*doobocha*	offer.food.to.the.deceased-PRS.IMPS.P

buikini-du,	buikini	sɪa-go-a-nɪ.
the.deceased-DAT	the.deceased	eat-PURP-OCM-3SG

Its name is a *doobocha*, which is offered to the deceased.

ǰi-dii	gurun	ŋaala	anaa	ǰi-dəsi	goan.
arrive-PRS.P	people	hand	not	arrive-NEG.PRS.P	certainly

Those who come to pay their condolences do not come empty-handed.

Bui-ki...	buikinəi-či...	buikini
die-PST.P	dead.person-DIR	the.deceased

ǰoog-čɪ-a-nɪ	ii-mi,	xəm	saorma	olbɪn-dɪɪ.
house-DIR-OCM-3SG	enter-SIM	all	*saorma*	bring-PRS.P

All of them bring *saorma* (offering for the deceased) and enter the house of the deceased.

Arkɪ-kaan	tukuru-du,	əpəkəən	—	gəə,	ui-du	xaɪ
vodka-DIM	bottle-DAT	bread.DIM		well	who-DAT	what

bi-i	osɪnɪ,	xəm	olbɪn-dɪɪ-čɪ	goan	čawa.
be-PRS.P	if	all	bring-PRS.P-3PL	certainly	that.ACC

They bring bottled alcohol, bread, or anything else.

Čaa,	čado=tanɪɪ	ii-xən	naɪ,	ii-mi,	təi	dərə-kəən
that.ACC	then=TOP	enter-PST.P	person	enter-SIM	that	table-DIM

ojaa-la-nɪ	olbɪn-kɪn-bɪ	sɪa-orɪ	ǰaka	nəə-rii,
surface-LOC-3SG	bring-PST.P-REFL	eat-PRS.IMPS.P	thing	put-PRS.P

totaraa	koči-čɪ	arkɪ-a	otokoo	ǰəwəri-rəə,
and.then	glass-DIR	vodka-ACC	a.little	pour.out-ANT

mɪxoraan-daa,	pəiŋən-či	tuu-rəə,	təi...	xaɪdu...
bow-ANT	knee-DIR	fall-ANT	that	where

bui-kin...	o-čɪn	naɪ-čɪ=tanɪɪ	un-dii-ni	goan:
die-PST.P	pass.away-PST.P	person-DIR=TOP	say-PRS.P-3SG	certainly

Whoever comes puts the food he brought on the table, pours some alcohol with a glass, kneels, and says to the deceased,

—	Gəə,	mii	simbiə	susuəči-ndə-xən-bi.
	well	I	you.ACC	see.off-INT-PST.P-1SG

"I saw you off.

Baa-roo	xoonɪ=daa.
take-2SG.IMP	how=ADD

Please take what I have offered to you.

Tui	xaŋgɪsɪ	ənə-i=dəə,	ǰooŋkan-bɪ,	bumbiwə	ajaǰɪɪ
that.way	away	go-PRS.P=ADD	family-REFL	we.ACC	decently

bi-wəən-duu=əm.
be-CAUS-IMP.2SG=REPO

Go far away, and let us including your family be safe.

Mii	sin...	sinči	buu-rii-wə	baa-roo.
I	you.DIR	you.DIR	give-PRS.P-ACC	take-2SG.IMP

Take what I have offered to you."

Totaraa	təi	arkɪ-kaan-dola	čumčuən-bi	tui	gɪda-la-raa,
and.then	that	vodka-DIM-LOC	finger-REFL	that.way	spear-VBZ-ANT

njaŋgaa	tuŋgən-bə-ni=dəə,	aŋma-nɪ	ǰakpa-wa-nɪ=daa
a.little	chest-ACC-3SG=ADD	mouth-3SG	vicinity-ACC-3SG=ADD

modorɪ-raa,	təi	arkɪ-kaan-ba=tanɪɪ	daaɪ	gurun	čado
smear-ANT	that	vodka-DIM-ACC=TOP	big	people	then

təə-si-i-du-ə-ni	čəktəri-i-ni	goan,
lie.down-DUR-PRS.P-DAT-OCM-3SG	spray-PRS.P-3SG	certainly

xəri-i-ni	čado.
treat-PRS.P-3SG	then

Then the guest dips his own finger into the alcohol, lightly rubs his chest and the vicinity of mouth, and sprays it where the deceased is lying as a sign of treatment.

Njaŋgaa	xəri-rəə,	pulə...	pulə-xən-bə-ni=tənii	tukuru-ə
a.little	treat-ANT	be.left	be.left-PST.P-ACC-3SG=TOP	bottle-ACC

xaŋgɪsɪ	nəəku-i.
away	put-PRS.P

After offering the deceased a little alcohol, he puts the remaining alcohol to one side.

Xaɪ-wa…	Xaɪ-wa=daa	olbɪn-kɪm	əpəkəən,	xaɪ…
what-ACC	what-ACC=ADD	bring-PST.P.REFL	bread.DIM	what

lala-kaan,	xaɪ-wa=daa	olbɪn-kɪm=daa,	sogdata-wa,
gruel-DIM	what-ACC=ADD	bring-PST.P.REFL=ADD	fish-ACC

pujuu-xəm=dəə,	čɪro-xam=daa,	čaa
cook-PST.P.REFL=ADD	roast-PST.P.REFL=ADD	that.ACC

olbɪn-kɪm=daa.
bring-PST.P.REFL=ADD

They also brought things like bread, gruel, braised fish, and baked fish.

— Təi	dooboča	njaŋgaa	nəučə-rəə=tənii,	totaraa,
that	*doobocha*	a.little	keep-ANT=TOP	and.then

xusəni	bui-ki-ni	osɪnɪ,	asɪ-nɪ,	ənini	čaa,
male	die-PST.P-3SG	if	wife-3SG	mother.3SG	that.ACC

ǰoog-do	bi-i	əkəsəl,	ǰapa-go-raa,
house-DAT	be-PRS.P	woman.PL	take-REV-ANT

oosɪ-go-ɪ-čɪ	goan.
remove-REV-PRS.P-3PL	certainly

After the *doobocha* was kept for a little while, and supposing a man died, the wife or mother of the deceased, or women in the house take and remove it.

Siluun	sɪaptaŋgɪ-wa	xəm	əm	boa-do	nəə-rii.
dry	food-ACC	all	one	place-DAT	put-PRS.P

All the dry foods are put in one place together.

Təi	arkɪ-wa=tanɪɪ	xəm	tukuru-ə	sii-rii-či	goan.
that	vodka-ACC=TOP	all	bottle-ACC	plug-PRS.P-3PL	certainly

Sii-rii.
plug-PRS.P

They close all the bottles with alcohol leftover with stoppers.

ǰoog-do	sɪa…	sɪa-rɪɪ-wa-arɪ
house-DAT	eat	eat-PRS.P-ACC-REFL.PL

doobo-ɪ	osɪnɪ,	čoolon=daa	bi-i,
offer.food.to.the.deceased-PRS.P	if	soup=ADD	be-PRS.P

boda=daa	bi-i.
boiled.cereal=ADD	be-PRS.P

If something to eat is offered to the deceased in the house, soup or boiled cereal is provided.

Təi	xəm	silə-ku-ni	goan.
that	all	broth-PROP-3SG	certainly

They are all liquid.

Təi	silə-ku	ǰaka-wa=tanɪɪ	goɪ	kalan-čɪ	jəwəri-i-či
that	broth-PROP	thing-ACC=TOP	other	pot-DIR	pour.out-PRS.P-3PL

dooboča-xam.
offer.food.to.the.deceased-PST.P.REFL

They offered the deceased the liquids which were poured in a separate pot.

Dooboča-xam	xəm	goɪ	alɪo-čɪ,
offer.food.to.the.deceased-PST.P.REFL	all	other	dishes-DIR

goɪ	kalan-čɪ	jəwəri-i-či.
other	pot-DIR	pour.out-PRS.P-3PL

They put all *doobočas* given to the deceased in separate dishes or pots.

Čaa=tanɪɪ	əm	boa-do	tui…	tui…,	ǰuər-bə
that.ACC=TOP	one	place-DAT	that.way	that.way	two-ACC

aoŋga-mɪ,	xumu-i	ini-či=ə	xəm	tui
spend.a.night-SIM	bury-PRS.P	day-DIR=MIR	all	that.way

nəə-rii-či goan.

put-PRS.P-3PL   certainly

They put the *doobochas* together in one place and pass the second night until the day when the deceased is buried.

Tui=dəə.
that.way=ADD

That is the way it goes.

Təi   gərbu-ni   «saorma»,   «saorma».
that   name-3SG   *saorma*   *saorma*

Its name is *saorma.*

Ilaačɪa   ini-du   o-čɪn   naɪ-wa,   niə-wu-i
third   day-DAT   pass.away-PST.P   person-ACC   go.out-TR-PRS.P

ǰuliə-lə-ni,   baaroolɪ-ɪ-čɪ.   Baaroolɪ-ɪ-čɪ.
front-LOC-3SG   put.on-PRS.P-3PL   put.on-PRS.P-3PL

On the third day, they clothe the deceased before they move him.

Mii   ənim   tui   gusərə-i   bi-čin:
I   mother.REFL   that.way   say-PRS.P   be-PST.P

— Baaroolɪ-mɪ,   gaksɪdaan   tətuə-wə
put.on-SIM   odd   clothing-ACC

tətu-wəən-buri=əm.
dress-CAUS-PRS.IMPS.P=REPO

My mother said, "The deceased should be dressed in an odd number of clothes."

Ui   saa-rɪɪ-nɪ,   poaktanɪ,   əsi   niru-məəri,   tui
who   know-PRS.P-3SG   some   now   write-SIM.PL   that.way

niru-əsi-l=kəə: «Xəm   xaɪ-ko...   gaksɪa-ko
write-NEG.PRS.P-3PL=CNTR   all   what-PROP   one.of.a.pair-PROP

tətuə-wə... tətuə-w... tətu-wəən-dii bi-či-l.
clothing-ACC clothing-ACC dress-CAUS-PRS.P be-PST.P-3PL

Who knows? Now, some people may write as follows: "Everyone do not put an odd number of clothes on the deceased.

Gaksıdaan osını, guči ui-wə=dəə məənǰiji ǰapa-ı
odd if again who-ACC=ADD oneself.INS catch-PRS.P

o-čın naı».
pass.away-PST.P person

The deceased will take someone with him if he puts on an odd number of clothes."

Ui saa-rıı, xoonı bi-i=nuu?
who know-PRS.P how be-PRS.P=Q

Who knows what they should do?

Mii ənim xısaŋgo-xan-ba-nı, gusərə-xən-bə-ni
I mother.REFL speak-PST.P-ACC-3SG say-PST.P-ACC-3SG

əǰə-xən-bi.
memorize-PST.P-1SG

I remember only what my mother said.

Əniə tui un-dii bi-či-ni goan, bui-kin
mother that.way say-PRS.P be-PST.P-3SG certainly die-PST.P

naı-a baaroolı-mı, gaksıdaan tətuə-wə
person-ACC put.on-SIM odd clothing-ACC

tətuə-uri=əm.
dress-PRS.IMPS.P=REPO

My mother said, "The deceased should be dressed in an odd number of shroud.

Balana tui bi-či=əm=dəə.

long.ago that.way be-PST.P=REPO=ADD
In the old days, that was the way it was."

Sənəǰii... Sinəǰii gurun bui-ki-ni osɪnɪ, ɪlaan tətuə.
poor poor people die-PST.P-3SG if three clothing
If a poor person die, he should be dressed in three articles of shroud.

Ilaan tətuə-dui oɪ-wa tətuə-wəsi.
three clothing-COMPR few-ACC dress-NEG.PRS.IMPS.P
Less than three articles of shroud is not dressed.

Təŋ bajan gurun=tənii ǰoan ɪlaan tətuə-wə
very rich people=TOP ten three clothing-ACC
tətu-wəən-dii bi-či=ə, un-dii. Əgǰi.
dress-CAUS-PRS.P be-PST.P=MIR say-PRS.P many
It is said that very rich people are dressed in shroud as many as thirteen.

Ojaa — ojaa-la-nɪ tətuə.
surface surface-LOC-3SG clothing
They are outer garments.

Təi naɪ=tanɪɪ təŋ əm xaɪ=maa daaɪ osɪ-ɪ-ni
that person=TOP very one what=SML big become-PRS.P-3SG
goan.
certainly
And that person becomes very big.

Xado tətuə-wə tətu-wəən-kin osɪnɪ, xado-ǰɪ
how.many clothing-ACC dress-CAUS-PST.P if how.many-INS
buniə-uri ojaa-la-nɪ.

cover-PRS.IMPS.P surface-LOC-3SG

However many articles of shroud the deceased might be made to put on, it was covered with the same number of covers.

Vot. Təi ojaa-la-nɪ buniə-čə=dəə ɪlaan osɪnɪ, ɪlaan;
R. well that surface-LOC-3SG cover-PASS=ADD three if three

toɪŋga osɪnɪ, toɪŋga buniə-čə; ǰoan ɪlaan osɪnɪ,
five if five cover-PASS ten three if

ǰoan ɪlaan.
ten three

If the number of them is three, three covers were put on, and for five, five covers, and for thirteen, thirteen covers.

Guči=tənii o-čɪn naɪ-a xəur-du
again=TOP pass.away-PST.P person-ACC coffin-DAT

nəə-rii-du-ji, pəgiə-lə-ni səktəpum səkčiə-uri,
put-PRS.P-DAT-REFL bottom-LOC-3SG mattress.ACC spread-PRS.IMPS.P

čiptun-gu-ə-ni=dəə nəə-uri.
pillow-DSG-OCM-3SG=ADD put-PRS.IMPS.P

When the deceased is placed in a coffin, a mattress is laid on the bottom and a pillow is placed on it.

Təi buniə-čə-du buniə-rii-du-ji, polta-ǰɪ
that cover-PASS-DAT cover-PRS.P-DAT-REFL blankets-INS

polta-la-waan-borɪ.
blankets-VBZ-CAUS-PRS.IMPS.P

The cover is covered with a blanket.

To ta-mɪ, polta-la-waan-dɪɪ-do-jɪ=tanɪɪ, təi
so do-SIM blankets-VBZ-CAUS-PRS.P-DAT-REFL=TOP that

polta ǰəilən-wə-ni bəgǰi-či-ə-ni nəə-uri.
blankets shamanic.caps-ACC-3SG leg-DIR-OCM-3SG put-PRS.IMPS.P

Bəgǰi-či-ə-ni	nəə-uri.
leg-DIR-OCM-3SG	put-PRS.IMPS.P

In doing so, the top of the blanket is to be placed toward the legs.

Bəgǰi-du	bi-čin-bə=tənii	ǰɪlɪ-čɪ-a-nɪ	nəə-uri.
leg-DAT	be-PST.P-ACC=TOP	head-DIR-OCM-3SG	put-PRS.IMPS.P

The bottom of it is to be placed toward the head.

Guči=tənii	xəur-du	(təi	buni-du	balǰɪ-go-a-nɪ),
again=TOP	coffin-DAT	that	otherworld-DAT	be.born-PURP-OCM-3SG

əi-du	xaɪ-wa	ta-xa-nɪ…	əi	boa-do
this-DAT	what-ACC	do-PST.P-3SG	this	world-DAT

naɪ-ǰɪ	balǰɪ-ɪ-do-jɪ	xaɪ-wa	ta-xa-nɪ	osɪnɪ,
person-INS	be.born-PRS.P-DAT-REFL	what-ACC	do-PST.P-3SG	if

təi	xaǰon-ba-nɪ	xəm	nəə-uri.
that	goods-ACC-3SG	all	put-PRS.IMPS.P

Whatever a person did in this world where he had been born, all of his things are put in his coffin for the afterworld.

Xuʒəni	oʒɪnɪ,	tunjəpu-n-gu-ə-ni	nəə-uri,
man	if	walk.with.stick-NMLZ-DSG-OCM-3SG	put-PRS.IMPS.P

buri-gu-ə-ni,	mɪočaan-ba=daa	əsi	nəə-rii=ə=l.
bow-DSG-OCM-3SG	gun-ACC=ADD	now	put-PRS.P=MIR=3PL

For a man, a stick is placed in the coffin, but now they also put his bow or gun.

Xəur-du	nəə-rəsi-l.
coffin-DAT	put-NEG.PRS.P-3PL

There is something that they do not put in the coffin.

Xaɪ-du… xumu-n-du nəə-rii-či goan.

what-DAT bury-NMLZ-DAT put-PRS.P-3PL certainly

Xaɪ=daa	xəm	xaǰon-ba-nɪ.
what=ADD	all	goods-ACC-3SG

They put these things in his grave.

Sɪa-orɪ	alɪo-sal-ba	nəə-rii,	kotaan-sal-ba,
eat-PRS.IMPS.P	tableware-PL-ACC	put-PRS.P	cup-PL-ACC

xonjaan-ba.
spoon-ACC

They put food, dishes, cups and spoons in the grave.

To	ta-mɪ	sarbɪ	ǰaka-wa=ragda	nəə-rəsi.
so	do-SIM	sharp	thing-ACC=LIM	put-NEG.PRS.P

But sharp things are not allowed to put.

Təi	sarbɪ	ǰaka	ačaasɪ=am:	naɪ-a	waa-rɪɪ
that	sharp	thing	not.appropriate=REPO	person-ACC	kill-PRS.P

ǰaka.
thing

It is said that the sharp things should not be put because they are used for killing people.

Totamɪ	kučəən-bə	čado	nəə-rəsi.
therefore	knife-ACC	then	put-NEG.PRS.P

Xaɪ-do…	xusəni-du	kučəəm	nəə-rəsi.
what-DAT	man-DAT	knife.ACC	put-NEG.PRS.P

Knives are not put for men.

Əktəni-du=tənii	gɪrsoo…	*tam…*	xaɪ-wa…
woman-DAT=TOP	knife.for.sewing	R. there	what-ACC

jaoko-a	nəə-rii=dəə,	xaǰa	nəə-rəsi.
graver-ACC	put-PRS.P=ADD	scissors	put-NEG.PRS.P

Knives for sewing are put for women, but scissors are not.

Xaǰa-čɪ-asɪ	osɪ-go-a-nɪ	ujuun	gurun-bə.
scissors-VBZ-NEG.PRS.P	become-PURP-OCM-3SG	living	people-ACC

Nəə-rəsi.
put-NEG.PRS.P

Scissors are not put so that they may not be used to cut living people.

Tui=dəə.
that.way=ADD

That is the way it goes.

Muə-wə	omɪ-go-a-nɪ	alɪo-go-a-nɪ,
water-ACC	drink-PURP-OCM-3SG	tableware-DSG-OCM-3SG

muksu-gu-ə-ni…
wooden.bowl-DSG-OCM-3SG

Xaɪ-wa=daa	xəm	xəm	nəə-rii	čado.
what-ACC=ADD	all	all	put-PRS.P	then

Tableware is put in the grave to let the deceased drink water.

Tui	ta-mɪ	xəur-ni	buə,	naanaɪ-du,	daaɪ-a
that.way	do-SIM	coffin-3SG	we	Nanai-DAT	big-ACC

aŋgo-ɪ-čɪ	goan.	Daaɪ	xəur-bə.
make-PRS.P-3PL	certainly	big	coffin-ACC

They make a coffin bigger than the ordinary Nanai person's frame.

Xəm	taosɪ	čɪkɪ-go-a-nɪ	xaǰon.
all	to.there	lie-PURP-OCM-3SG	goods

The purpose was to place things in the coffin.

Nəə-rii-či xaǰon xəm čıkı-go-a-nı.
put-PRS.P-3PL goods all lie-PURP-OCM-3SG

They put and place them there.

Balana təi ambaan-sal-ba xaı-rasɪ... osɪ-g...
long.ago that demon-PL-ACC do.what-NEG.PRS.P become

njoančı saa-rasɪ osɪ-go-a-čɪ, naı ǰoog-ǰıaǰı
they know-NEG.PRS.P become-PURP-OCM-3PL person house-ABL

o-čın naı-a... naı niə-wu-i-wə-ni,
pass.away-PST.P person-ACC person go.out-TR-PRS.P-ACC-3SG

bui-kin naı-a uikə-lə niə-wu-wəsi bi-čin.
die-PST.P person-ACC door-LOC go.out-TR-NEG.PRS.IMPS.P be-PST.P

In the old days, the deceased was not carried out through the door of the house to prevent ghosts from being aware of his death.

Paawa-la, paawa nuuči-ni osını=tanıı, korıan-ba
window-LOC window small-3SG if=TOP timbered.wall-ACC

əmǰiə kaltaaǰıa-la-nı xaı-rıı... bojalı-ı,
one (of the pair) side-LOC-3SG do.what-PRS.P break-PRS.P

xəur-bə niə-wu-i.
coffin-ACC go.out-TR-PRS.P

The coffin is carried out through the window, and if the window is too small, a wooden board from the wall is broken to make space for the coffin.

Xaı... naı xəur-du nəə-uxən naı-a
what person coffin-DAT put-PST.IMPS.P person-ACC

niə-wu-i.
go.out-TR-PRS.P

The deceased who was put in the coffin is carried out.

Totapɪ=tanɪɪ,	korɪan-ba	bəun-du-ə-ni	nəəku-rəə,
after.that=TOP	timbered.wall-ACC	place-DAT-OCM-3SG	put-ANT

xəm	modorɪ-go-ɪ	čadu.
all	grease-ITER-PRS.P	then

Təi	ini=ə=tul	modorɪ-go-ɪ	goanɪ.
that	day=MIR=EXCL	grease-ITER-PRS.P	certainly

Afterwards, on the very same day, the wooden board is restored to its original place and greased completely.

Naɪ,	xumu-pi,	ǰoog-čɪ	močogo-ɪ	xəm,	ǰoog-do
person	bury-COND.IMPS	house-DIR	turn.back-PRS.P	all	house-DAT

mojɪn	oosɪ-go-go-a-nɪ.
intact	remove-REV-PURP-OCM-3SG

After burying the deceased, people return home and clean the house.

Tui=dəə	goan.
that.way=ADD	certainly

That is the way it goes.

Niɔ-wu-i=dɔɔ,	bɔgǰi-ǰi-ɔ-ni	ǰulɔsi	niɔ-wu-i
go.out-TR-PRS.P=ADD	leg-INS-OCM-3SG	forward	go.out-TR-PRS.P

boa-čɪ	ǰoog-ǰɪaǰɪ.
outside-DIR	house-ABL

When they carry the deceased out of the house, they let the legs out in the first.

Əsi	poaktanɪ	un-dəsi-l=kəə,	ǰɪlɪ-ǰɪ-a-nɪ	ǰuləsi
now	some	say-NEG.PRS.P-3PL=CNTR	head-INS-OCM-3SG	forward

niə-uri=əm=dəə.
go.out-PRS.IMPS.P=REPO=ADD

Some people now may say that the head of the deceased should go out first.

Ui	saa-rɪɪ?
who	know-PRS.P

But who knows?

Balana=kaa	mii	ənin-bi,	mii	saa-rɪɪ-jɪ	daaɪ
long.ago=CNTR	I	mother-REFL	I	know-PRS.P-REFL	senior

gursəl	tui	un-dii	bi-či-ni	goan:
people.PL	that.way	say-PRS.P	be-PST.P-3SG	certainly

ǰoog-čɪ-jɪ	ǰɪlɪ-ǰɪ-jɪ	ǰuləsi	ii-gu-uri,
house-DIR-REFL	head-INS-REFL	first	enter-REV-PRS.IMPS.P

niə-gu-u-mi=tənii,	bəgǰi-ǰi-jɪ	ǰuləsi
go.out-REV-TR-SIM=TOP	leg-INS-REFL	first

niə-gu-uri=əm=dəə.
go.out-REV-PRS.IMPS.P=REPO=ADD

In the old days, my mother and some elders whom I know said, "The legs should be let out first because he entered the house with his head first."

Tui	ta-mɪ	o-čɪn	gurun-bə	bəgǰi-ǰi-ə-či
that.way	do-SIM	pass.away-PST.P	people-ACC	leg-INS-OCM-3PL

niə-wu-i.
go.out-TR-PRS.P

So the deceased is carried out with his legs first.

Tui	ǰuər-bə	aoŋga-mɪ,	naɪ	əgǰi	pulsi-i.
that.way	two-ACC	spend.a.night-SIM	person	many	frequent-PRS.P

For two days, many people visit.

Kukpun=dəə	əgǰi	osɪ-ɪ	goanɪ	təi	xaɪ…
litter=ADD	many	become-PRS.P	certainly	that	what

xaɪ-wa=daa	xəm	sɪa-orɪ-a	ta-orɪ,	goɪ
what-ACC=ADD	all	eat-PRS.IMPS.P-ACC	do-PRS.IMPS.P	other

ǰaka-sal	ta-orɪ.
thing-PL	do-PRS.IMPS.P

A lot of trash accumulates, for all the food and other things should be prepared.

Təi	kukpun-bə=tənii,	təi	o-čɪn	naɪ	ǰoog-do
that	litter-ACC=TOP	that	pass.away-PST.P	person	house-DAT

bi-i-du-ə-ni,	boa-čɪ	niə-wu-wəsi	bi-čin.
be-PRS.P-DAT-OCM-3SG	outside-DIR	go.out-TR-NEG.PRS.IMPS.P	be-PST.P

While the deceased was in the house, the trash was not brought out of the house.

ǰoo	doo-la-nɪ	xapolɪ-ɪ,	əm	boa-čɪ,	əm
house	inside-LOC-3SG	sweep-PRS.P	one	place-DIR	one

ǰokon-čɪ	xapolɪ-raa,	xapol-ǰɪ	dasɪ-raa,	tui
inner.corner-DIR	sweep-ANT	broom-INS	cover-ANT	that.way

nəuči-uri.
gather-PRS.IMPS.P

It is swept with broom and gathered to one place or a corner of the house and covered.

Naɪ-a,	naɪ	bəjə-wə-ni	boa-čɪ
person-ACC	person	body-ACC-3SG	outside-DIR

niə-wu-pi=məə,	ǰoog-ǰɪaǰɪ	niə-wu-pi=məə,	təi
go.out-TR-COND.IMPS=CON	house-ABL	go.out-TR-COND.IMPS=CON	that

kukpun-bə	boa-čɪ	niə-wu-i=dəə	aja.
litter-ACC	outside-DIR	go.out-TR-PRS.P=ADD	OK

Only after the deceased is brought out of the house is the trash allowed to be taken out of the house.

Boa-čɪ	niə-wu-rəə,	əm	boa-du	xəm
outside-DIR	go.out-TR-ANT	one	outside-DAT	all

xaɪ-worɪ...	xumu-uri	təi	kukpun-bə.
do.what-PRS.IMPS.P	bury-PRS.IMPS.P	that	litter-ACC

All of the trash taken out of the house is buried in one place.

Təi=dəə	xaɪ...	xaɪmaarɪ	tui	ta-ɪ-čɪ?
that=ADD	what	why	that.way	do-PRS.P-3PL

Why do they do so?

Xaɪ-wa=daa	boa-čɪ,	o-čɪn	naɪ	ǰoog-do
what-ACC=ADD	outside-DIR	pass.away-PST.P	person	house-DAT

bi-i-du-ə-ni,	niə-wu-wəsi.
be-PRS.P-DAT-OCM-3SG	go.out-TR-NEG.PRS.IMPS.P

When the deceased is in the house, nothing is taken out of it.

Goɪ	gurun-bə	orkɪn	osɪ-asɪ	osɪ-go-a-nɪ.
other	people-ACC	bad	become-NEG.PRS.P	become-PURP-OCM-3SG

The purpose is not to harm any other person.

ǰoog-do	njoanɪ=ragda	bi-əsi-ni	goanɪ.
house-DAT	he=LIM	be-NEG.PRS.P-3SG	certainly

It is not only the deceased who is in the house.

Guči	goɪ	gurun=dəə	bi-i:	puril-ni=dəə	əǰi-ni,
again	other	people=ADD	be-PRS.P	children-3SG=ADD	husband-3SG

asɪ-nɪ	—	goɪ	gurun	tui	bi-i.
wife-3SG		other	people	that.way	be-PRS.P

Other people such as children, the deceased's husband or the deceased's wife are also in the house.

Balana o-čɪn naɪ-wa sirəktə xətuli-i bi-čin.
long.ago pass.away-PST.P person-ACC thread cut-PRS.P be-PST.P

In the old days, a ritual of breaking off relations (thread) with the deceased was performed.

Təi xərəktə... sirəktə xətuli-məəri=tənii, duilə,
that buff thread cut-SIM.PL=TOP in.the.forest

xumu-i boa-du, xumu-n ǰakpa-do-a-nɪ ta-ɪ
bury-PRS.P place-DAT bury-NMLZ next-DAT-OCM-3SG do-PRS.P

bi-čin.
be-PST.P

In the old days, the ritual of breaking off relations with the deceased was performed in the forest, that is, near the grave where the deceased was buried.

Əsi=tənii, boa-čɪ niə-wu-məəri, boa-la, tuliə-du
now=TOP outside-DIR go.out-TR-SIM.PL outside-LOC yard-DAT

ta-ɪ təi sirəktə xətuli-uri-ə.
do-PRS.P that thread cut-PRS.IMPS.P-ACC

Now, the thread cutting ritual is performed in the yard of the house when the deceased is carried out.

Təi sirəktə-wə=tənii xoonɪ xətuli-i-či?
that thread-ACC=TOP how cut-PRS.P-3PL

How do they break off relations?

Balana, saman-sal bi-i-du-ə-ni, xəur ǰakpa-do-a-nɪ
long.ago shaman-PL be-PRS.P-DAT-OCM-3SG coffin next-DAT-OCM-3SG

saman təə-rii, buikini ŋaala-wa-nɪ əm
shaman sit-PRS.P the.deceased hand-ACC-3SG one

ŋaala-ǰɪ-jɪ ǰapa-ɪ.
hand-INS-REFL take-PRS.P

In the old days when there were shamans, they sat down next to the coffin, took the deceased's hand with his own one hand.

Buikini ŋaala-do-a-nɪ əm kurkə kupən-bə-ni
the.deceased hand-DAT-OCM-3SG one reel.of.thread thread-ACC-3SG
ǰapa-waan-dɪɪ.
take-CAUS-PRS.P

He makes the deceased take a reel and thread in the hand.

Totaraa məən ŋaala-ǰɪ-jɪ tui bələči-i-ni goanɪ
and.then oneself hand-INS-REFL that.way help-PRS.P-3SG certainly
təi ǰapa-čɪ-ɪ-wa-nɪ.
that catch-FR-PRS.P-ACC-3SG

And he helped take it with his own hand.

Təi kupən duə-wə-ni=tənii, xusəni bui-ki-ni osɪnɪ,
that thread end-ACC-3SG=TOP male die-PST.P-3SG if
asɪ-nɪ, puril-ni, ənini, amɪnɪ njoanɪ əm
wife-3SG children-3SG mother.3SG father.3SG he one
ǰooŋkanɪ təi duə-wə-ni ǰapa-ɪ.
family.3SG that end-ACC-3SG catch-PRS.P

If the deceased is a man, members of his family like his wife, children, mother, and father grab the other end of the thread.

Əktəni bui-ki-ni osɪnɪ, əǰi-ni, puril-ni,
female die-PST.P-3SG if husband-3SG children-3SG
ənini, amɪnɪ… *tam…* ǰooŋkanɪ ǰapa-ɪ.
mother.3SG father.3SG R. there family.3SG catch-PRS.P

If the deceased is a woman, members of her family like her husband, children, mother, and father grab the other end of the thread.

Təi=tənii xoonɪ ta-ɪ-čɪ?
that=TOP how do-PRS.P-3PL

What did they do?

Təi saman ə… əmǰiə ŋaala-do-jɪ təi
that shaman one one (of the pair) hand-DAT-REFL that

buikini ŋaala-wa-nɪ kupən kurkə…
the.deceased hand-ACC-3SG thread reel.of.thread

kurkə-ǰi-ə-ni ǰapa-čɪ-ɪ.
thread-INS-OCM-3SG take-FR-PRS.P

In one hand, the shaman takes the hand of deceased with the reel and thread.

Əmǰiə ŋaala-do-jɪ=tanɪɪ xaɪ-wa… moo-kaan-ba
one (of the pair) hand-DAT-REFL=TOP what-ACC wood-DIM-ACC

ǰapa-čɪ-ɪ. Moo-kaan-ba ǰapa-čɪ-ɪ.
take-FR-PRS.P wood-DIM-ACC take-FR-PRS.P

In the other hand, he takes a piece of wood.

Təi kupən duə-wə-ni ǰapa-xan naɪ-a… naɪ-a
that thread end-ACC-3SG catch-PST.P person-ACC person-ACC

ǰapa-waan-daa=tanɪɪ, un-dii-ni goan: — Gəə,
take-CAUS-ANT=TOP say-PRS.P-3SG certainly well

sii asɪ… asɪ-sɪ=daa (sii əǰi-si=dəə), sii
you wife wife-2SG=ADD you husband-2SG=ADD you

puril-si=dəə, gəə, simbiə susuəči-i=ə.
children-2SG=ADD well you.ACC see.off-PST.P=MIR

After making the family take the end of the thread, he says, “Well, your wife, (your husband) and your children see you off.

Sii ənə-i=dəə, əmuučəkəən ənə-ruu, un-dii.
you go-PRS.P=ADD alone.DIM go-2SG.IMP say-PRS.P

Ui-wə=dəə	əǰi	ǰapa-ra.
who-ACC=ADD	not	take-INF

You should leave alone without taking anybody with you."

Tui	un-dii-du-ji=tənii	moo-ǰɪ	masɪ-ǰɪ
that.way	say-PRS.P-DAT-REFL=TOP	stick-INS	strong-INS

paačɪ-la-ɪ-nɪ	goan	təi	kupən-dulə.
mallet-VBZ-PRS.P-3SG	certainly	that	thread-LOC

While saying this, he strikes the thread hard with a stick.

Təi	kupən=tənii	xətu	ənə-i.
that	thread=TOP	torn	go-PRS.P

The thread goes torn.

Təi	moo-ǰɪ	paačɪ-la-ɪ-do-a-nɪ,	kupən	tui…,
that	stick-INS	mallet-VBZ-PRS.P-DAT-OCM-3SG	thread	that.way

tui	paačɪ-la-ɪ-do-a-nɪ,	moo-ǰɪ	tui
that.way	mallet-VBZ-PRS.P-DAT-OCM-3SG	tree-INS	that.way

paačɪ-la-ɪ-nɪ	goanɪ,	kupən	xətu	ənə-i-ni	goan.
mallet-VBZ-PRS.P-3SG	certainly	thread	torn	go-PRS.P-3SG	certainly

The shaman strikes it with the stick in that way, and the thread goes torn.

Təi	kupən	xətu	ənə-i-wə-ni=tənii	təi	asɪ-nɪ=daa,
that	thread	torn	go-PRS.P-ACC-3SG=TOP	that	wife-3SG=ADD

əǰi-ni=dəə,	piktə=dəə	xaŋgɪsɪ	ǰoog-čɪ
husband-3SG=ADD	kid=ADD	away	house-DIR

pagǰɪala-go-mɪ=tanɪɪ,	təi	kupəm	turgən	naŋgala-ɪ.
run.away-REV-SIM=TOP	that	thread.ACC	fast	throw-PRS.P

Turgən	naŋgala-ɪ	naa-čɪ.
fast	throw-PRS.P	earth-DIR

When the thread goes torn, the wife or husband and children of the deceased quickly throw the thread away and run to the house.

Mənə=tənii, xamasɪ əm ičə-gu-ə-mi, ǰoog-čɪ-jɪ
oneself=TOP back not see-ITER-INF-SIM house-DIR-REFL

čuul tutu-gu-m, ii-gu-i.
directly run-ITER-SIM enter-REV-PRS.P

They ran directly to their own house and enter it, not looking back.

Tui ǰɪa ǰɪa-warɪ tui
that.way companion companion-REFL.PL that.way

xaɪ-rɪɪ-čɪ goan, təi buni-či ənə-i
do.what-PRS.P-3PL certainly that otherworld-DIR go-PRS.P

naɪ əmuučəkəən ənə-gu-wəən-i, ǰooŋkan-ba ǰapa-asɪ
person alone.DIM go-REV-CAUS-PRS.P family-ACC catch-NEG.PRS.P

osɪ-go-a-nɪ.
become-PURP-OCM-3SG

In that way, the family have the deceased go to otherworld alone, not with its family.

ǰooŋkan-ba xorɪ-čɪ-maari, tui ta-ɪ-čɪ.
family-ACC protect FR-SIM.PL that.way do-PRS.P-3PL

To protect the family, they do so.

Taja-čɪ ta-orɪ-du, xumu-uri-du bəjə-du
that.place-DIR do-PRS.IMPS.P-DAT bury-PRS.IMPS.P-DAT body-DAT

bi-i əkəsəl-bə bi-wəən-buwəsi čadu.
be-PRS.P woman.PL-ACC be-CAUS-NEG.PRS.IMPS.P then

Pregnant women are not allowed to attend the burial.

Bəjə-du bi-i əkəsəl niə-rədəəsi=ə,
body-DAT be-PRS.P woman.PL go.out-NEG.PRS.P=MIR

ičə-ədəəsi=ə taja-čɪ bi-i ǰaka-sal-ba;

see-NEG.PRS.P=MIR that.place-DIR be-PRS.P thing-PL-ACC

They do not go outside, and do not look at things that are facing that direction.

naɪ xumu-i-du-ə-ni=dəə, ənə-ədəəsi=ə.
person bury-PRS.P-DAT-OCM-3SG=ADD go-NEG.PRS.P=MIR

Doo-ko, doo-la-nɪ naɪ — piktə balǰɪ-ɪ.
inside-PROP inside-LOC-3SG person child be.born-PRS.P

Those who have a baby in their womb do not go to the burial.

Tui ta-mɪ naɪ xumu-n-du-ə-ni bəjə-ǰi... bəjə-du
that.way do-SIM person bury-NMLZ-DAT-OCM-3SG body-INS body-DAT

bi-i əktə-wə xaɪ-rasɪ... bi-wəən-buwəsi.
be-PRS.P woman-ACC do.what-NEG.PRS.P be-CAUS-NEG.PRS.IMPS.P

In that way, a pregnant woman is not allowed to be at the burial.

Totaraa xumu-n-bə... xaɪ... xəur-bə bui-kin naɪ-čɪ
and.then bury-NMLZ-ACC what coffin-ACC die-PST.P person-DIR

too-bo-ɪ-čɪ goanɪ xumu-n baaro-nɪ.
go-TR-PRS.P-3PL certainly bury-NMLZ direction-3SG

Afterwards, they carry the coffin in which the deceased was put to the grave.

Xumu-n-bə ələ xulə-xən.
bury-NMLZ-ACC already dig-PST.P

A grave was already made.

Xumu-n doo-la-nɪ=tanɪɪ kərən-bə aŋgo-ɪ-čɪ
bury-NMLZ inside-LOC-3SG=TOP wooden.chamber-ACC do-PRS.P-3PL

goan, kərən-bə.
certainly wooden.chamber-ACC

They build a wooden chamber inside it.

Balana=tanɪɪ	moo-wa	xaɪ…	poo-maarɪ,	tujəə tujəə	bi-i
long.ago=TOP	wood-ACC	indeed	saw-SIM.PL	so.much	be-PRS.P

waa-mɪ	moo-ǰɪ	čikə-lə-i-či	xəm.
catch-SIM	tree-INS	base-VBZ-PRS.P-3PL	all

In the old days, they sawed or collected lots of wood, laying a wood foundation.

— Xəm	təi	xumu-n	doo-wa-nɪ,	əmutuu	ǰoo=maa,
all	that	bury-NMLZ	inside-ACC-3SG	as.if	house=SML

aŋgo-ɪ	bi-či-či	goan	čadu.
make-PRS.P	be-PST.P-3PL	certainly	then

And they made the inside of the grave just as that of a house.

Pəgiə-lə-ni=dəə	undəxən-bə	nəə-rii.
bottom-LOC-3SG=ADD	board-ACC	set-PRS.P

Boards are laid on the floor.

Totapɪ=maa	təi	kərən	doo-la-nɪ=maa,
after.that=CON	that	wooden.chamber	inside-LOC-3SG=SML

təi	doo-čɪ-a-nɪ	xəur-bə	nəə-rii	bi-či-či	goan.
that	inside-DIR-OCM-3SG	coffin-ACC	set-PRS.P	be-PST.P-3PL	certainly

They placed the coffin in the wooden chamber at last.

Xəur-bə	xumu-n-či	nəə-rii-wəri	ǰuliə-lə-ni	xaɪ-wa-nɪ…
coffin-ACC	bury-NMLZ-DIR	set-PRS.P-REFL.PL	front-LOC-3SG	what-ACC-3SG

dasɪ-ko-wa-nɪ	dasɪ-ɪ	bi-či-či	goan.
cover-PROP-ACC-3SG	cover-PRS.P	be-PST.P-3PL	certainly

Before putting the coffin in the grave, they put a lid on it.

Dasɪ-ko-wa-nɪ	dasɪ-ɪ-do-arɪ=tanɪɪ,			
cover-PROP-ACC-3SG	cover-PRS.P-DAT-REFL.PL=TOP			
tukpən-gu-i-či	goanɪ	təi	xəur	komtaan-ba-nɪ.
nail-ITER-PRS.P-3PL	certainly	that	coffin	cap-ACC-3SG

When they put a lid on the coffin, they drive nails into the lid.

Xaɪ…	əm…	əm	modan	paačɪ-la-orɪ	tukpən-bə.
what	one	one	time (turn)	mallet-VBZ-PRS.IMPS.P	nail-ACC

Əm	modan	paačɪ-la-orɪ	tukpən-bə.
one	time (turn)	mallet-VBZ-PRS.IMPS.P	nail-ACC

Each nail should be struck just once.

Xəmtu	tukpən=tənii	ba…	xaɪ	anaa…	budər	anaa.
all	nail=TOP	pair	indeed	not	pair	not

The nails are not even-numbered.

Budər	anaa:	nadaan,	xujun,	ǰoan	əmun	—	budər
pair	not	seven	nine	ten	one		pair

anaa	tukpəm	tukpən-dii-du-ji.
not	nail.ACC	nail-PRS.P-DAT-REFL

When they drive nails, they are not even-numbered: seven, nine, eleven and so on.

Gəə,	xaɪ-čɪ…	xumu-n-či	tugbu-i,	nəə-rii	təi
well	what-DIR	bury-NMLZ-DIR	fall-PRS.P	set-PRS.P	that

xaɪ-wa…	xəur-bə	—	naɪ-wa.
what-ACC	coffin-ACC		person-ACC

The coffin with the deceased is lowered and set into the grave.

Totaraa	təi	xəur	ojaa-la-nɪ=tanɪɪ	guči	moo-wa
and.then	that	coffin	surface-LOC-3SG=TOP	again	tree-ACC

dəri-gu-i-či.

spread-ITER-PRS.P-3PL

After that, they spread pieces of wood out over the coffin.

Xəm=dəə	dasɪ-go-ɪ-čɪ	moo-ǰɪ.
all=ADD	cover-REV-PRS.P-3PL	tree-INS

All are covered with trees.

Totapɪ=tanɪɪ	təi	pulə-xən,	xəur-či	ii-rəsi	xaǰon,
after.that=TOP	that	be.left-PST.P	coffin-DIR	enter-NEG.PRS.P	goods

waaɪča-orɪ	xaǰon	bi-i=dəə,
hunt-PRS.IMPS.P	goods	be-PRS.P=ADD

poawanɪ	xəur	pəgiə-lə-ni,	poawanɪ	xəur	ujə-lə-ni
some	coffin	bottom-LOC-3SG	some	coffin	top-LOC-3SG

nəə-rəə,	naa-ǰɪ	xumu-gu-i-či	goan.
put-ANT	earth-INS	bury-REV-PRS.P-3PL	certainly

And if there are any items or hunting equipment left, some of them are put under the coffin, and others over the coffin, and these are covered with soil.

Taosɪ	too-xan	gurun=tənii	xəm...	xə...	xoroačɪ-maarɪ
to.that.place	go-PST.P	people-TOP	all	all	hold.fist-SIM.PL

naa-wa	təi	xumu-n	doo-čɪ-a-nɪ	naŋgaačɪ-ɪ.
earth-ACC	that	bury-NMLZ	inside-DIR-OCM-3SG	throw.away-PRS.P

Those who went to that place takes a handful of soil and throw it into the grave.

Təi	ərin-du=tənii	mamaarɪ-sal...	Əm	mama	siun
that	days-DAT=TOP	old.woman-PL	one	old.woman	sun

garpa-ɪ-nɪ	kaltaaǰɪa-la	tawa	ɪwan-dɪɪ.
rise-PRS.P-3SG	side-LOC	fire	burn-PRS.P

At that time, an old woman makes a fire in the direction of the sun rising.

Goɪ	mama=tanɪɪ	xumu-n-ǰiə…	xumu-n	ǰakpa-do-a-nɪ,
other	old.woman=TOP	bury-NMLZ-ABL	bury-NMLZ	next-DAT-OCM-3SG

siun	tuu-gu-i-ni	kaltaaǰɪa-la	ǰuəjəčiə
sun	sink-ITER-PRS.P-3SG	side-LOC	second

tawa	ɪwaŋ…	ɪwan-go-ɪ.
fire	burn	burn-ITER-PRS.P

Another old woman makes the second fire in the direction of the sun setting beside the grave.

Siun	garpa-ɪ-nɪ…	garpa-ɪ-do-a-nɪ	taawo-oxan
sun	rise-PRS.P-3SG	rise-PRS.P-DAT-OCM-3SG	light.up-PST.IMPS.P

tawa	—	təi	tawa	ujuun	gurun	tawa-čɪ.
fire		that	fire	living	people	fire-3PL

The fire in the direction of the sun rising is that of the living people.

Ujuun	gurun	tawa-čɪ.
living	people	fire-3PL

It is fire of the living people.

Tadu	nuuči	gurun,	naonǰoan	gurun,	masɪ	gurun
then	small	people	young	people	strong	people

—	Xəm	bi-i-či	čadu.
	all	be-PRS.P-3PL	then

All the small, young, and strong people exist.

Əi…	əi	siun	tuu-gu-i-ni	xaɪ-do-a-nɪ…
this	this	sun	sink-ITER-PRS.P-3SG	what-DAT-OCM-3SG

bado-do-a-nɪ	taawo-xa-či	tawa=tanɪɪ
opposite.side-DAT-OCM-3SG	light.up-PST.P-3PL	fire=TOP

—	bui-kin	naɪ	tawa-nɪ.
	die-PST.P	person	fire-3SG

The fire in the direction of the sun set is that of the deceased.

Siun tuu-gu-i-ni=məə, naɪ tuu-rii-ni goan
sun sink-ITER-PRS.P-3SG=SML person fall-PRS.P-3SG certainly

čadu bu-mi.
then die-SIM

At that time, if a man die, as the sun sets, he falls.

Gəə, təi buikini tawa-nɪ.
well that the.deceased fire-3SG

Well, it is the fire of the deceased.

Gəə, təi tawa-wa ɪwa-čɪ-ɪ əktə — təŋ urun-ku,
well that fire-ACC heat-FR-PRS.P woman very mind-PROP

otolɪ-ɪ əktə.
know-PRS.P woman

The woman who makes that fire is very thoughtful and wise.

Xaɪmɪ?
why

Why is it so?

Təi tawa-du təi saorma, naɪ olbɪačɪ-xa-nɪ
that fire-DAT that *saorma* person carry-PST.P-3SG

sɪa-orɪ ǰaka.
eat-PRS.IMPS.P thing

This was because people brought *saorma*, that is, food to the fire.

Guči dooboča-oxan sɪa-orɪ ǰaka:
again offer.food.to.the.deceased-PST.IMPS.P eat-PRS.IMPS.P thing

čoolon, boda, uliksə, əpən, lala — xaɪ=daa xəm,
soup boiled.cereal meat bread gruel what=ADD all

arkɪ — xəm təi tawa-čɪ nəə-mi, ǰəgǰi-či-uri čadu.
vodka all that fire-DIR set-SIM burn-FR-PRS.IMPS.P then

All the *saorma* such as soup, boiled cereal, meat, bread, gruel, drinks and so on had to be thrown into the fire and burned.

Čaa xəm ǰəgǰi-či-uri.
that.ACC all burn-FR-PRS.IMPS.P

All of them should be burned.

Poanɪ xaǰon — čaa=daa xəm bojačɪ-ɪ, gudə-či-i
rest goods that.ACC=ADD all broken.VBZ-PRS.P tear-FR-PRS.P

ta-mɪ, təi tawa-du ǰəgǰi-uri.
do-SIM that fire-DAT burn-PRS.IMPS.P

The leftover items are also smashed and split apart, and had to be burned down in the fire.

Otolɪ-asɪ-nɪ təi tawa ǰəgǰi-či-i osɪnɪ, təi
understand-NEG.PRS.P-3SG that fire burn-FR-PRS.P if that

naɪ silə-ku ǰaka-wa: boda-wa, čoolon-ba
person broth-PROP thing-ACC boiled.cereal-ACC soup-ACC

— taosɪ jəwərsu-i-du-ə-ni, tawa
to.that.place pour.DUR-PRS.P-DAT-OCM-3SG fire

guup-čii-ə... tawa guup-čii-əri.
be.extinguished-PRS.P-REFL.PL fire be.extinguished-PRS.P-REFL.PL

If an unwise person makes the fire, it may be extinguished when he pours fluid food, for example, boiled cereal or soup.

Gəə, təi təŋ orkɪn ǰaka. Təŋ orkɪn ǰaka.
well that very bad thing very bad thing

This is a very ominous sign.

Təi buikini tawa-nɪ guup-čii-əri osɪnɪ,

that the.deceased fire-3SG be.extinguished-PRS.P-REFL.PL if

balana tui un-dii bi-či-či goan: təi orkın.
long.ago that.way say-PRS.P be-PST.P-3PL certainly that bad

In the old days, they said, “It is an ominous sign if the fire of the deceased go out by itself.

əi ǰooŋkan-dola guči naı bu-dii=jəm=dəə.
this family-LOC again person die-PRS.P=REPO=ADD

If this happens, another member of the family die.”

Tui tamaarı čadu təŋ otolı-ı naı-a
therefore then very understand-PRS.P person-ACC

təə-wəən-dii bi-či-či goan, təi tawa tul tul
sit-CAUS-PRS.P be-PST.P-3P certainly that fire always

ǰəgdə-gu-ə-ni.
light.up-PURP-OCM-3SG

For that reason, they had a very wise woman sit and keep the fire smouldering the whole time.

Təi xaı-wa... təi saorma-wa, xaǰon-ba
that what-ACC that *saorma*-ACC goods-ACC

ǰəgǰi-či-i-du-əri=tənii, xumu-n-ǰiəǰi... xumu-n-ǰiəǰi təi
burn-FR-PRS.P-DAT-REFL.PL=TOP bury-NMLZ-ABL bury-NMLZ-ABL that

tawa-čı tui xurmi-kuukəən pokto-kaan=maa xulə-i
fire-DIR that.way small-EXTR pathway-DIM=SML dig-PRS.P

bi-či-či goan.
be-PST.P-3PL certainly

When the *saormas* and items were burned down, they dug a small stream like pathway from the grave to the fire.

Təi pokto-kaam=tanıı xaımaarı tui xulə-i bi-či-či?
that pathway-DIM.ACC=TOP why that.way dig-PRS.P be-PST.P-3PL

Why did they dig the pathway in that way?

Tui	un-dii	bi-či-či	goan
that.way	say-PRS.P	be-PST.P-3PL	certainly

They said as follows:

— Əidu	ǰəg…	ǰəgǰi-či-i-uxən	xəm	taosɪ
here	burn	burn-FR-PST.IMPS.P	all	to.that.place

ənə-i=əm,	xumu-u…	xumu-uxən	naɪ-čɪ.
go-PRS.P=REPO	bury-PST.P	bury-PST.P	person-DIR

"Everything that is burned here will go to that place, that is, the deceased.

Xumu-uxən	naɪ	xəm	baa-rɪɪ	čawa.
bury-PST.P	person	all	take-PRS.P	that.ACC

The deceased will take those things away."

Təi	«xuməgdəm»,	gərbiə-si-i	bi-čin.
that	ritual.stick.ACC	call-DUR-PRS.P	be-PST.P

«Xuməgdəm=dəə,	gərbiə-si-i	bi-čin.
ritual.stick.REPO=ADD	call-DUR-PRS.P	be-PST.P

That was called *xumegden* (a ritual stick).

Tui=dəə.
that.way=ADD

That is the way it goes.

Tota…	Totapɪa	xaɪ-rɪɪ-do-arɪ…	tok…
a.little.later	later	do.what-PRS.P-DAT-REFL.PL	go.up

tookpaačɪ-ɪ-do-arɪ=tanɪɪ,	təi	xuməgdən-dulə
go.up-PRS.P-DAT-REFL.PL=TOP	that	ritual.stick-LOC

boda-wa, xaɪ-wa… muə-wə jəwərsu-i bi-čin
boiled.cereal-ACC what-ACC water-ACC pour.DUR-PRS.P be-PST.P

goanɪ, buikini baa-go-a-nɪ. buikini
certainly the.deceased take-PURP-OCM-3SG the.deceased

baa-go-a-nɪ.
take-PURP-OCM-3SG

When someone goes up the grave in the later, he pours the boiled cereal or water along the *xumegden* so that the deceased may take it.

Gəə, čadu xəm tui ta-raa, əlkəǰiəni ǰoog-čɪ
well then all that.way do-ANT gradually house-DIR

mutə… močogo-ɪ goan.
be.able.to return-PRS.P certainly

Well, after everything is done, they finally return home.

Balana=tanɪɪ xumu-n baaroa-nɪ əm pokto-la too-rɪɪ.
long.ago=TOP bury-NMLZ direction-3SG one road-LOC go-PRS.P

In the old days, they took some way to go to the grave.

ǰoog-čɪ xumu-n-ǰi-ə-či=tənii goɪ pokto-l əu…
house-DIR bury-NMLZ-INS-OCM-3PL=TOP other road-LOC descend

əu-gu-i bi-čin.
descend-REV-PRS.P be-PST.P

They took a different way to descend from the grave.

Əsi=tənii əm pokto-l too-rɪɪ, əm pokto-l əu-gu-i.
now=TOP one road-LOC go-PRS.P one road-LOC descend-REV-PRS.P

Now they take the same way to go and descend.

Tui ta… ta-ɪ-čɪ goan.
that.way do do-PRS.P-3PL certainly

They do like that.

Gəə, tui=dəə.
well that.way=ADD

Well, that is the way it goes.

Naanaɪ, naɪ osɪ-očɪa-nɪ, ɪlaan xərgən-bə ta-ɪ.
Nanai person die-COND-3SG three funeral.repast-ACC do-PRS.P

When a person die, Nanai performs funeral repasts three times.

Niə-wu-xən-bi ini-du, ɪlaačɪa ini-du, — xərgən.
go.out-TR-PST.P-REFL day-DAT third day-DAT funeral.repast

There is a funeral repast on the third day of moving the coffin out.

Toɪŋgɪačɪa ini-du — xərgən.
fifth day-DAT funeral.repast

There is a funeral repast on the fifth day.

Nadaačɪa ini-du — xərgən.
seventh day-DAT funeral.repast

There is a funeral repast on the seventh day.

Gəə, tui bi-i gɪan.
well that.way be-PRS.P principle

That is a principle.

Tui nadaan ini-du naɪ buikini ǰoog-do
that.way seven day-DAT person die-PST.P-3SG house-DAT
tul tul ixərə ǰəgdə-i-wə-ni gələ-uri.
always lamp-ACC light.up-PRS.P-ACC-3SG ask.for-PRS.IMPS.P

For those seven days, a lamp always has to be lighted up in the house where someone died.

İİxərə	guup-uri	osɪnɪ,	balana	tui
lamp	be.extinguished-PRS.IMPS.P	if	long.ago	that.way

un-dii	bi-či-ni	xərgən-du,	burpuun-du	ixərə
say-PRS.P	be-PST.P-3SG	funeral.repast-DAT	mourning-DAT	lamp

ǰəgdə-əsi-ni	osɪnɪ,	əi	ǰooŋkan	əlkəǰiəni	xəm
light.up-NEG.PRS.P-3SG	if	this	family	gradually	all

aba-na-ɪ=am=daa.	Xəm	bu-dii=jəm.
not-VBZ-PRS.P=REPO=ADD	all	die-PRS.P=REPO

In the old days, it was said that if the lamp was ever off during the funeral repasts and the period of mourning, the family would gradually vanish and everyone would eventually die out.

Tui tamɪ	tul tul	ixərə	ǰəgǰi-či-i-uri
therefore	always	lamp	light.up-FR-PRS.IMPS.P

bi-či-ni	goan.
be-PST.P-3SG	certainly

For that reason the lamp is always kept on.

Gəə,	tui	ta...	tawa	bodo-ɪ.
well	that.way	fire	fire	consider-PRS.P

Fire is thought as follows:

Naanaɪ	tawa	təŋ	maŋga-ǰɪ	bodo-ɪ	bi-či-ni
Nanai	fire	very	hard-INS	consider-PRS.P	be-PST.P-3SG

goanɪ.
certainly

“Nanai people think fire is very powerful.

Iwačɪ-orɪ tawa, ixərə tawa-nɪ,

heat-PRS.IMPS.P fire lamp fire-3SG

xaɪ... siun=dəə əmutuu tawa=maa bi-i.
indeed sun=ADD as.if fire=SML be-PRS.P

Hot stove, a lighting lamp, and even the sun is considered to be just as fire.

Təi... čawa xəm bodo-ɪ bi-čin goan.
that that.ACC all consider-PRS.P be-PST.P certainly

All of them are considered like that."

Nuučikəənǰuən-bə=dəə xəm tui aloosɪ-ɪ bi-čin.
children-ACC=ADD all that.way teach-PRS.P be-PST.P

Even all of our children are taught in that way.

Gəə, xərgən=dəə xaɪ?
well funeral.repast=ADD what

Well, what is the funeral repasts?

Arkɪ-kaan-ba omɪ-ɪ, sɪa-orɪ-kaam sɪa-rɪɪ.
vodka-DIM-ACC drink-PRS.P eat-PRS.IMPS.P-DIM.ACC eat-PRS.P

The living people drank alcohol and ate food.

Sɪa-orɪ-kaam naɪ tuju-xən-bə-ni,
eat-PRS.IMPS.P-DIM.ACC person treat-PST.P-ACC-3SG

nəə-xən-bə-ni=tənii tui un-dii-či bi-či-ni goan:
set-PST.P-ACC-3SG=TOP that.way say-PRS.P-3PL be-PST.P-3SG certainly

About the food which was offered to and was put down for the deceased person, they said as follows:

Naɪ xaɪ-wa nəə-xə-ni osɪnɪ, otokoo=daa xaɪ-wa=daa
person what-ACC set-PST.P-3SG if a.little=ADD what-ACC=ADD

xəm, xəm čala njaŋgaa, čala njaŋgaa, čala

all all on.the.spot a.little on.the.spot a.little on.the.spot

njaŋgaa xəm ǰapa-mɪ, sɪa-orɪ=m=daa.
a.little all take-SIM eat-PRS.IMPS.P=REPO=ADD

"All the living people should take and eat all food offered to the deceased on the spot, however small it may be.

Tui sɪa-rasɪ-so osɪnɪ, əsi goɪ boa-čɪ,
that.way eat-NEG.PRS.P-2PL if now other place-DIR

buni-či, ənə-xən naɪ sɪa-orɪ-a xəm
otherworld-DIR go-PST.P person eat-PRS.IMPS.P-ACC all

baa-rasɪ=am.
take-NEG.PRS.P=REPO

If the living people do not eat the food, the deceased person who went to the otherworld would not take all the food."

Naanaɪ tui un-dii bi-či-ni goan:
Nanai that.way say-PRS.P be-PST.P-3SG certainly

— Naɪ bui-kin=dəə, buni-či ənə-pi,
person die-PST.P=ADD otherworld-DIR go-COND.IMPS

əmutuu ujuun=məət, balǰɪ-ɪ=jam=daa.
as.if living=SML be.born-PRS.P=REPO=ADD

Nanai people said, "If a person die, he will go to otherworld and live just as he lives in this world."

Xaɪ... tui tamaarɪ, gəə, xaǰon-go-a-nɪ əgǰi-ə
indeed therefore well clothes-DSG-OCM-3SG many-ACC

tətu-wəən-dii bi-či-či goan.
put.on-CAUS-PRS.P be-PST.P-3PL certainly

Čado bi-i=dəə, tuə=dəə bi-i, ǰoa=daa bi-i,
then be-PRS.P=ADD winter=ADD be-PRS.P summer=ADD be-PRS.P

njəŋnjə=dəə bi-i, bolo=daa bi-i.
spring=ADD be-PRS.P autumn=ADD be-PRS.P

For that reason, they dressed the deceased in lots of clothes. There are also winter, summer, spring and autumn there.

Gəə,	xaǰonɪ	xəm	bi-i-ni	osɪnɪ,	gəə,	tui
well	clothes.3SG	all	be-PRS.P-3SG	if	well	that.way

balǰɪ-ɪ-nɪ	goan.
live-PRS.P-3SG	certainly

If the deceased have these clothes, he lives in that way.

Gəə,	tui	un-dii	bi-či-či	goan:
well	that.way	say-PRS.P	be-PST.P-3PL	certainly

Nanai people said,

—	Buə	murči-i-pu	naɪ	bui-ki-ni.
	we	think-PRS.P-1PL	person	die-PST.P-3SG

"We think of a person's death.

A,	bui-ki-ni	xaɪ?
R. but	die-PST.P-3SG	what

What is death?

Təəm	ərsi-əsi-ni.
only	breathe-NEG.PRS.P-3SG

It means the person just does not breathe.

Təəm	ərsi-əsi-ni,	bunǰi	gəsə	bi-əsi-ni.
only	breathe-NEG.PRS.P-3SG	we.INS	together	be-NEG.PRS.P-3SG

The person just doesn't breathe and is not with us.

Njoanɪ	goɪ	boa-čɪ	ənə-xən.
he	other	place-DIR	go-PST.P

The person went to another place.

Goɪ boa-du… goɪ boa-du balǰɪ-ɪ.
other place-DAT other place-DAT be.born-PRS.P

The person lives in another place."

Tui un-dii-l.
that.way say-PRS.P-3PL

Nanai people say like that.

Čuu xamoroɪ xərgən=tənii əm aɪŋanɪ-du,
most last memorial.ceremony=TOP one year-DAT

aɪŋanɪ sii-učiə-ni=ə.
year pass-COND-3SG=MIR

The last memorial rituals is performed after one year passed from the funeral.

Poaldoanɪ ɪlaan aɪŋanɪ=daa sii-rii=jə.
sometimes three year=ADD pass-PRS.P=MIR

Təi kasaa-wa aŋgo-ɪ-čɪ.
that memorial.service-ACC make-PRS.P-3PL

Sometimes a memorial service is performed after three years passed.

Kasaa — daaɪ xərgən. Daaɪ
memorial.service great memorial.ceremony big

xərgən.
memorial.ceremony

This memorial service is a big ritual.

Təi kasaa-wa=tanɪɪ nəə saman aŋgo-ɪ.
that memorial.service-ACC=TOP certainly shaman make-PRS.P

Saman aŋgo-ɪ.
shaman make-PRS.P

A Shaman conducts this memorial service.

Təi ərdəŋgə xəsə. Xaɪ… xərgən.
that interesting word what memorial.ceremony

There is an interesting word.

Təi xərgən-du, təi kasaa-du əgǰi
that memorial.ceremony-DAT that memorial.service-DAT many

naɪ osɪ-ɪ.
person come-PRS.P

Lots of people come to this memorial service.

Əmun naɪ-wa manjaa=daa
one person-ACC only=ADD

kasaata-wasɪ=a.
perform.a.memorial.service-NEG.PRS.IMPS.P=MIR

This memorial service is not held for just one person.

ǰuər naɪ, ɪlaan naɪ, xado naɪ…
two person three person how.many person

It is held for two, three, many people.

ǰɪxa əgǰi gələ-i-ni goanɪ=a.
money many need-PRS.P-3SG certainly=MIR

Lots of money is needed.

Naɪ=daa əgǰi ǰi-dii-ni.
person=ADD many come-PRS.P-3SG

Many people come.

Tui ta-mɪ	maŋga	kasaata-orɪ.
therefore	expensive	perform.a.memorial.service-PRS.IMPS.P

Therefore, a lot of money is needed to hold the memorial service.

Samam	gələ-uri.
shaman.ACC	request-PRS.IMPS.P

It requires shaman.

Saman	xoda-nɪ=daa	maŋga.
shaman	price-3SG=ADD	expensive

The cost of shaman is high.

Tui tamaarɪ,	gəə,	sinəǰii-ləə	bi-i	gurun,
therefore	well	poor-SUFF	be-PRS.P	people

ba...	bui-ki-ni	baar-nɪ	ɪsɪ-očɪa-nɪ
first.anniversary	die-PST.P-3SG	first.anniversary-3SG	arrive-COND-3SG

mutə-gu-əsi-či	goanɪ.
be.able.to-ITER-NEG.PRS.P-3PL	certainly

Therefore, somewhat poor people are unable to perform a memorial service themselves for one year.

Totamaarɪ	xalačɪ-ɪ-čɪ	goan	goɪ	gurun-bə.
so	wait-PRS.P-3PL	certainly	other	people-ACC

So they wait for other person.

Totaraa	goɪ	gurun-ǰi	gəsə	kasaa	ta-ɪ-čɪ.
and.then	other	people-INS	together	memorial.service	do-PRS.P-3PL

And they perform a memorial service with other people.

Gəə,	kasaa	ta-paa...	kasaa-wa
well	memorial.service-ACC	do-COND.PL.IMPS	memorial.service-ACC

ta-paa...	ta-waa...	ta-waa...
do-COND.PL.IMPS	do-COND.PL.IMPS	do-COND.PL.IMPS

kasaa-wa	ta-paarɪ=maat,	ba...	təi
memorial.service-ACC	do-COND.PL.IMPS=CON	first.anniversary	that

taja-čɪ-a-nɪ	xərgən-bə	xaɪ-wa=daa
that.place-DIR-OCM-3SG	memorial.ceremony-ACC	what-ACC=ADD

ta-asɪ.
do-NEG.PRS.P

Ever since they perform the memorial service, they do not hold a memorial ritual for the deceased.

Guči=tənii	təi	nad...	nadaačɪa	ini-du	xərgən-bə
again=TOP	that	seven	seventh	day-DAT	memorial.ceremony-ACC

ta-paarɪ,	panjoo-wa	aŋgo-ɪ-čɪ.
do-COND.PL.IMPS	wooden.figure-ACC	make-PRS.P-3PL

When they perform the memorial ritual on the seventh day, they make a *panyoo* (wooden figure).

Panjoo-kaan	tujəə	bi-i.
wooden.figure-DIM	like.that	be-PRS.P

Panjoo shapes like that.

Panjoo-kaan-ba	aŋgo-ɪ-čɪ	goan	moo-ǰɪ,	əmutuu
wooden.figure-DIM-ACC	make-PRS.P-3PL	certainly	wood-INS	as.if

naɪ-kaan=maa=daa.
man-DIM=SML=ADD

They make *panyoo* with wood like a human.

Təi	naɪ-kaan-ba=tanɪɪ	təi	naɪ	bi-či-ni	nakan-du,
that	man-DIM-ACC=TOP	that	man	live-PST.P-3SG	heated.floor-DAT

təi	bəun-du-ə-ni	nəučə-i-či.
that	place-DAT-OCM-3SG	keep-PRS.P-3PL

They keep the *panyoo* on their heated floor where they live.

Ao-xa-nɪ	xaǰon-ba-nɪ	xəm	namo-raa,	təi	namo-ča
sleep-PST.P-3SG	goods-ACC-3SG	all	fold-ANT	that	fold-PASS

ǰuliə-lə-ni=tənii	təi	panjoo-kaan	bəun-gu-ə-ni
front-LOC-3SG=TOP	that	wooden.figure-DIM	place-DSG-OCM-3SG

undəxə-kəən-bə	nəə-rəə,	təi	panjoo-kaan-ba	nəə-rii-či.
board-DIM-ACC	put-ANT	that	wooden.figure-DIM-ACC	put-PRS.P-3PL

They fold the bedding, put a board as the place of *panyoo* in front of the bedding, and put the *panyoo* there.

Sɪa-rɪɪ-do-arɪ,	təi	panjoo-kaam	sɪa-waan-dɪɪ.
eat-PRS.P-DAT-REFL.PL	that	wooden.figure-DIM.ACC	eat-CAUS-PRS.P

When they eat, they feed it.

Akpan-go-ɪ-do-arɪ,	təi	panjoo-kaam
lie.down-REV-PRS.P-DAT-REFL.PL	that	wooden.figure-DIM.ACC

akpan-go-waan-dɪɪ.
lie.down-REV-CAUS-PRS.P

When they lie down, they lay it down.

Təə-gu-i-du-əri,	təi	panjoo-kaam	təə-u-gu-i.
sit-ITER-PRS.P-DAT-REFL.PL	that	wooden.figure-DIM.ACC	sit-TR-ITER-PRS.P

When they sit down, they sit it down.

Əmutuu	aja	balǰɪ-ɪ	naɪ=maat,	ujuun	naɪ=maat
as.if	good	live-PRS.P	person=SML	living	person=SML

nəučə-i-či.
keep-PRS.P-3PL

As if the *panyoo* were a living person, they keep it.

Gəə,	tui	un-dii-či	goan	təi:
well	so	say-PRS.P-3PL	certainly	that

They say as follows:

—	Njoanɪ	bui-ki-ni	bi-əsi=əm.
	he	die-PST.P-3SG	be-NEG.PRS.P=REPO

“He does not die.

Kasaa	ta-orɪ-čɪ=a,	njoanɪ	bunǰi	gəsə
memorial.service	do-PRS.IMPS.P-DIR=MIR	he	we.INS	together

bi-ə=m.
be-PRS=REPO

Until we hold the memorial service, he is with us.

Buə	xɪsaŋgo-ɪ-po=a=daa	njoanɪ	xəm	doolǰɪ-ɪ.
we	talk-PRS.P-1PL=MIR=ADD	he	all	hear-PRS.P

He hear all that we say.

Buə	un-dii-pu=ə=dəə	xəm	otolɪ-ɪ.
we	say-PRS.P-1PL=MIR=ADD	all	understand-PRS.P

He understand all that we say.

Bunǰi	gəsə	balǰɪ-ɪ-nɪ.
we.INS	together	live-PRS.P-3SG

He lives with us.”

Kasaa	ta-paarɪ=tanɪɪ,	təi	panjoo-wa
memorial.service	do-COND.PL.IMPS=TOP	that	wooden.figure-ACC

ǰəgǰi-gu-i.
burn-ITER-PRS.P

They burn the *panyoo* after the memorial service.

Təi	panjoo-wa	ǰəgǰi-gu-i	aba-na-go-a-nɪ.
that	wooden.figure-ACC	burn-ITER-PRS.P	not-VBZ-PURP-OCM-3SG

They burn the *panyoo* to make it disappear.

Gəə,	čado=maat	un-dii:
well	then=CON	say-PRS.P

After that, they say as follows:

—	Gəə,	bortɪ	ənu-xən	bunǰiəǰi.
	well	permanently	go.away-PST.P	we.ABL

"The deceased left us forever.

Gəə,	əsi	bunǰi	njoanɪ	aba.	Aba.
well	now	we.INS	he	not	not

Now the deceased is not with us."

Tui	osɪ-go-i.
that.way	become-ITER-PRS.P

It become in that way.

Balana	naɪ-wa	naa-du	xumu-əsi	bi-čin.
long.ago	person-ACC	earth-DAT	bury-NEG.PRS.P	be-PST.P

Naa-du	xumu-əsi	bi-čin.
earth-DAT	bury-NEG.PRS.P	be-PST.P

In the old days, the deceased was not buried in the ground.

Kərəm	aŋgo-raa,	əmutuu	ǰoo=maa=daa,
wooden.chamber.ACC	make-ANT	as.if	house=SML=ADD

təi	kərən-du	nəə-rii	bi-či-či
that	wooden.chamber-DAT	put-PRS.P	be-PST.P-3PL

goanɪ	xaɪ-wa…	bui-kin	naɪ-wa	xəur-du.	Xəur-du.
certainly	what-ACC	die-PST.P	person-ACC	coffin-DAT	coffin-DAT

They made a wooden chamber like a house, and laid the coffin and the deceased in it.

Təi	kərən=tənii	əmutuu	ǰoo=maa	bi-i.
that	wooden.chamber=TOP	as.if	house=SML	be-PRS.P

Əmutuu	ǰoo=maa	bi-i.
as.if	house=SML	be-PRS.P

The wooden chamber looks like a house.

Kərən-du	nəə-rii	bi-čin.
wooden.chamber-DAT	put-PRS.P	be-PST.P

In the wooden chamber the coffin was put.

Əi	loča-sal	agbɪn-bo-očɪa-nɪ=a	(loč…	loča-sal=tanɪɪ
this	Russian-PL	appear-TR-COND-3SG=MIR	Russian	Russian-PL=TOP

mənə	bui-kin	ǰɪasɪl-b…	xəm	naa-du
oneself	die-PST.P	companion-REFL.PL	all	earth-DAT

xumu…	xumu-i-či	goanɪ);	naanaɪ-sal=daa	naa-du
bury	bury-PRS.P-3PL	certainly	Nanai-PL=ADD	earth-DAT

xumu…	xumu-lu-xə-či	naɪ-sal-ba.
bury	bury-INCH-PST.P-3PL	person-PL-ACC

After Russians came (they bury the dead in the ground), Nanai people also began to bury the deceased.

Paɪdan=daa	balana	aba	bi-čin.
grave.mark=ADD	long.ago	not	be-PST.P

In the old days, there was no grave mark either.

Naa-du	xumu…	xumu-i=dəə,	xumu-rəə,	xumu-n-du=tənii
earth-DAT	bury	bury-PRS.P=ADD	bury-ANT	bury-NMLZ-DAT=TOP

moo-kaan	suuktu-kəən-bə-ni	moktolɪ-raa,	gɪda-la-ɪ
wood-DIM	branch-DIM-ACC-3SG	break-ANT	spear-VBZ-PRS.P

bi-či-či goan.
be-PST.P-3PL certainly

They break branches off a small tree and just stick them into the grave after burial.

Gəə, təi... čaa=tanɪɪ tui un-dii bi-či-či goan:
well that that.ACC=TOP so say-PRS.P be-PST.P-3PL certainly

Nanai people say,

— təi moo-kaan, daaɪ moo osɪ-mɪ, urə-i-ni osɪnɪ,
that wood-DIM big tree become-SIM grow-PRS.P-3SG if

təi uləən.
that good

"If the small tree grow up to be a big one, it is good.

Təi bui-kin naɪ oroondolanɪ goɪ naɪ
that die-PST.P person instead.of other person

balǰɪ-go-ɪ.
be.born-ITER-PRS.P

Another person is born in place of the deceased.

Goɪ naɪ balǰɪ-go-ɪ.
other person be.born-ITER-PRS.P

Another person is born."

Tui un-dii bi-čin.
that.way say-PRS.P be-PST.P

Nanai people said so.

Təi paɪdan=tanɪɪ — təi=dəə loča-sal ičə-wəən-ki-či
that grave.mark=TOP that=ADD Russian-PL see-CAUS-PST.P-3PL

goanɪ.
certainly

Russians showed their grave mark.

Loča-sal paɪdam aŋgo-ɪ.
Russian-PL grave.mark.ACC make-PRS.P

Russians make their grave mark.

Naanaɪ=daa əsi paɪdam aŋgo-lo-xa-čɪ.
Nanai=ADD now grave.post.ACC make-INCH-PST.P-3PL

Now Nanai people also make their grave mark.

Balana əčiə aŋgo-a bi-čin.
long.ago not make-INF be-PST.P

In the old days, Nanai did not make their grave mark.

Nuučiku naɪ bu-dii-ni osɪnɪ, baar-bɪ
little person die-PRS.P-3SG if one.year-REFL

ɪsɪ-go-asɪ piktə bu-dii-ni osɪnɪ, balana
arrive-ITER-NEG.PRS.P child die-PRS.P-3SG if long.ago

naa-du xumu-əsi bi-čin piktə-wə.
earth-DAT bury-NEG.PRS.P be-PST.P child-ACC

In the old days, if a little baby under the age of one died, it was not buried in the ground.

Gəə, mii gusərə-čə-i=kəə, təi… xaɪ…
well I say-PASS-1SG=CNTR that what

I was told as follows:

gɪamata tətuə-du-ə-ni, xamɪa-la-nɪ, moo.
wedding dress-DAT-OCM-3SG back-LOC-3SG tree

"There is a tree on the back of a wedding gown.

Təi ǰaagda moo-wa-nɪ naɪ ulpi-i bi-čin
that pine tree-ACC-3SG person embroider-PRS.P be-PST.P

goan.
certainly

Someone embroidered the pine."

Təi moo-do=tanɪɪ… xaɪ-wa… niičəəkəə-səl-bə aŋgo-maarɪ,
that tree-DAT=TOP what-ACC bird-PL-ACC make-SIM.PL

ulpi-i bi-či-či.
embroider-PRS.P be-PST.P-3PL

They made the birds and embroidered them on the tree.

Gəə, tui un-dii bi-či-či goan: — Nuuči piktə,
well so say-PRS.P be-PST.P-3PL certainly little child

baar-bɪ əčiə ɪsɪ-go-a piktə, — niičəəkəən.
one.year-REFL not arrive-ITER-INF child bird

niičəəkəən.
bird

They said that a baby under the age of one was a bird.

Totamaarɪ bui-ki-n… baar-bɪ əm ɪsɪ-go-a-mɪ
so die-PST.P-3SG one.year-REFL not arrive-ITER-INF-SIM

bui-kin piktə-wə, xəm baaroolɪ-raa,
die-PST.P child-ACC all dress-ANT

toɪksa talo-ǰɪ tui xuku-rəə,
birch.bark.of.special.treatment birch.bark-INS so wrap-ANT

duisi ɪra-ɪ bi-či-či goan.
to.the.forest carry-PRS.P be-PST.P-3PL certainly

Therefore, they dressed the baby who died under the age of one in all of its clothes, wrapped with birch barks, and took it into the forest.

Totaraa=tanıı moo gara-nı aldan-do-a-nı, moo gara-nı
and.then=TOP tree bough-3SG gap-DAT-OCM-3SG tree bough-3SG

aldan-do-a-nı tui kapıra-maarı,
gap-DAT-OCM-3SG so attach-SIM.PL

tui čadu dərəǰi-gu-wəən-dii bi-či-či goan, uilə. Uilə.
so then stay-ITER-CAUS-PRS.P be-PST.P-3PL certainly above above

And they tied it up between the branches of a tree, and had it maintained high.

Xaımaarı tui ta-xa-čı?
why so do-PST.P-3PL

Why did they do?

Balana naı tui un-dii bi-či-či goan:
long.ago person so say-PRS.P be-PST.P-3PL certainly

In the old days, they said as follows:

— Nuuči piktə, baar-bı əčiə ısı-go-a piktə —
little child one.year-REFL not arrive-ITER-PRS child

niičəəkəən. niičəəkəən.
bird bird

“A baby under the age of one is a bird.

Njoanı dəgdə-gu-i=əm=dəə.
he fly-REV-PRS.P=REPO=ADD

It will fly.

Mənə dəgdə-gu-i.
oneself fly-REV-PRS.P

It will fly itself.

Totapɪa	njoanɪ=tanɪɪ,	goɪ	piktə	osɪ-go-m,
later	he=TOP	other	child	become-ITER-SIM

baljɪ-go-ɪ.
be.born-ITER-PRS.P

In the later, it will be born again as another baby.

Goɪ	piktə	osɪ-go-m,	baljɪ-go-ɪ.
other	child	become-ITER-SIM	be.born-ITER-PRS.P

It will be born as another baby."

To	ta-mɪ	tui	un-dii	bi-či-či	goan:
so	do-SIM	so	say-PRS.P	be-PST.P-3PL	certainly

Furthermore, they also said as follows:

— Nuuči	piktə	bu-dii-du-ə-ni,	bur-bučiə-ni,
little	child	die-PRS.P-DAT-OCM-3SG	die-COND-3SG

saɪ-orɪ=am=daa.
mark-PRS.IMPS.P=REPO=ADD

"If a baby died, it should be marked."

Bəgji-kəən-du-ə-ni=dəə,	ŋaala-kaan-do-a-nɪ=daa,
leg-DIM-DAT-OCM-3SG=ADD	hand-DIM-DAT-OCM-3SG=ADD

oŋbo-kaan-do-a-nɪ=daa,	darama-kaan-do=daa,
buttock-DIM-DAT-OCM-3SG=ADD	back-DIM-DAT=ADD

bəjə-du-ə-n...,	xai-do=daa...	bəjə-du-ə-ni=dəə	aja.
body-DAT-OCM-3SG	what-DAT=ADD	body-DAT-OCM-3SG=ADD	good

Marking its legs, hands, buttocks, back, and body is good.

Sɪalta-jɪ	saɪ-ča	aŋgo-orɪ.	Saɪ-ča.
charcoal-INS	mark-PASS	make-PRS.IMPS.P	mark-PASS

The marks should be made with charcoal.

Tui=dəə aja, tui=dəə aja, tui kəəndəli-m=dəə
that.way=ADD good that.way=ADD good that.way surround-SIM=ADD

aja, sɪalta-ǰi modorɪ-orɪ, uləən modorɪ-orɪ
good charcoal-INS smear-PRS.IMPS.P well smear-PRS.IMPS.P

saa-or... saa-orɪ-ǰɪ, ičə-uri-ǰi
know-PRS.IMPS.P know-PRS.IMPS.P-INS see-PRS.IMPS.P-INS

modorɪ-orɪ.
smear-PRS.IMPS.P

It is all right to mark around its body thoroughly with charcoal to know and see it later.

Totapɪ, ui-du=dəə piktə balǰɪ-go-ɪ-nɪ osɪnɪ,
after.that who-DAT=ADD child be.born-ITER-PRS.P-3SG if

jarsɪ-ɪ-čɪ goanɪ, taja-čɪ bi-i
examine-PRS.P-3PL certainly that.place-DIR be-PRS.P

saɪ-ča ui-du=dəə aba=noo=m=daa.
mark-PASS who-DAT=ADD not=Q=REPO=ADD

If a baby is born to someone afterward, they examine it to see if it had the marks of the deceased baby or not.

Taja-čɪ bi-i saɪ-ča ui-du=dəə ičə-i-wəri
that.place-DIR be-PRS.P mark-PASS who-DAT=ADD see-PRS.P-REFL.PL

osɪnɪ, un-dii-či goan: — Gəə, təi piktər... bui-kin
if say-PRS.P-3PL certainly well that child die-PST.P

piktə oroondolanɪ sikuun piktə balǰɪ-go-xa-nɪ.
child instead.of new child be.born-ITER-PST.P-3SG

If the marks that were on the deceased baby was found on a new baby, they said, "The new baby was born in place of it."

Tui un-dii bi-či-či goan.

that.way say-PRS.P be-PST.P-3PL certainly

They said so.

Xaɪ-wa… muələn-kin naɪ-wa=tanɪɪ balana naɪ-ǰɪ
what-ACC drown-PST.P person-ACC=TOP long.ago person-INS

gəsə, gərəən naɪ xumu-i-ǰi-əri gəsə,
together lots.of person bury-PRS.P-INS-REFL.PL together

xumu-əsi bi-či-či goanɪ.
bury-NEG.PRS.P be-PST.P-3PL certainly

In the old days, they did not bury a person who drowned in the same way how they buried other persons.

Paaǰɪ xumu-i bi-či-či goan.
separately bury-PRS.P be-PST.P-3PL certainly

They buried him differently.

Xaɪ-do baogo-xan osɪnɪ, təi baogo-oxan bəun
what-DAT find-PST.P if that find-PST.IMPS.P place

bado-do-a-nɪ muələn-kin naɪ-wa xumu…
opposite.side-DAT-OCM-3SG drown-PST.P person-ACC bury

xumu-i bi-či-či goan čadu.
bury-PRS.P be-PST.P-3PL certainly then

If they discovered a person who had drowned, they buried him at the opposite side of the place where they discovered him at that time.

Tui=dəə.
that.way=ADD

That is the way it goes.

Gəə, ələ.
well enough

That is all.

3

Translation of the Russian Version of the Nanai Speech Materials

3.1. Childhood education and child rearing rituals

Long ago, the Nanai people believed that families with many children were the happiest families. This is because, though many children were born, many children also died. At times, there would only be one or two children left. That is why families with many children were believed to be happy families, and these people were envied. When a child was born, it was a joyous occasion for the family. This is because a son would succeed the clan and inherit the father's work. In other words, because a son was able to continue whatever his father did, a son was the happiness of a family. They were also happy when a daughter was born. This was because after raising a daughter, though she was married off, and this, of course, meant she was leaving the clan, if someone wanted to take the daughter, he had to pay the *tori* (bridewealth). In other words, a daughter also improved the family's fortune to a certain extent. A *tori* given to a potential bride included things like clothes, shoes, bowls, various household necessities, and fur. If the potential groom were from a rich family, it even included gold and silver products.

Families did not teach their children anything in particular. They did not do as they say to do nowadays, that children must learn this and that. Sons just did exactly what their brothers and father did. If the father caught fish, the son also played fisherman. After the son grew up a little, when he was four or five years old, the father would take his son along when he went fishing. And the son did not just follow, he was to carry all that he was able to the boat. For example, he would carry things like the *soopon* (water bowl), and if he was rather big child, he would carry the pail or the fishing net. Daughters did exactly as their mothers did. They did things like cook, clean, make clothing, embroider, or make patterns. In other words, everything for a lifestyle, that is, what children need to know while living their lives, what they need to learn, is what they were taught.

The basis of a Nanai family was group work. If someone is working, it was absolutely unacceptable for someone else to just sit or lay around. Whether it was a son or a daughter, this was absolutely unacceptable. Everyone must work all together. The only people who could not work were the sick or injured. If someone was injured, he (or she) lied down or sat, but this is because he could not work. Everyone else must do some work. This is how they grew up to be hard-working people. Therefore, when children grew up and became adults, they became hard-working people just like their parents. And if their children were born, those children would also become like them. This is because their lifestyle itself fostered diligence. Without diligence, no one is able to make living for himself (or herself). This was the very foundation of education.

In order to teach children how to be grateful, and for the sake of instilling future diligence, parties were often held. They were held in the form of praises. If a six or seven year old son went fishing, and was able to catch and bring back even a small fish by himself, a party was prepared at home. Using that fish, traditional Nanai foods were cooked like *tala* (sliced raw fish) in the summer, *piarmaa* (frozen fish) in the winter, fish soup and so on. Old relatives, respected people, and people close by gathered, and the guests all brought presents to give to the child. While eating the food made using that fish, the elder people who came to the party would praise the son. They praised him, saying "This is delicious! The *tala* is really delicious! The fish soup is really delicious! I've never eaten anything this good before. You did well! You did very well! When you grow up, you'll become someone who can feed us and take care of us!" When the child hears these words, he is happy and motivated, thinking "I should go out tomorrow, I should catch one again," and in his heart, he wants to receive praise again. In this way, this becomes motivation for him to want to become a respectable fisherman. Tools necessary for fishing were usually given as gifts to the son for catching his first fish. Of course they were tools for children, but for example, they gave supplies necessary for fishing as presents like fishing rods, fishing line that his grandfather made himself, poles which are not just sticks that he broke but were well-polished, and rope made of hemp or nettle. This is how they encouraged children. If the son caught a rabbit on a hunt as his first catch, once again a party was held. In the same way, food was prepared with that rabbit, and the son was praised. Supplies used for hunting were given as presents. Things like bows, arrows, traps, and skis were given. The child liked it when he received his gift, and dreamed that he would become a praiseworthy hunter like his father when he grew up. This sort of method of encouragement was a means of cultivating children into praiseworthy hunters and praiseworthy fishermen.

In the same way, daughters were also encouraged. If they made clothes well, or embroidered well, they were given presents. For example, things like thread (and long ago there was no thread, so it was hand-made using fish skin or animal veins, threads of different thicknesses made and twisted in different ways), needles made from bones, thimbles, (leather thimbles, in order to protect the girls' fingers because fingers get pricked while doing needlework on leather), were given as presents. When they play with dolls, they do not just play, but copy what their mother and father do exactly. In other words, while playing, they familiarize themselves with their parents' skills. Like this, they train and familiarize themselves with their parent's skills.

When raising a child, moral education was the most important thing. The most important point in moral education is that you can never take someone else's things. No matter how much you want something, it is not allowed because it is not ours, but someone else's. If you want it badly, you ask for them to give it to you, or ask if you can have it, and if you get permission, you can have it. If you do not get permission, you absolutely must not, in any circumstance, even touch it. Even a two or three year old child, although he (or she) does not know what is someone else's and what is not, if he really wants something and is with his mother or grandmother, the mother or grandmother will take him into the owner's house. For example, if the child sees a cucumber growing in the vegetable field, the mother or grandmother takes him to its owner and says "My child wants this cucumber so very much." Then, if the owner says, "Pick it and take it with you!" then the mother or the grandmother picks the cucumber and gives it to the child and thanks the owner, telling her "We also have cucumber, but this is only because the child wants it so much, and so we will return one later." Of course the lady of the house says "There's no need to return with it," but the mother or grandmother says "No, we will return with it." This is because the child must clearly know. If you take what is someone else's, you must return it.

This is one example of moral education. You must not take what is another's. That is why for our people, though it must be the same for Korean people, there was nothing we would call thievery at all. What is another's is another's, what is yours is yours. That is why, in the past, there were no locks at all. When you left the house, you could just close the door and leave. Later, when settlers appeared in the Far East, the Nanai people indicated that all the people left and nobody was home by standing a stick at the door. This meant that nobody was home. It was after the twentieth century that locks appeared. Before then, there was no such thing as a lock, and there was also no thievery.

Another thing of great concern was helping children from a young age get used to being considerate of the elderly and the sick. It is making them understand that helping elderly people is a natural duty. For instance, when fishing, you can go with just your family, but if the father were with someone else, such as the owner of the net and the owner of the boat, and these two following the father got on the boat and rowed the oars together, after catching fish, they would divide the catch amongst themselves into four, and the three people would take one each, and the fourth portion was left for an elderly, sick person who could not catch fish for himself. Rather than the adult, the child would then deliver it in person. In this way, the child was taught to be considerate of the elderly. Nowadays, there are things like various nursing homes and veterans homes. But, long ago, there was nothing like these, was there? People who could work supported their clan and their village. Long ago, because the village was not big, sickly people amongst the people who lived in the village were supported. Children growing up understood that, and even if nobody asked them to, they knew by themselves that looking after incapable people was their duty. Hunters were the same. When they brought back their catch, they shared it with elderly and sick people without fail. It was believed that, because god was observing everything, taking care of elderly and sick people brings happiness and fortune, which is granted to those who take care of the sick and elderly. It is this point that was considered important for a child's education. Nowadays, though children are told to do this and that, and though they are scolded when they do not do them, and while there were also lazy children back then, in those days, all children clearly knew their respective, personal duties.

What is important is diligence, and the awareness that this is an issue for the child to figure out for himself [or herself], and not something he does because someone told him so, is instilled in the child. It is having the child do something himself, even if no one tells him to do so. Diligence is "law" for young people. It is "law" for the young. It is thought that god is observing everything from above, and that he will make them happy and lucky people. The gods know which people needed what sort of attention. They believed that if they work hard and be considerate and respectful of elderly people, this brings luck, health, happiness. In moral and ethics education, another important thing is honesty and truth. Another important thing is humility. You must not boast about yourself or stand out. This is very important. This is why there is a proverb like this for the Nanai people. "Do not praise yourself, it is by observing you that others will know what sort of person you are."

Every night, when children were going to bed, they really liked listening to bedtime stories. If mother or grandmother did not tell us a story, we did not fall asleep. Mother and grandmother knew this. That is why as soon as we laid down to sleep, they sat next to us and told us a story. Then young children fell asleep right away, while older children wanted to hear at least a little bit more. Mother and grandmother sat next to us and told us a story. Although bedtime stories were for children, these were all stories that, after hearing them, allowed children to build real character within themselves. To tell you a bedtime story, though many different characters appear, amongst them the male main character *Mergen* is the most fortunate young man, being the handsomest, the strongest and the bravest of them all. The female main character also is the prettiest, the most fortunate, and is a person that has all the good points that the male main character has, and is successful and first place in everything she does. What purpose did these stories serve? Of course, because children come to like these main characters, they grow up wanting to be like them, and strive to develop the same character as the main characters. That is why they wanted to hear the story tomorrow and the day after, and finally, through oral tradition, children developed character.

Another significant thing in childhood education was play. Playing was not simply for amusement, once again it also built character that children needed when they became adults. So how did young boys play? It was none other than shooting arrows. Long ago, because there were no targets, they put up objects and hit those. This is how they had archery contests. Otherwise, they saw who could ride skis the quickest, who could come down best on skis after climbing a mountain. Or when spring came and the snow melted and the ice in the river melted and started to break, they would play and have contests on boats. The slightly older thirteen or fourteen year old children take the eight to ten year old children on the boat, and they ride the boat between the ice pieces, avoiding spaces where the ice can squeeze the boat. If it feels like there is a big piece of ice approaching, they would quickly get on the ice, grab the two sides of the boat, bring it to a place with water and rode the boat again all the way to the riverside. Playing like this developed agility and courage, and it developed skills that allowed them to pull through even difficult situations that may arise when men go fishing or hunting.

Young girls also played. Even when they played simple games, for example when they played with dolls (See Fig. 12 on page xii above), which in Nanai we call *akoan,* they followed what their mothers did exactly. Nowadays there are even talking dolls, but in those days, the dolls, of course, could not talk, and we made the dolls ourselves. What the mother does, the doll follows exactly. The doll even cooks and cleans. If the mother scolds the child, then the mother doll also scolds her, and for the baby doll, she speaks to it as the mother would to a baby. When she has to cry, the doll cries, and it also does things like carry firewood, build fires, and boil food. In other words, play itself is a means of education.

That is why elderly people always said, "While we raise our children we must teach them everything we know how to do. We must teach our every skill and everything we are able. Not only this, but we must tell children all the legends and tales that we know while we are alive. This is because legends and tales contain all of the history of a clan and a people. If children do not know this, it disconnects the "thread" of time, the "thread" of generations. If that happens, how would they be able to live without knowing our laws, our customs and our traditions?" That is why now, when we work to preserve our language, our customs, and culture, we try to make our children and adults very interested in it. For example, there is something I always talk about. "Our writers are talking about this or that in their works. Please, read this. Please, read that." This is very important. Our ancestors always said as follows. "If we cannot pass down what we know, what we know through legends and tales, the children can never know our traditions and manners, and they cannot continue their livelihoods and they cannot pass down the customs and traditions, the characteristics of our clan and people." As I see it, this is extremely important. This is the "golden thread" that goes through traditional childhood education. This is why children continued to soak up what had been passed down for generations. In this way, children grew up to become praiseworthy hunters, praiseworthy fishermen, praiseworthy experts in sewing, praiseworthy experts in leather making, and so on, to become good people who respect one another, honest people. Traditional education, not only the Nanai, but for all the indigenous people, is reflective, and because it is rich in content, I want to emphasize how important succession and restoration is. Speaking as a pedagogue, in Russian pedagogy there is the concept of "folk pedagogy". This concept is directly referring to traditional pedagogy.

In our Khabarovsk kraj, there is a school that is promoting the revival of this very "folk pedagogy". For example, there is a school in a town called Nizhnie Khalby in the Komsomolsk district, a big school with not many students, a school with about a hundred students, and even there "folk pedagogy" is being brought back. This is a good thing.

3.2. Birth rituals

In the past, there was no medicine whatsoever. That is why, as a substitute for medicine, wood chips (*saori*, See Fig. 11 on page xii above) made from thinly sawed trees were used. This was everywhere in homes with women. And for the sake of birth rituals, medicine was made from wood chips sawed from, not just any tree, but a special tree. They were made, for instance, from Filipendula and the trunk of a violet willow, and the mother would use it when giving birth. Wood chips were given to the mother as gifts after she gave birth. The reason wood chips, of all things, were given is that they are an indispensable necessity for the mother. Mothers of the Nanai people gave birth to her child squatting in a temporary home made for childbirth, and if there was difficulty in the delivery of the baby, a midwife or the mother-in-law did as follows. What they did was extend their legs and sweep down the mother's back from top to bottom using the soles of their feet, making motions as if they were pushing the baby out of the mother's body, to help make the delivery of the baby faster. This was a special kind of ritual, in which they did the motion without actually touching the back with the feet, doing it as if they were pushing the baby out of the mother's body, and this helped support a quick birth for the mother. When the baby was born, they immediately laid it on a temporary cradle made of birch bark (See Fig. 9 on page xi above). The birch bark was boiled very thoroughly, prepared carefully until it was completely soft. The cradle is made so that it has absolutely no knots — it was made so that it did not hurt or cause discomfort to the baby. The reason I am talking about knots is there are the sides and the bottom of the cradle, and all of them were connected with string, woven with either thin vine or roots. If the vine was short, for example, if it was two meters long and it could possibly not be enough to connect everything, then there was no choice but to tie two ends somewhere. If knots were formed like this, then all of them were always taken out to the exterior without letting any remain in the interior, and it was made so that lying in the cradle did not hurt the baby. And of course, to make the place the baby lies down softer, woods chips were spread out on the bottom of the cradle, and especially bactericidal wood chips were spread. Cloth was draped over the top. Long, long ago, when there was no cloth, very carefully processed fish skin was set down. In the past when there was no cloth, fish skin was used to create underwear. Therefore, imagine how well one would need to process fish skin, especially when using it for a baby. Then after about five or six days, the baby was laid in a regular cradle. This cradle is bigger because it is made with what is commonly called "expectations of future growth". As per usual, it was made with birch bark and the rim and bottom was made tougher so that it did not crack or break even if the baby shuffled around or kicked it.

In the past, no, even until the nineteenth century, when cutting the umbilical cord after giving birth was used. It was a sharp blade used to cut leather or cloth when making clothing. It was a small blade, and the edge was small too, but it was a very sharp blade. The cord was cut after boiling the blade. A sterilizing powder made from trees was sprinkled on the mother's side of the umbilical cord, and this powder was found in every home that had young women. It was turned into powder by thinly cutting, then grinding acacia (*waarangkola*). This was sprinkled on the baby's side of the cord as well, and the cut umbilical cord (*chungguru*) was taken, dried, wrapped in fish skin long ago, and later in cloth, and after placing it in a pouch and stitched shut, it was stored in the mother's sewing box. Because a woman was always with her sewing box, and though the umbilical cord dried up completely from being placed there and broke apart, the umbilical cord was always with the woman. This is important never to lose. This is because it was believed to come from the baby and contained the baby's spirit soul. This is why this tradition was rather strictly observed. The umbilical cord that was cut like this was stored there in the box. Another important thing has to do with why it was kept in the sewing box. Because there are pointy needles in a sewing box, when evil spirits appear, these needles, by protecting the umbilical cord, protects the baby from them. This carried a lot of meaning.

When moving back from the temporary home back to the regular home, it could be the day after, three days after, or even up to ten days after the baby is born. It differed based on different childbirth situations. At home, the very best spot, the warmest spot, right next to the fire pot was the mother and baby's spot. There was even a special bowl set aside and prepared for the mother. Of course the objective was hygiene. And for a rather long time, the mother ate the root of Angelica Gigas Nakai (*eukhekhin*) that was dried, sliced and powdered or small pieces of it. This root promotes uterine contractions after birth, and heals any bad effects of pregnancy within the mother's body. The mother was also made to drink water infused with rose hip. In this way, the mother was carefully looked after. Wood chips made from a different tree, called bird cherry, were used for the mother's hygiene as well. Near the end of autumn or in the winter, bird cherry branches were cut, and sawed, which must be done at home in the winter. Because the branches have a good fragrance, it spreads throughout the house, and has a sterilizing effect for the air in the house. It has the effect of killing all the germs in the house. This is why women use wood chips made from this tree after childbirth without fail. This is very, very important.

Another important thing is, for over half a year after childbirth, the mother's breast is massaged almost every day. Because it hurts, it is hard not to let out a groan, but groaning for our Nanai women is forbidden. That is why no matter how much it hurt, women had to endure it, even if it meant groaning alone in secret. The reason for the massage was to increase the amount of breast milk. For Nanai women, breastfeeding their children until they were two or three year was a given, and some were even breastfed until they were five years old. My mother said at some point, children play outside with other children of similar age, then they come in and breastfeed. Even though they were able to eat like adults they drank breast milk and they were breastfed until the child himself (or herself) refused to drink breast milk any longer. Breast milk was considered medicine for children, and so they were thought to be healthy while they drank breast milk, and breast milk actually has remedial qualities when a child is sick. This is very important.

Cleaning up for the mother like bathing, changing underwear, wiping down with wood chips and so on for the first time was done three days after giving birth. People were not permitted to go anywhere and just dispose of the bathing water, water from washing underwear and wiping down with wood chips and so on. A hole was specially made in the ground, and this water was poured in and covered in dirt. Outsiders were not allowed to touch the puddle. Whether it was a dog or a person, no one was allowed to touch it. This was considered a rite to protect the lives of the mother and baby. The second thing that was done to keep clean was ten days after giving birth. They did things like laundry, and afterwards the woman washed and dried the underwear she wore when giving birth and various other items, then wrapped it and put it away so that no eyes would be laid upon it. Not only men, but everyone was not allowed to see it. Because all these items were either worn or used when bringing the baby into this world, it was believed that this could be inauspicious or even cause harm to the baby. This is why these items were protected, so that no one could see them.

Though not everyone does it, mothers who wanted to know the destiny of their child held a certain ceremony (*solbon*). After the child is born and the woman returned home from the temporary home together with her child, a willow branch was twisted and made into a round hoop, and the mother holding her child passed through it. The head was not to touch the top portion, and she must pass without letting her shoulders and arms touch the sides. Someone would hold the hoop and the woman would pass through. If the woman passed through without touching anything, then a future of good fate awaited the mother and her child, but if she touched anything, it was believed that something bad awaited them. Because they were worried that they would make a mistake, and to disallow anyone from knowing beforehand and interfering, many people did not do this ceremony. Why would we want to disappoint anyone?

There was always a lot of interest in the newborn baby. This was because a baby was something every Nanai family wanted, and it was considered a big blessing. There were many instances in which a baby did not survive, and because the infant mortality rate was high, families did everything they could to protect the baby's life. There were many methods that were used to protect the baby's life. For example, amulets were made for the baby. As I already said in Nanai, if a baby cried heavily, it was thought that the baby could have been the only one born of what were originally twins, and to calm the baby, and also to have the baby not cry so much and so often, a twin was made for the baby. It was made mainly using straw that was not rough or grass that grew on mounds in bogs. It was thin and soft so it did not prick the baby, and the form of a person was made with hay or grass, and this “twin” was placed inside the cradle. It was placed near the baby’s pillow without letting it touch its body, and this amulet was always with the child like a twin. Sometimes this had an effect to a certain extent and the baby was placated, and parents were satisfied. It was also thought that evil spirits or demons knew that the baby was born and wanted to take it, steal it from the parents in some way. The following amulet was made to scare these evil spirits and demons. When a pike was caught then it was boiled and made into food, and the jawbone was removed from the head and it was dried with the teeth intact and hung on the arch near the front of the cradle. The cradle was an ellipse like this and above the head, there was an arch made from a bent willow branch, and like how a rattle is hung above cradles, this kind of amulet was hung. Hanging the jawbone of the pike on the arch of the cradle was used as a way to scare evil spirits. Another possible amulet was the claw of an animal. For example, the claw of a bear or a field mouse was removed while taking apart an animal, then it was dried and hung on the arch of the cradle. This is not simply a toy for the baby to look at, but an amulet that protects the baby from evil spirits and demons.

One did not talk about the birth of a child to a lot of people. Only people who were close like relatives were told. This is because if this was widely known then not only people, but evil spirits would come to know, and it was not told so that evil spirits would not know of the birth. For this purpose, it was forbidden to prepare items for the baby before it was born, so that evil spirits did not know of it beforehand.

After the baby was born, while the mother was at the temporary house, the women of the home immediately started to sew clothes for the baby quickly.

This kind of ritual existed. From what I understand, the birth ritual was the effort of parents to protect the life of their child. The birth ritual is called *iliochiori* in Nanai, which means "make him (or her) stand on his own feet", and it was also called *nai osiweemburi* or "the making of a person". "Making someone stand on his (or her) own feet" is raising a child until they become young adults, and the "making of a person" is making the son or daughter understand and discern in the way their parents, older brothers, or older sisters do, and teaching the son or daughter how to do whatever he or she needs to anything.

The following methods of preserving life were used. When a child died once before (for example, there is a case in which a women gave birth to sixteen children and all of them died save for one daughter), when a baby is born in a family in which a child has died before, the family negotiates with someone else not part of their clan, a person of a different clan who birthed and raised a healthy child who grew up well, and the baby that was just born was given to that other family to be raised. This was not because the baby was not needed, but because the baby was absolutely necessary. After being raised in the other home for about three years, then when it was raised strong and healthy, the baby was returned. There was this method, and another is one in which the family would borrow the cradle of a woman who had a baby who lived healthily and did not die. The Nanai people did not make a new cradle every time a baby was born. They made a strong and pretty cradle once, and when the baby grew up and was able to walk, it was placed carefully where it did not gather dust or break. Cradles made with birch bark like this was usually made so that it can be used for many years. Families in which an older brother or an older sister once died would borrow cradles like this from families in which a baby grew up healthy and the cradles would be used for a given period of time. Families believed that if a baby grew up healthy in that cradle once before, that very cradle may help their baby grow up to be healthy as well.

If someone is holding the baby or the baby is elsewhere, it was forbidden to rock the empty cradle. There were many times when a woman, while making something with her hands, rocked the cradle with her feet to help the baby fall asleep. She would rock the cradle with her feet almost unconsciously, and this was not allowed when the cradle was empty, when the baby was not inside. This was because it was believed that this meant one wished death upon the baby. Doing this was not allowed because there was no baby inside an empty cradle. It was also forbidden to leave, outside, items of children who were not yet a year old. For example, even if you have to dry wet laundry, you only hung and dried it during the day while the sun is out, and when the sun begins to pass by, you gather everything and bring it inside of the house and hang it inside. These rules and traditions continued until the child grew up and became independent. Remembering when I was growing up, when the sun began falling below the horizon, the mothers of every house would come out and call their sons and daughters home, saying, “The sun is setting, the sun is setting.” And from what I remember, in the morning, even if I want to sleep some more, even if I want to sleep more in the morning from listening to old stories at night, when the sun rose, we were made to wake up. We had to wake up with the sun, and sleep together with the sun. Why was this? “This was because if you liked to sleep for a long time, then you could be stepped on by everyone who woke up and was walking around, and so you can get hurt or bad things can happen to you." Why is playing or running around outside not allowed after the sun sets? "This was because everyone returned to his (or her) home, and only evil spirits and ghosts were roaming around. It was because they could grab you." The reason for all of these traditions was to protect the lives of children and to maintain a regular lifestyle. From what I remember, my mother goes out to gather wood in the woods three times before the sun even rises. Long ago, the woods were right behind the house. She rode a sled that was pulled by one dog to collect wood. And when the sun rises, we also rise.

There was also this method. For example, scraps of clothing were obtained from the elderly. Because fish skin was always available, there was always scraps, and later when fabric came out, it was used to make a *khalat* (outer robe), and the resulting scraps were collected. These scraps were attached together to make children's clothing, and scraps were always collected from the elderly. These clothes were also a kind of protective amulet. This is because if the fish skin or fabric was already worn by someone who has already lived for a long time, these clothes would also look after the child's life for a long time. Once again, the clothes made of these scraps themselves were amulets for the child. Things like bracelets were sewed and also made with these clothing scraps and put on children's wrists. Nowadays, if we're talking about going abroad, when Valentina (the daughter of the narrator) went to a temple in India, a bracelet made of string was put on her wrist there, and it is said she was told not to take it off for three years. She was to keep wearing it night and day, even when she washed herself, and after three years, it would fray and come off by itself. In the past, the Nanai people used a similar method. Using those clothing scraps, children's bracelets were made and put on their wrists, and they became amulets for the children. As for the skull of a bear, one was obtained from a hunter who had been hunting for a long time, or who hunted well, or who lived a long time. After a bear was caught, there was a ritual in which there was a bear ceremony and the bear's head was eaten, and many people preserved the bear's skull carefully afterwards. It was dried and hung on the wall as an amulet to wish health upon the whole family. It was hung like one would hang a mask, though of course nowadays masks are not amulets but mainly ornaments. After obtaining a bear skull, it was hung on the wall until the child was two or three, up to five years old, and families prayed to it, saying "As you had protected the lives of that house, its children and the families of that clan, please help us. Please protect our family, our children." Therefore it was not just obtained and hung up on the wall without thought, but everyone made wishes to and respected the bear skull.

For the Nanai, considering the naming of children as a protective practice was a widely practiced custom, as well as tradition. First, like how one did not tell of the birth of a child to everyone, one also did not name her child immediately. A name could be given a month or even three months after birth. In most cases, old people like the child's grandmother or grandfather, who had lived for a long time, would select the name, but if they were not present, a person who had lived a long time, like a relative or even someone of a different clan, would name the child. This is why it was common to see people with names that did not seem like names. For example, there was one woman I knew personally who lived a long time, and her name was *Gara,* which means "tree branch". This woman lived her whole life with this name. There was a man whose name was *Dongsya,* which means "limping leg". And there was the name *Budike,* which means "dying", and this was the name of a young boy. The purpose of naming a child like this was so that evil spirits would not covet the child, even if they were to find out about the baby's birth and growth. The evil spirits thought "what's the use of a child that is dying, he will die soon anyway," "what's the use of a tree branch" and would avoid those children. And often names like this also had the meaning of a protective amulet for Nanai people. Of course, in addition, there were other good names for children of families who grew up safely.

In these ways, children were human beings who were raised and given all the best things by their parents and people close to them — they were raised to be safe and loved. And what is important is this was not simply done just to protect the child, because it had meaning for the succession of the clan. Having many children meant having many people in the clan and this meant prosperity for the clan. And because the clan was diverse, big clans were considered strong and enduring, and this being big meant the clan became wealthy, because it meant a comparable that much increase in manpower.

3.3. Wedding rituals

Long ago, marrying off a daughter mainly depended on the father's wishes. There were more of this kind of marriage than other kinds. There was a wide variety of ways to arrange marriages. During Chum salmon season, or in other words, during autumn when it is time to catch Chum salmon, men and women go out, and the men catch fish with their nets and the women prepare the fish that are caught. People from the entire village gathered at the fishing site. Sometimes, people from other villages came to the site too. Those people also caught fish, and some people came with the purpose of finding out if there was a daughter who was available for marriage. Suppose a certain person had a son whose time to marry had come, and naturally, because he wanted to bring home a good daughter-in-law, he would purposefully go to the place where all the men of the village had gathered. This person tries talking to this person and that person, and he gradually finds out if there was a daughter who is available for marriage. He also finds out how someone was living, what his daughter is like, whether she is hard-working, if she is good with her hands, or if on the contrary, she is lazy. Of course, this is to choose the best daughter-in-law. When the person is finished with finding things out through other people in this way, and after fishing season is over, he takes his wife and about three to five older people from his family and they return to the village together. They go to the house of the person that has a daughter to marry off, the house with the daughter about whom there are many good rumors spreading around. They bring a ceramic bottle filled with liquor, food, and presents. The owner knows what is going on, but asks anyway. When he asks, "For what have you come?", they reply, "We are hoping to find a potential bride for our son, and we have come to understand that there is a wonderful daughter in this honorable family. Please allow your daughter to be married off to our son." This is the "request" phase. In other words, it is the step to find out the parent's thoughts about whether they agree or not to marry the daughter off to the son.

One particular detail is what the father of the potential bride did if he did not agree. He also did not just sit around. Because he knew that during the fishing season there was someone who came from somewhere to talk with certain people and find things out, if that person were to come to his house, then that person would be coming with a set agenda, and therefore the father of the daughter also found out ahead of time about that person, things like what kind of person he is, what kind of person his son is and so on. He is not just sitting with his arms crossed. This is because from his perspective, he must give his daughter away. That is why, if there is something that he does not like about that family, or if there is a particularly negative aspect about that family, that person and his family who come to his house are rejected. In this situation, they do not open or even receive the bottle of liquor. Even if he does not say, "I will not give you my daughter," if he does not receive the bottle of liquor, then this already signifies rejection, then those people have no choice but to turn around and leave. If the father of the daughter receives the bottle of liquor and entertains the guests, even inviting other relatives to come, this means that the family of the son got approval for the daughter to be married off to the son. This is the first phase, the "request" phase (*medeliku*).

If the family of the son returns home after getting approval from the daughter's family, they deliberate on everything that had happened, tell the son, then call together the elders of the family and have a discussion. Afterwards, they announce when they would like to go visit the parents of the potential bride for the second time. Once again they come bringing presents, food, and, of course, the bottle of liquor, but this second time is the second phase known in Nanai as *yengsi*. At this time, both sides agree upon the terms of the *tori* (bridewealth), which is the amount for the bride that the father of the bride requests. A *tori* include things like fur, clothes, various household necessities, and gold and silver products, and if the son's family is a rich family with a lot of money, then even money is requested. A variety of fabrics is also requested, and in the past, because a lot of silk was brought in from Manchu, requests were made in the form of asking for certain amounts of silk or whatever fabric. Negotiations about "how much of what" are done clearly and precisely. This is a *tori* for their daughter. The son's family stayed for about two days, discussing in this way and eating together. Afterwards, a long time would pass by. For some people, in some cases it takes a year or even longer. This is because if the *tori* was large in scale, the son's family must gather for it. They must obtain everything from somewhere. If they need fur, for example, they can not just kill a marten and bring the hide, but they must do things like process it by skinning and drying it, and it must be of the highest quality. This is why it takes a long time to gather things for the *tori*. Meanwhile, they settle on exactly when they would take the *tori* to the daughter's family. Of course, a rich family prepares it quickly, in three to four months or half a year. In any case, the daughter's family knows exactly when the potential groom's parents would come for the third stage. In the case that the son's family cannot prepare it all at once, even if the *tori* cannot be fully prepared, as per a request from the groom's parents to the bride's parents, the bride's parents can agree to give their daughter for marriage. For instance, the groom's family brings half at the moment, and brings the remaining half when the daughter gets married. Or the groom's family gives a third of it later. If the amount of the *tori* was too much for the groom's parents to handle, then there were even times when they had no choice but to give up on the potential bride.

The third phase is called *degbeliku* in Nanai, or in other words, the "uncorking". Once again, the potential groom's side brings the bottle of liquor and food as expected, and the important thing is they bring the *tori*. At this time, many of the clan's relatives come together. The potential bride and her mother also participate. This time, the potential groom also comes together, and people greet the potential groom. If the potential groom and the potential bride are from different villages, this is finally the time that the potential groom and the potential bride greet one another for the first time. If they are from the same village, this is a different issue of course... And so, though it is not the formal wedding ceremony, a large wedding celebration is held. A wedding is defined as when the girl leaves her original home and goes to the groom's home. As such, a joyous celebration is held, one worthy of being called the first portion of a wedding ceremony. It is a joyous celebration in which the daughter is married off, the potential groom is to everyone's liking, and they are happy because the *tori* is brought correctly. On this night, the potential groom and the potential bride are allowed to sleep together. In other words, now there is no doubt that the two will become husband and wife. However, even when the third phase ends, the potential bride is not taken away yet, and the potential groom and his parents leave for home. The potential groom has to prepare and gather for everything, including the *tori*.

The potential bride has to prepare the dowry (*mirue*). First, a special boat (*gila*) that the bride is sent off in is made.

Above the seat for bride in the middle of a large boat with eight to twelve oars, is something like an awning created out of birch bark, and patterns are put in. The entire boat is decorated with patterns — it is a boat for the wedding ceremony. Eight to twelve people who will row the oars ride the boat, and the bride sits in the middle. Also, houses meant to store the contents of the dowry are built. This is because, once again, there is a formidable dowry as well, including things like clothes, shoes, bowls, and household necessities. No matter how poor the parents of the potential bride are, they prepare as much as possible, and this is because only what the bride takes with her to her husband's home belongs to her. These are her possessions. She has no right to any other item in the husband's home. This is why she brought everything from needles to thread to the husband's home. There was a boat filled with the dowry, and there were boats carrying people who were following along, and so there were many boats. It takes a long time to prepare all of these things. Because they had to ride boats, wedding ceremonies were usually held in the summer. They set the date to a day when the weather was good — it could not be raining nor could the wind even be blowing. This is because it was the day the bride was leaving her parent's home and they can go by riding a boat. Though having a wedding during the winter was exceptionally rare, in this case a sled was made for the bride to ride and go in.

Dowries are given in proportion to the size of the *tori*. If much was asked of the potential groom's parents for the *tori* and much was brought, or had been agreed to be brought, the dowry given in return is made to be appropriate compared with the *tori*. If the *tori* is small, so is the dowry. In some cases, the groom could be from a poor family that does not own anything. Of course, they may go hunting and catch a lot of animals, but this sort of thing is nothing. However, let's say in this case, the potential groom is honest, conscientious, and hard-working. In this case, because the young woman and young man are often people of the same village, their parents know each other's families. In other words, when the time came to get married, the potential bride's parents already knew well what kind of person the young man was, and they knew that though he was poor, he was a good person, that he was honest, hard-working and trustworthy. It can be a situation in which the parents are old, and therefore are unable to provide for the son. In addition, if the young woman liked the young man, her parents liked for the young man to marry their daughter and approved of it — even though the son's family was not able to bring a *tori* at all, they approved of it. Like Russian "matrilocality", it was something like matrilocality, which is when the family of the potential bride accepts the potential groom into their home. There was something like that for the Nanai people as well. In other words, the empty-handed young man would go to the potential bride's house with nothing on him. However, in return for the trust of allowing him to marry the bride without a *tori*, like the Russians say, he worked "to death". He did whatever that was asked of him, work that needed to be done. Whether it was hunting, fishing, or housework, whatever the potential bride's father told him to do, he did. In short, he repaid the marriage debt by being the main worker in the house. Although there were cases like this, they were very rare.

It is almost impossible to find a love marriage. If two people loved each other and the man took the woman and secretly ran away from the village, the entire village, people from the entire clan would go out, search for and find them. At the very least, they suffered severe punishments, and at the extreme, would be killed. This is because they debased the honor of the clan. It is because they went against the clan's order, custom, and tradition. There were cases like these.

When the arranged time to take the bride from her parent's home arrives, they gather all of the dowry and pack it, then they dress the bride. First, her hair is washed and made from that of a maiden to that of a bride. Her hair is braided into two parts, and three ornamental cords twisted with many different colors braided in together, and this hair is wrapped around and raised, like what is known nowadays as a crown, and the ends are sent over the top and made to fall behind the ears, together with the ends of the twisted cords, and this all is made to hang down to the shoulders. To adorn the back of the head was a neck-flap (*apito*) which nowadays is affixed with a pin, made of embroidered cloth that is made and attached, covering the back of the head. And of course, a hat used for wedding ceremonies was put on her.

The outfit consisted of the following things. First are the undergarments (*enggeregde*). In the past when there was no cloth, all of this was created using fish skins. Fish skin is specially worked and made to be as soft as silk and not be prickly. Over this, a long *khalat* made in one layer (*pokto*), a light *khalat* for the summer, was worn. Over this, something similar to a child's bib was wrapped around, and throughout the border, round metal disks were hung and when the bride walked the disks come in contact with each other making a jingling noise. It was believed that this noise chased away evil spirits from the bride. This is not ornamental. This is because it was not visible when over it, another wedding robes was worn. It was worn just to produce the sound. The bridal robes was very beautifully embroidered (See Fig. 8 on page x above). Though it was embroidered over every seam, the most important portion is the back. On the back, above the waist, a design of the Three Worlds that make up the universe was embroidered in. The Upper World is the world of gods, the Middle World is the place where people, animals, the ground, water, mountains and so on exist, and the Lower World is the underworld, the world beneath the waters, the world of the dead. The Three Worlds were expressed on the design on the bridal robes.

Below the waist, until the hem, the middle has a long opening, so the border was once again embroidered — it was embroidered on both sides with the world tree and the family tree. The family tree showed which clan the bride was a part of and which region the clan was from (See Fig. 4 on page viii above). If it was a mountainous region, then mountains in the form of waves were embroidered, and if it was the lowlands, then a tree with a straight line below it that has nothing like hills was embroidered. Below the tree near the root portion, animal totems were embroidered. Animals like the elk, the deer, and the Manchurian wapiti were embroidered, and the Lower World was represented using animals like the turtle, the scorpion, and the frog. On the tree trunk, the shape of a snake coiling around and climbing it was embroidered, and there were also insects. This is the world in which humans and animals reside. The family tree did not just express the clan but also the universe, and the Upper World is the crown of the tree, where the gods reside. According to Nanai mythology, there are 9 domains of the Upper World. Each domain has a reigning god, and each god serves different functions. Of them, two domains are ruled by goddesses and they protect womankind. They also do things like allow children be born in houses without children. And birds are embroidered on the branches near the top of this tree to symbolize the spirits of yet to be born infants. Because there will definitely be a child in the future for the bride who is just now leaving to her groom, this embroidery foretells the child who is to be born in the future. Instead of leaves, metal ornaments are hung and shaken by the wind, making sounds and even falling to the ground. According to legend, if you pick up these fallen metal disks, then you become a shaman.

And so if you visit our folk museum, these round metal disks, large ones, are hanging there. These are later put on the chests of shamans. They reveal the path that a shaman was supposed to tread. In this way, the bride was dressed in this rich bridal robes, and if it was a little cold, an *amiri* (outer coat) made of fish skin was put on her, and scholars nowadays say that the *amiri* is also a part of the bridal robes, but I personally think it is not. The reason they assert that it is part of the bridal robes is because the bride just wears it on the day she leaves or because it was always included in the dowry. Originally, this piece of clothing was absolutely necessary, it just blocked the cold and the wind. Women wore this clothing during the winter. They wore it when they went fishing and also when they went to gather wood. Although the bridal robes made of cloth and embroidered was only worn on the day of the wedding, the outer coat made of fish skin was worn nearly every day. On the chest portion of the bridal robes or the *amiri*, a half-moon silver ornament (*selke*) was put on, and the bride put on bracelets, rings, and earrings. The earrings were special, so women have them on later, not just during the wedding ceremony. They were called *largyuka* and small fragments were hung on the bride's ear, and it made a sound when she walked. The bride was dressed up in this way.

Before the bride left her house, she kneeled in front of her parents, received their blessings, and cried. This is because she was leaving the home that she was born in and grew up in, and was now leaving for someone else's home. However, crying a lot while sending the bride off was not allowed. Because it was believed that shedding many tears was not good for the daughter's life ahead, tears were held back tightly. The bride poured liquor into a small wineglass (*kochi*) and gave it out to different people. First, she gave it to her mother, then to her father. When she presented the glass while sitting on her knees, the mother kissed her daughter's two cheeks. This was done because of tradition. We never kiss on the lips — we only kiss the cheeks. Then, the bride offered a glass to all the people present who were seeing her off. Another significant thing was that in every house of the Nanai people, there was a *sewen* standing in a corner across from the door, and the *sewen* takes many forms (See Fig. 11 on page xii above). What I am talking about now is the *Juulin*, which takes the shape of a face and has no legs, and is made roughly from a tree stump using an axe. It stood there in order to protect the family, and had no legs, while the lines of the face are made coarsely by carving out the cheeks like this. There were many types of *Juulin* — some were not very big while some were about 70 centimeters tall. These *Juulin* stood in the corner of every house and protected the house and the family. Even when going out hunting, hunters kneeled in front of it and made offerings of things like food and liquor, and during the winter, they used to hunt for three to four months, and they pleaded to the *Juulin* for it to protect and keep the house and family safe while they were out hunting and not home, for everything to be as it was originally when they return. It was as if they were leaving it in their stead when they left, as if it were a member of the family. When the bride left for marriage, she did not bid farewell or say anything to the *Juulin*. This is because she was not just simply leaving the home, but she was leaving the clan and becoming someone of a different clan. In other words, getting married means becoming a member of a different clan.

To give an example, my family had four brothers and sisters. So my parents had two daughters and two sons: my sister and myself, and two brothers. When I was growing up, if a Russian guest came and stayed the night, he (or she) would look at us and say "Sergey, your children grew up very well," and my father would reply "Yes, they grew up very well. However, the only children I have here are sons." Then the guest, who seemingly did not understand this very well, would ask "Then your daughters are not your biological daughters?" "They are my daughters, but they will eventually become someone else's daughter, after all." If the guest asks "how do they become someone else's daughter," then our father replies "when they marry, they will become people of a different clan and become strangers." That is why I kept my maiden name "Kile" (inheriting my father's surname), and so my father was happy. So my father's surname was "Kile", and I kept the name even after marriage. I am a part of the "Kile" clan. These types of things were our customs.

The bride did not bid farewell to the *Juulin*, The bride's mother picked up a flint right before the daughter left the house. What purpose did this serve? Like I mentioned before, when a woman leaves her clan and goes to a different clan, all the bride's possessions were just the dowry and what she was taking from her parent's home. However, according to our customs, everyone at any given time must have "one's own fire". "One's own fire" was a requirement. This is why the mother, when the bride was leaving, put the flint in a small pouch and packed it inside the waist of her clothes for her. Long ago, because there were no matches or lighters, the flint was given so that she could make a fire anytime, so that she can have "her own fire", so that she does not have to rely on anyone and use "her own fire" to warm her body and boil food, and tinder was given as well. This was very important.

There was a ritual that the bride performed before leaving her home. A cast iron pot was commonly included in the *tori,* and there were big ones and small ones, and they were firmly fixed onto a furnace. When you enter an old Nanai house, immediately there is a furnace burning. In that furnace, there is a large pot, in which fish, meat, or whatever was boiled. Aside from this, there were pots with small handles attached. There were pots like this. The groom brought pots for the *tori*, and the bride brought her own pots from her parent's home as part of the dowry. Because the pots that the groom brought already belonged to the bride's parents, they were left inside the home, and outside the threshold were pots that the bride was going to take to the groom's home. The bride, while leaving her parent's home, first stepped on the pots that the groom brought over, then passing over the threshold, she stepped on the pots on the outside. If the pots do not shake during this ritual, then the bride's life will be good, but if even one of them shook, then it was not good. As the elderly said, if a family is wealthy, because they did not want the bride's life to not be good because of a shaking pot, the bride would make multiple attempts by switching out different pots and doing it until the pots did not shake. This was a ritual to foresee the future of a young woman after marriage.

If the bride is able to leave the house over the threshold after stepping on the pots, a staff is put in her right hand. The staff was also specially carved, and wood chips were put on and draped like ribbons as decorations for the head portion of the staff. The bride held this staff in her right hand. In the past, houses were not far from the riverside, or the waterside. The boats were there as well. Three sticks that were not very thick were made to stand on both sides of the street, and the top of those sticks were decorated with wood chips and they indicated the road that the bride was to walk to the riverside. The bride had to follow this road while holding a staff in her hand, and on this road, nobody was allowed to get ahead of her. The bride was to follow the clean road that has not been trodden by anybody yet until the boat. Behind the bride, usually three "friends" followed her, but they were only called "friends", when actually they were aunts. These people also wore appropriate clothing. Behind them, anybody seeing the bride off followed this wedding parade. Though anybody was allowed to follow until the boat, only after the bride was sitting in her seat on the boat were they allowed to go down. The bride, by herself, had to get on the large boat with eight to twelve oars and the awning made of birch bark that blocks the sunlight. Afterwards, there was the boat that was loaded only with the dowry, if there was not much then everything was put on one boat, and if there was a lot, it was put on two or three boats. Everyone who was coming along rode on the last boat. That is, neither the groom nor his parents came to take the bride. Only close relatives came. The groom and his parents waited by their own riverside.

There were many routes that the bride could take. If the young lady was marrying a man from the same village, the bride would still ride the boat on the riverside near her parent's home and circle around to a certain extent, and then return. At this time, before arriving at the waterside near the groom's home, they disembarked on a riverside in the middle and the bride made sure to make a fire, bring back a lit firebrand to her seat, and put it in a metal bowl in the middle of the boat. This is because the boat was made of wood and the awning made of birch bark can catch fire in an instant. What did this signify? First, the bride was to take "her own fire" to the groom's house. The flint that the bride received from her mother must at some time make a fire, and there must be fire at home at all times. Next, because the bride is going to live at the groom's house, she has to join "her own fire" with the husband's fire, with the fire of her husband's clan. By doing so, by joining "her own fire" with the fire of her husband's clan, the bride becomes a part of the husband's clan. Only after this does the boat leave once more, and when they almost arrive at the riverside of the man's side of the village, arrows were shot toward the water from the stern of the boat. When there were no guns, they shot arrows, and when guns were introduced, they fired guns. By doing this, they scared the evil spirits and chased them away from the bride. These things were done so that the bride would able to reach the groom's house safely and in good health. They believed that evil spirits may see all the people gathered and all the noisiness and think "My, I can live here. It must be a rich family's young lady," and in order to protect the bride, they frightened and chased the evil spirits away by shooting arrows.

When they arrive at where the groom lives, the groom, his parents, and his relatives prepare everything and go out to meet the bride. As soon as the bride arrives, while still wearing her bridal robes, she goes to the stream and collects two buckets of water, then goes to the yard to pick up firewood and puts it in the furnace. In other words, as soon as the bride passed over the threshold of the groom's parent's home, she had already begun the work of the groom's clan. The bride also did the "passing over the threshold and stepping on the pots" at the groom's home as well. Some people did it, some people didn't, but in any case, something like this existed. The bride's work for the first day finishes at around this point. A wedding banquet was held that people gathered for and took part in, and if the bride came from a different village, it was the first time they were seeing her and so they observed her carefully. The second day was known as the "Bride's Day". The bride was the first to wake up, and she collected water and filled the pot completely, filled the water pail, made a fire in the furnace, prepared food, that is, after she finished everything, she went outside and unpacked the bags, unwrapped the things that were wrapped up, untied the things that were tied up from the dowry she brought and she hung everything on a specially made large rack. She hung a lot of her own *khalat*, but the reason she had a lot of *khalat*, was that when a woman got married, she had to work, watch the children, help and attend to the husband, and so because she thought she would have no time to make things with her hands, a lot of *khalat* was prepared before getting married. One part of all those *khalat* can even be used for a funeral. She hung all of her many *khalat*, beddings, blankets, and even rugs. Everything was beautifully embroidered with many different designs. She also put out all of the bowls made of birch bark, wood bowls, and even animal hides that she brought in a kind of exhibition (See Fig. 10 on page xi above). In this way, the people of the village, all the people of the groom's clan could see what she brought, and show them that she did not come empty handed. At this time, people could not only immediately see how much of what she brought, but also judge how skillfully and beautifully everything was made. The wedding ceremony continued for until the third day, and afterwards, everyday life began.

Another thing I want to mention about wedding rituals is what the position of women was like in the family. Many women lived sufficiently happily, and they were satisfied with their lives. When a child was born, the child usually brings stability to the family. It is possible to meet a good husband, someone who is calm and wise. Then the family was normal and everyone was satisfied. On the other hand, it was not uncommon for the bride to come to the groom's house and see that the husband was a violent person. He would insult or hit her, whether or not there was a child, and if there was no child, it was worse. There were also cases of adultery. That is why there were cases of women asking to be taken away from the husband's family and husband's clan. In these cases, she usually asked the brother of her mother. The father's side married her off, but she asked the mother's side relatives, who she was more comfortable with, to taken her away. This was uncommon but did happen. When the uncles came, they explained the whole story. If the husband apologized and promised not to bother her and live peaceably, they convinced their niece to stay, and the bride remained there.

There were many possible reasons women asked relatives to take them away. The husband can cheat on them, treat them badly, hit them, or their in-laws can treat them poorly. In these cases, she asked her relatives for help, and the mother's side relatives came and took her back without any investigation or ruling. This was in rare cases. Normally, the elders of both clans met, fully grasped the situation, and decided whether or not to allow a divorce. Divorce procedures were complicated — for example, if the woman left the clan because of the husband's wrongdoing, the husband had to pay an additional recompense, and if it was the woman's fault, her dowry was taken from her and was not even given her child. The child stayed with the husband's family. In other words, there are two solutions: either the relatives figure it out themselves, or there is this sort of ruling. It was not possible to object to the ruling and all were required to follow it.

There were many kinds of marriages. The one I talked about is the one in which the parents came to an agreement. Another case is when two families each have a son and a daughter, and the fathers of the two families negotiate and agree to exchange daughters with one another. In other words, it was the type in which one would marry off his daughter to the other, and the other would marry off his daughter to the first. In the case of this kind of exchange (*Juechin*), there was no need for a *tori*. There was this kind of marriage. In my case, it is as follows. If two sets of parents have a very good relationship, and if to one family, a daughter is born, and to the other, a son is born, after about two years have passed, or one year, or one and a half years have passed, the two fathers come to an agreement and decide to marry the two children. If the fathers negotiated sincerely, then a ritual was performed. The *khalat* of the son and the daughter are put into a jar made with clay, and a cover made of leather is used to cover it, then it is immured with mud. In today's terms, this was an engagement. When the children grow up, they know they are to become husband and wife. I, too, was engaged to a boy in this way. However, the time of the Soviet Union came, and the marriage was unfulfilled. That boy grew up to be a good person, attending the Herzen State Pedagogical Institute (Leningrad), but when he returned, I was already married. That man protested "You were to be my wife, but why did you not obey our tradition." Something like this happened. There was this kind of marriage and other kinds of marriages as well. There was also a case in which a family asked for a *tori* that was so big that the potential husband could not gather up enough for the daughter, and the daughter could not marry for her entire life. This kind of potential bride is known as a *kaarmaajin.* Normally, this was because the daughter of a very rich family that asked for a very large *tori,* but the result of this was the daughter remained alone.

3.4. Funeral rituals

From olden times, Nanai people believed the following about death. When someone got sick, could not recover and died, they believed that his (or her) soul was taken away by spirits. If someone, for whatever reason, committed suicide — and this was rare, a very rare occurrence — then it was said that the soul left on its own volition. If someone died of an unlucky accident, though it was the case that an unlucky accident occurred, it was believed that it was not just an unlucky accident, but that it was the scheme of evil spirits. Even so, in any case, Nanai people thought that when a person died, his soul left him. When he stopped breathing, seeing, moving, or feeling, they believed it was his soul that left. However, it was believed that the soul was somewhat alive, that is, that what dies is the outer shell of the body. Though when a person dies, his body breaks down, this is only the outer shell of the body, and it was believed that the soul lives for a long time. This is why before a dead person is sent to that world, he was treated like he was alive. This is the attitude that relatives, close friends, and people of the village took toward the dead person.

So what was done first if someone died at home for whatever reason? Before anything else, the person was laid down according to the customs. In the past, there was a *kan*, but we called it *nakan*. There were no stools, and in the left side of the house, there was a two-sided *kan*, a four-sided *kan* if it was a big house. In the left side of the house, two boards were laid on the ground. Or if a wide board is available, then one wide board was laid on the ground. This was so that the deceased was not just placed on top of the board. On the board, something like a mattress was placed, and this was called *sektepun* in Nanai. A pillow, then the deceased was placed on top, and the arms and legs of the deceased were straightened alongside the body. The feet were gathered and tied up with a white cloth so that they did not separate. In the past, the face was covered with a piece of cloth, but in the twentieth century, due to Russian influence, the face was no longer covered and was kept uncovered. Of course, older people followed old customs for a long time and therefore covered the face, though they did allow younger people who were accustomed to not covering the face to do so. However, they claimed it would be better to cover the face.

If a husband died, his wife wrapped her head in a white bandana or band and her arms with a white cloth. All relatives were also marked with white cloth. This is because white was the color of mourning for the Nanai people. After this, all relatives and close friends were told that someone had died. While some family members notified everyone about the death, other family members put away all the tools for hunting or fishing into the shed (*takto*). In the past, every house had a shed next to it, and some men had a special shed to keep these kind of tools. If there was this sort of shed, everything was placed there, and during the three days that the deceased remained at the house, no one was allowed into the shed. Later, when sheds began to disappear, the hunting and fishing tools were gathered in one spot in the house and no one was allowed near them. The wife made the shroud for the burial ritual. She prepared clothes, shoes, coverings, and bowls. All these things were hung above where the deceased was lying. Two knots were made with rope, and a pole used for pushing off of shore in a boat was put through the knots, and things like the shroud and coverings were hung on the pole.

Aside from this, things that were going to be burned after

the funeral at the graveyard and during the burial rituals were gathered and things that were going to be given away were packed. If someone contracted a serious disease and knew he (or she) was soon going to die, he gave away things to friends, close friends, and relatives himself, but if he died without giving everything away, everything was given away. Giving things away was not considered a sin or a violation of tradition, somethings were burned and one or two things worthy of remembrance were kept. The rest was removed. Everything that could be hung on the pole was hung, other objects were gathered and put in a special place. What these other objects were was bowls. It was believed that the deceased, after leaving for next world, behaved as they would in this world, doing activities such as eating, hunting, fishing, etc. All the things required for this, including bowls, were chosen and set aside. After everything was chosen, some things were placed in the coffin, some beneath or above the coffin in the grave, and the things to be burned were gathered separately. During the three days that the deceased was at home, everything was gathered separately.

Bearing in mind that the soul was alive, while the deceased was at home, he (or she) was treated the same as a living person. Food was given to the deceased the same number of times that the family ate — if the family ate three times, then he was given food three times, if they ate twice, then twice. A small table was placed next to the deceased, a special bowl was prepared, and a little bit of food was put in it and placed on the table right next to him. So that the deceased could eat, a special bib was sewn. This is called a *lelue*. On it, the simple likeness of a stomach, esophagus, and intestines, in other words the path that food takes, was embroidered on. Small metal disks like coins, smaller than a shaman's rings, were hung on the edges of the bib. On the very bottom of the bib, a jade ring was sewed on. The jade ring was taken off of women's earrings, and all women had earrings made of jade rings. It was around two centimeters in diameter and there was a large hole in the middle. This ring was hung on the bib, and a long thread, longer than two meters, was threaded through the jade ring, and a bead was attached to the other end. A table was set for the lying deceased, and when food was placed on the table, the bead was dipped into the food. For example, if the deceased is presented with boiled rice *boda*, the bead was dipped in the *boda*, if he is given something to drink, like water, then the bead was dipped in water. It was thought that the food would travel through the string, go through the jade ring, and be transferred through to the stomach and bowels. For this reason, the bib was embroidered as such. In Nanai, this was called *eeriptun*, meaning that the deceased continued to breath, eat food, and drink water.

For what reason was the thread so long? During the funeral, after burying the deceased, the bead at the end of the thread was kept exposed outside the grave and placed on top of it. This is because after the funeral, during the post-funeral rituals, when people visited the grave, they fed and gave water to the deceased, and once again, they dipped the bead into the food and water. This custom still continues now, but now, the thread is made short. The thread with the bead is about half a meter long, just enough for the chest of the deceased to be connected to the table set up right next to him, and the bead is taken and dipped in the plate or bowl. The food was not placed there for long, about five minutes, then put away, and after the bead is rinsed clean, it is placed on the deceased's chest. This food that is placed on the table and given to the deceased is called *doobocha* in Nanai. It refers to the food offered to the deceased while he (or she) remains lying at home.

During this time, close relatives and acquaintances come to visit. In the past, because Nanai villages were small, if someone died, the entire village, male or female, all came to offer their condolences when they were able. Only pregnant women are not allowed to go to offer their condolences. Pregnant women cannot go to the grave either. I understand that it is the same in Korea. When offering condolences, people bring a bottle of wine or vodka, and though in the past there was no vodka — this was brought in by Russian people — everyone brings liquor nowadays. There was no need to bring a large bottle — people even bring those only about a quarter of a liter. In the past, people brought things like bread, boiled fish, and *yukola* (dried fish), and nowadays they mainly bring things like pieces of salami, crackers, chocolate and so on. The bowl in which food is given to the deceased is always clean. If anything was put in the bowl, it is immediately taken, cleaned, wiped and put back. People offering their condolences placed the food they brought down, poured vodka into a small glass and offered it to the dead, but instead of the lips, they offer it on the chest. This is because the bib with the stomach embroidered on it is on the chest. Then, they dip their index finger in the vodka to get a few drops and they can sprinkle it on the chest. And they say the following. "I have come to bid farewell. I have always revered you, but it is a shame you had to leave us." They made sure to also say the following. "But since you are leaving us in any case, please go alone. Please do not take anyone with you." These words of protection had to be said, for saying this protects the remaining people, the living people, and especially the family. This continues for three days, and every person who comes to offer their condolences must observe these traditions. If someone older than the person who came to offer their condolences was next to the deceased, the younger person made sure to offer a drink and showed respect. If any vodka is left over, it is not thrown out, but the bottles are stopped with corks, and leftover foods are collected in a separate bowl. Nowadays, crackers or chocolate can be put into bags, but in the past, if boiled or dried foods were brought, they were put in separate pots. This is because no one was to take any away with them.

That was how they bade farewell. On the third day, the funeral is performed. Before the deceased is brought out, he (or she) was clothed, but there were two differing opinions. Some people said that the deceased must be clothed in an even number of articles of clothing. The idea was that if the deceased was clothed in an odd number of articles of clothing, then in order to fulfill pairs, someone else would be taken as well. From what I remember, my mother said the following. "The deceased was always clothed in an odd number of articles of clothing. Then, the number of coverings matches the number of articles of clothing. No matter how poor someone is, at least three articles of clothing were put on the deceased. The richest people even put on thirteen articles of clothing. The deceased was clothed in a *khalat*, pants, gaiters, shoes and so on, and therefore the body became much bigger. This is because clothes were put on over other clothes. The important thing is that whatever season the funeral was held, whether summer, spring, autumn or winter, the deceased was always also clothed in winter clothing. A fur hat, boots (*untii*), winter *bialoochi* and mittens were put on as well. This is because when a dead person goes to the afterlife, he (or she) will live in the same way, and therefore believed that he will need clothes for all four seasons. That is why the deceased was clothed in this way. There number of coverings were the same as the number of articles of clothing. On the very bottom, a mattress, known as a *sektepun* was placed, and in the past, everyone had this mattress, which was about the same size as those used in traditional Korean villages. Two layers of this sort of mattress that were embroidered were placed lengthwise into the coffin, and the deceased was laid on this. The coverings were placed backwards. The deceased was covered backwards, with the side that covers the head going to the feet and the side that covers the feet going to the head. All sorts of cloth were put on top of the covers, either his own cloth or those brought by people who came to offer condolences, but in any case, the number of coverings had to match the number of articles of clothing. For women, all her tools were placed in the coffin. Sewing tools, embroidery tools, and such were put in the coffin together, but scissors were not allowed to be included. This is because it was thought that the deceased would use the scissors to cut through, and cause harm to the living. For men also, all the things they need in that world were put in the coffin. Bowls were put in for both men and women. At this point, all the items that went into the coffin had their ends cut off a little. For example, when a bowl is put in, the edges are broken in a little, and if spoons are put in, the ends of the handle are purposefully a little damaged, by breaking them a little. A cane (*tunyepun*) was always placed next to the right hand for old men. This is why the coffin was made large and strong. It was made, not like nowadays with thin planks that collapse when covered in dirt, but with strong half-beams. The coffin had a rectangular shape, but the leg portion was slightly narrower. While the coffin is left outside, the deceased was clothed. While he (or she) was still on the board and the coverings were laid in.

In this state, a ritual called *tuyunbe anaori* in Nanai was performed. It means "forcing out the reception (food)", or in other words, bringing the food out of the home. There was a special person entrusted with making the food for the burial (funeral) rituals. Porridge was always included in the food, and there is also boiled soybeans, boiled kidney beans, thinly sliced baked bread placed in a bowl, and of course there is vodka or wine. After the porridge is put in a bowl, the middle is dug in a little and oil is poured in. In the very front, someone pours liquor into a glass, then behind that person, the women, holding the food, stand in line one-by-one in order. Starting from the eldest person, each person, excluding the children, puts the vodka or wine to his (or her) lips and tastes a little bit of the food in order with their hands or their spoons. After all the food is put away, in the past, after the deceased is clothed and placed in the coffin inside the house, all the necessary items are put in the coffin and then it was all brought outside. How is it brought outside? In the past, leaving through the door was uncommon, and people left through the windowsill. If the window was too small, they dug into the wall next to the window and after leaving through the opening, the men quickly pasted up and restored the wall. This is done so that the evil spirits would think that because no one left through the door, no one had died. According to my mother, when a person first enters the house, the head enters first and the feet follow through the door afterwards, and when he (or she) leaves the house, the legs must exit first followed by the body. Therefore, she said that when the deceased is brought out, the legs must be brought out first. Gaer (1991) also refers that the legs of the deceased must be brought out first. However, many Nanai people believe that the deceased must be brought out head first. It is difficult to judge who is correct. A lot of time has passed, and nowadays, the deceased is brought out this way and that way.

Another ritual during the funeral is "thread cutting", which in Nanai is called *sirektewe khetuliuri*. For the remaining living people, this is a way to protect them from evil spirits, and it is a ritual to prevent the dead from causing harm to the remaining people. So how is it performed? Not so long ago, it was not so long ago that all our shamans have died out (See

Fig. 11 on page xii above). For example, for my husband's funeral, there was a woman shaman. This ritual was performed by a woman shaman, and the shaman sits next to the coffin. In the past, this was done next to the grave in the burial grounds, but nowadays, it is performed in the yard of the house. The coffin with the deceased is brought out and placed on two stools, and the shaman sits next to this. The shaman grabs the deceased's hand in her hand and a ball of thread is put in the hands of the deceased. The shaman does it to make it seem like the deceased is holding the ball of thread. If the deceased is a man, his wife first grabs the end of the thread, and afterward it is given to the children. If they want to, friends may also participate. The person holding onto the end of the thread quickly turns away from the deceased and runs toward home. At this point, the shaman is holding a stick in her hand. When the string becomes tight, the shaman strikes down with the stick and cuts the thread. The person that ran with the thread must toss it away and, without turning back, run into the house. This ritual is done to protect living people from the deceased, so that the deceased may leave alone and not cause any harm to the family. In the past, it was done at the grave, but now it is done in the yard.

After this ritual is performed, to where is the coffin with the deceased taken? In the past, the funeral was conducted close-by, for example, in the garden. In the past, Nanai people did not bury the coffin, but built a wooden chamber (*keren*) and placed the coffin on top of it. But afterwards, they began to bury it. But in the 1940s, in a village called Kagdaga, coffins were buried in people's own gardens. There was no separate burial ground, and all their relatives were buried in their own gardens. Now, because there are burial grounds, the deceased are brought to the burial ground. In the past, the path to go to the graveyard and the one to leave it were differentiated. Even if the road back from the garden was 50 meters long, a different path was taken. Nowadays, there is only one road to the burial grounds, so people return on the same path, but this is a broken tradition. The reason the road to and from the burial grounds is differentiated is to confuse evil spirits. When taking the coffin and going to the graveyard, water and food is packed to go, and all the food that, for three days, people who came to offer their condolences brought is separated — the dry foods into separate pails or pots from the *boda* and other liquids, which is separately packed and brought. Not a lot of liquor is brought. Only a bottle or two are brought. All the relatives also follow to bid farewell. When covering the coffin, an odd number of nails were hammered in. Not many nails about nine to eleven. If the deceased was not very tall, nails were hammered in the four corners and one or two more, but if the deceased was tall, even more were nailed in. When hammering a nail, it was not allowed for someone to have many tries. It was considered to be very good if a nail was hammered in one try. If the coffin was large, the grave was dug to be large. When the dead were no longer buried in the log structure, it was built at the gravesite. Using logs with a diameter of about twelve centimeters and about two meters long, it is built as a square and the logs are piled up until it is a little taller than the coffin. Nowadays, hunting and fishing tools are slightly broken then can be put at the bottom of the grave and the coffin placed on top of them. Or the items can be left unbroken and burned later. Over all this the coffin is placed on top and the *keren* is covered with logs. This is to protect the deceased. After many years, the coffin will rot quickly. Because of the weight of the dirt, the coffin can mold (our coffin does not mold. The wood is quite strong.) But even so, this log structure helps to maintain the state of the coffin and to prevent the dirt from collapsing in. Though it has been many years since my parents passed away, when I visit, the grave looks like it was just built. The top is covered with grass, and the log structure is still there.

While the grave was being dug, two highly experienced people prepare everything, and with dry firewood and birch bark, they light two bonfires. One is lit toward the east, the side in which the sun rises, one is lit to the west, the side the sun sets, and the bonfire on this side is burned near the grave. The bonfire lit toward where the sun rises is the "fire of the living", and the one lit toward where the sun sets is the "fire of the deceased". When the sun sets, it becomes dark, and this is so because a person's life ended. The bonfire to the east just burned, and people stood around it, feeling its warmth, and did things like share stories, while at the "fire of the deceased", all the food that was gathered for three days was burned. There are not only dry foods, but also soup and *boda*. The reason it is necessary for a man or a woman to sit near the fire is that he or she can prevent the fire from going out and watch the fire carefully. If the bonfire goes out before everything is burned, it is a very bad omen. It meant the future of the family is now in danger. If dry foods were put in the fire, then a little bit of the liquids was poured on, then once again dry foods were put in, and this continued in this way until everything was burned. Objects were also burned, but before they were, they were ripped or broken a little. They were not to be burned while unbroken. Although this tradition is no longer observed, not too long ago, just 30 to 40 years ago, it was. A small ditch, hole, was dug from the grave to the bonfire, and the ditched was made slanted toward the grave. While the food and the objects were being burned, the liquid flowed to the grave. Therefore, the deceased received everything that was coming out of the bonfire. There was this kind of funeral tradition.

During the three days the deceased was at home, he (or

she) was never left at home alone, and a few people other than relatives were always there, and everyone did not sleep, sat around, and held conversations. Making people laugh was not prohibited. This is because though the deceased's outer shell of the body died, it was believed that his soul was alive. I remember one time, when I was working at the village party apparatus, there was something called the State Committee of Health and Safety — now it's known as Department of Health, but at the time it was the State Committee of Health and Safety. This committee was inspecting our one Nanai village, and at the time, there happened to be someone who died and these committee members came in, and they saw the scene of everyone gathered around, talking, joking, and laughing, and they recorded this and wrote a report. It said something about sacrilege while the deceased laid there. This stemmed from ignorance about traditions. In a house with someone who died, for 7 days, the light was not to be put out. Why for 7 days? According to Nanai tradition, the first post funeral ritual was conducted on the third day after death. In other words, right after the funeral is conducted, everyone returned home and performed a post funeral ritual. The second post funeral ritual was performed on the fifth day, and the third post funeral ritual was performed on the seventh day. During these 7 days, at night, putting out the light was not allowed. During the day it was bright because of the sunlight, but when it got darker, the light was turned on and it was kept on throughout the night. If the light goes out at some moment, it is a bad omen. The life of the house can go out. This is in spite of the remaining people.

This kind of custom existed. If the head of the house died, to prevent the house from faltering, as soon as he dies, a man of a different clan would take a thick rope, go around the house, and tie it below the eaves. The rope was pulled tight and the knot was made near the door. This rope is untied after the post funeral rites for the deceased are performed. Why was this rope tied? If the head of the house died, the family can falter and collapse. This symbolizes how the family can possibly collapse. The rope is tied to prevent this. Afterwards, the rope was untied and thrown away, and was not buried in the grave. It was just thrown away. If the rope is left at the grave, then this was considered a bad omen. Because it is a rope that was tied around the house of someone who died, it could not left together with that very person. That is why this rope was just thrown away. Nowadays, this is not done. Each family does not live in their own home, but live in homes with many households, and therefore the rope cannot be tied around the house.

On the seventh day, during the third post funeral ritual, a *panyoo* was made, which was a wooden doll that held the soul of the deceased. Even if someone dies, it is the outer shell of the body that dies, but the soul remains. The *panyoo* is a wooden person, and the head is carved and up to here, it is made like a thin stele. It is made on top of a square base, and until the shaman performs the big ritual, *kasaa*, or in other words the ritual to send the deceased to the other world, this *panyoo* was made to stand where the deceased had once lived, where he (or she) slept. It was stood up against the wall of where the deceased used to sleep, or it stood on the base nearby. When the family ate, they put a table and food in front of the *panyoo*, gave it things to eat, and when they slept, they put out bedding and the *panyoo* was laid down like a living person. When the *kasaa* was held, the shaman sent the soul to the other world, then the soul left for the other world, and afterwards the *panyoo* was burned, and post funeral rituals were no longer performed for that person.

If a baby who did not reach a year old died, it was not buried in the ground. It was clothed and wrapped using wrapping paper carefully made from birch bark and it was taken to the woods, where a tall, sturdy tree was chosen and it was affixed firmly between the branches of that tree. When I spoke about wedding rituals, I talked about how on the wedding *khalat*, there were embroidered birds on the tree of the clan symbol. It was thought that children under a year old were not yet people, but were birds. If an infant died, the soul becomes a bird and flies away, and the bird's soul enters a woman, and she gives birth to the baby. A different baby is born in place of the original baby. In order to confirm that this different baby was born to the woman in place of the original baby, during the preparation of the funeral ritual for the dead infant, marks are made. Cold coal was taken out of the oven and used to draw the form of a bracelet on the arm. Marks were sometimes made on the legs or the body. They were made so that they could be easily visible. It was made clearly visible. When a baby was born in that village, the baby was always carefully checked. If markings are found on the baby's body in the same spot as they were on the dead baby's body, then it was said that the soul of the dead baby had returned to this baby.

4

Glossary

Remarks:

(1) Items in this glossary are arranged in the following order: a(aa) b č d ə(əə) g ɪ(ɪɪ) i(ii) j ǰ k l m n ŋ o(oo) p r s t u(uu) w x.

(2) Derivational suffixes are also given with roots in 4.1, separated by hyphen.

(3) Nanai verbs are ended in hyphen.

4.1. Lexical forms

4.1.1. Nanai-English

Aba	not
aba-na-	not-VBZ
aba-na-go-	not-VBZ-ITER
abolɪ-	depart this life
ačan-	meet
ačaŋkora	filbert
ačaasɪ	inappropriate, not.appropriate
ačo-	remove
ačoa-	get rid of
adoo	twins
adoo-ko	twins-PROP
aag	elder brother
agbɪn-	appear
agbɪn-bo-	appear-TR

agda-	be glad
agda-nasɪ-	rejoice-REP
aɪŋanɪ	year
aɪŋanɪ-sɪ-	year-VBZ
aɪsɪma	made with gold
aɪsɪn	gold
aja	good, OK
aja-na-go-	good-VBZ-REV
ajaǰɪɪ	well, decently, safely
ajapo-	love
ajasɪ-	be suitable
akoačɪ-	doll.VBZ
akoan	doll, toy
akpan-	lie down
akpan-go-	lie down-REV
akpan-go-waan-	lie down-REV-CAUS
aldan	gap
alɪo	tableware, dishes
aloosɪ-	teach
altama	basin
ama	father
ambaan	fairly
ambaan	ghost, demon
amda-	imitate
amɪn	father
amɪnaa	fathers
amɪrɪ	robe
amta	tasty
ana-	push
anaa	without, no
anda	friend
anjaa	feast, holiday
anjaara-	celebrate
aaŋgɪa	right
aŋgo-	make, do
aŋgo-go-	make-REV
aŋgo-lo-	make-INCH
aŋma	mouth
aŋpa	father-in-law

ao-	sleep
aojan	groom
aon	day
aoŋga-	spend a night
aoŋga-čɪ-	spend a night-FR
apɪto	neck-flap
aapon	hat
arakɪ	alcoholic drink, vodka
arčokaan	girl
argala-	deceive
arkɪ	alcoholic drink, vodka
asɪ	wife
asɪa	female
aso	so much
Baa-	find, get, take
bado	opposite side
baɪ	only, just
baɪbɪɪ	just, ordinary
bajan	rich
bajan-laa	rich-SUFF (somewhat rich)
baakɪ	lazy
balana	long ago
balapčɪ	ancient
balǯɪ-	live, be born
balǯɪ-go-	be born-ITER
banɪxa	thanks
banjaala-go-	thank-ITER
baogo-	find
baar	first anniversary, one year, year
bargɪ-	prepare
baaro	direction
baaroa	direction
baaroolɪ-	dress, put on
bəgǯi	foot, leg
bəjə	body
bəjun	elk, animal, beast
bələči-	help

bəun	place
bɪa	month
bɪaŋsa-	spend time
bi-	be, lie, live
bi-gilə-	be-OBLG
bi-wəən-	be-CAUS
biǰərə	perhaps, likely
boa	place, heaven, outside, world, god
boačaan	island
boakɪa	outside
boatoačɪ-	hunt
boatoŋgo	hunter
boda	fluid food, fluid soup
bodo-	consider
bojaa-	break
bojačɪ-	broken.VBZ
bojalɪ-	destroy, break
bolo	autumn
bolookto	meadowsweet
boŋgo	first
boŋnan	fishing rod
borakta	firestone
bortɪ	permanently
boso	fabric, cloth
bota-	cast a net, catch a fish
bu-	die
buu-	give
buu-gu-	give-REV
budər	pair
buə	we
bui-	die
buikini	the deceased
bumbiwə	we.ACC
bundu	we.DAT
buni	underworld, otherworld
buniə-	cover
bunǰi	we.INS
bunǰiəǰi	we.ABL
bur-	die

bur-bu-	die-TR
buri	bow
burpuun	mourning
busəsi-	endeavor
busuəktə	willow
buu-wəən-	give-CAUS
Čaa	that.ACC
čado	then, at that time
čadu	then
čaagǰan	white
čakpa-	soak
čala	on the spot
čaalı-	cut
čəktəri-	scatter, spray
čıa	behind
čıkı-	lie
čımana	tomorrow
čıro-	roast
čısa-	sail
čıxala-	agree
čikəli-	base
čiptun	pillow
čiun	flint
čoča-go-	run-REV
čoolon	soup
čooro	hut
čowoo	thief
čuu	most, very
čukin	bad
čuul	directly
čumčuən	finger
čuŋguru	fallen away navel
Dada	aunt (maternal, elder)
daaı	large, big, adult, great, grown-up, senior
daaı-əkə	grand-female
daaı-ǰıma	big-SEL

daaɪ-laa	large-SUFF (somewhat large)
daaɪ-ookaan	big-EXTR (very big)
daaɪn	grandmother
daamɪn	grandfather
daoko	loaded
darama	backbone
daramɪ	wide
dasɪ-	cover up, close, cover
dasɪ-go-	cover-REV
dasɪ-ko	cover-PROP
dawa	salmon
daxala-	follow
daxala-mǰɪ	follow-AGT (bridesmaid)
dəgbəli-	open
dəgbəliku	uncorking
dəgdə-gu-	fly-REV
dəəŋgurə	slingshot
dəŋsi-	serve
dərə	table
dərəǰi-	stay
dərəǰi-gu-wəən-	stay-ITER-CAUS
dərəl	face
dəri-	spread
dəri-gu-	spread-ITER
doo	inside
doo-ko	inside-PROP
doobo-	offer food to the deceased
dooboča	food offered to the deceased
dooboča-	offer food to the deceased
dookɪa	inner, inside
doolaa	quietly
dolbo	night
dolɪn	half
doolǰɪ-	hear
doolǰɪ-waan-	hear-CAUS
dosɪǰa-	listen
duə	end
duəntə	taiga
duərə-	step

duilə	in the taiga, in the forest
duin	four
duipə	taiga (here and there)
duisi	to the taiga, to the forest
dujə	taiga side
duri	baby bed

Əčiə	not
əədən	fool
əgǰi	much, many
əgǰi-ləə	many-SUFF (somewhat many)
əi	this
əikə	elder sister
əjə	here, near
əǰə-	memorize
əǰən	owner
əǰi	husband
əǰi	not
əǰi-lə-ndə-	get husband-VBZ-INT
əkəsəl	female.PL, woman.PL
əksən	uncle (paternal, younger)
əktə	female, woman
əktəni	female, woman
ələ	enough, already
ələə	soon
əlkə	gradual, quiet
əlkəə	quietly
əlkəə əlkəə	very quietly
əlkəǰiəni	gradually
əm	not
əm	one, same
əm-ǰimə	one-SEL (one of two)
əmbə	rarely
əmǰiə	one (of the pair)
əmuučən	alone, lonely
əmuə	cradle
əmukəəkəən	only one
əmun	one

əmuni	one person
əmusi-	move gently
əmutuu	as if
əndur	god
ənə-	go
ənə-gu-wəən-	go-REV-CAUS
əniə	mother
əniənəə	mothers
ənin	mother
əninəə	mothers
ənjuə	pot
ənu-	go, return, go away
ənuu	illness
ənuu-ku	disease-PROP, illness-PROP
ənu-lu-	get ill-INCH
ənu-lu-wəən-	get ill-INCH-CAUS
ənusi-	illness.VBZ
əŋgərəgdə	underwear
əŋpə	mother-in-law
əpən	bread
əər	time
ərdələ-	produce
ərdən	custom
ərdən-ku	method-PROP
ərdəŋgə	interesting
ərdəŋgə-si-	interesting-VBZ
ərgən	soul
ərin	time, days
əəriptun	funeral bib
ərsi-	breathe
əsəli-	put
əsi	now
əsii	just now
ətəxi-	take care
ətuu-	protect, guard
əu-	descend
əu-gu-	descend-REV
əukən	sister-in-law
əusi	this way

əuxəxin	angelica
Gaksıa-ko	one of a pair-PROP
gaksıdaan	odd
gara	oarlock, bough, little branch
garpa-	rise
gəə	well, OK, good
gəkči-	freeze
gəkčiun	frost
gələ-	need, request, want, invite, search, ask for, ask, seek
gələ-gu-	ask for-REV, seek-REV, want-REV
gərbiə-si-	call-DUR
gərbu	name
gərəən	people, lots of
gərəəni	people
gəsə	together
gəun	empty
gıamata	bride, wedding
gıan	rule, principle
gıda-la-	spear-VBZ
gıla	wedding boat
gıol	oar
gıolı-mǰı	row-AGT, rower
gıraan-	tread
gırmaksa	bone
gırsoo	knife for sewing
goaon	quant, pole
goı	other
goı-ǰıma	other-SEL (the other)
goı goı	various
goıda-	last long
gookoǰı	politely
golǰon	stove
golo	ethic group
gormaxon	rabbit
goro	distant, long time, far
goropčı	long

gučəkə	uncle (maternal, younger)
guči	again
guči guči	again and again
gučkuli	beautiful, pretty
gudə-či-	tear-FR
guičə	roof
guisə	box, wardrobe
gujiə-si-gu-wəən-	mercy.VBZ-ITER-CAUS
gujiələ	poor
gujiən	mercy
guup-	be extinguished
gursəl	people.PL
gurun	people
gusərə-	tell, say
gusərə-gu-	tell-ITER
gusərəəndu-	talk
gusin	uncle (maternal, younger)
gusinəə	uncles

Ilaačia	third
ılaan	three
ılaanı	three peoples
ılga	embroidery
ılga-ko	pattern-PROP, picture-PROP
ılga-la-	embroidery-VBZ
ılı-sı-	stand-DUR
ılıačıa	third
ılıočı-	save a child's life
ında	dog
ıŋsoo-	lend
ıŋsoo-čı-	lend-FR
ıra-	carry, bring
ırbası-	dislike
ısı-	reach, arrive
ısı-go-	arrive-ITER
ıwa-čı-	heat-FR, kindle-FR
ıwan	kindle
ıwan-	burn

ɪwan-go-	burn-ITER
ɪxon	village
ɪxonkaan	village residents
Ii-	enter, lay
ii-gu-	enter-REV
ii-wəən-	enter-CAUS
ii-wu-gu-	enter-TR-REV
ičə-	see, show
ičə-gu-	see-ITER
ičə-ndə-	see-INT
ičə-wəən-	see-CAUS
ičəǰə-	look, watch
ičəuči-	show
ičuən-	show
iduǰi	in turn
ini	day
inoksa	snot
ixərə	lamp
Jaoko	graver
jaotaan	awning
jara-	navigate
jarako	net
jarsɪ-	examine
jək	to end
jəŋsilə-	match
jəwəri-	pour
jəwərsu-	pour.DUR
joso	locker
J̌aagda	pine
ǰaka	thing, affair, goods
ǰakpa	around, next, vicinity
ǰakpon	eight
ǰapa-	take, catch
ǰapa-čɪ-	catch-FR, keep-FR, take-FR

ǰapa-go-	take-REV, bring-REV, take away-REV
ǰapa-waan-	take-CAUS
ǰapača-	grab
ǰəgdə-	burn, light up
ǰəgǰi-	burn
ǰəgǰi-či-	burn-FR, light up-FR
ǰəgǰi-gu-	burn-ITER
ǰəilən	shamanic caps
ǰəjəku	blade
ǰələči-	betray
ǰəəri-	spread
ǰəuŋgiə	left
ǰɪa	friend, companion
ǰɪaja	next
ǰɪǰa	near
ǰɪǰan-	approach
ǰɪlgan	voice
ǰɪlɪ	head
ǰɪxa	money
ǰi-	come, arrive
ǰiǰu-	come back
ǰipərə-	patch
ǰirkəgu-	lay in state
ǰoo	house
ǰoa	summer
ǰoan	ten
ǰobo-	work
ǰobo-lo-go-	work-INCH-ITER
ǰoboso	hardworking
ǰoog	house
ǰoǰa-go-	judge-ITER
ǰoǰa-n	judge-NMLZ
ǰokon	inner corner
ǰool-	swell
ǰooŋgo-	come to mind
ǰooŋkan	family
ǰuə	two
ǰuəčin	exchange
ǰuəjə	second

ǰuəjəčiə	second
ǰuəni	two people
ǰuər	two
ǰukə	ice
ǰuki-	bewitch
ǰuki-či-	bewitch-FR
ǰulə	front
ǰuləsi	forward, first
ǰuulgəən	fate, fortune
ǰuliə	front
ǰuulin	Juulin
ǰului	first
Kagba	crock
kaıran	pity
kalan	pot
kaltaaǰıa	region, crack
kamalı-	forbid
kan	heated floor, *ondol*
kaokaa	quietly
kapıra-	attach
kaarmaaǰin	the most beautiful daughter
kasaa	memorial service
kasaata-	perform a memorial service
kəčəri-	turn
kəəndəli	around
kəəndəli-	go up, surround
kəndərxiən	threshold
kəndərxin	threshold
kərəl-	take care of
kərən	wooden chamber
kərgiən	felly
kəsi	luck, happiness
kəsi-ku	happiness-PROP
kətən	stern
kısıako	misfortune
kičə-	make efforts, be diligent, try
kidu-	respect

kirim	stationary
kočalı-	hinder
kočı	wineglass, glass
kolaan	insect
kolı	custom
komtaan	cap
koŋgırı-	ring
korıan	timbered wall
korpı-	finish, be in time
koorxıǰı-	be injured
kota	esophagus
kotaan	cup
kučəəli-	pierce
kučəən	knife
kuuči-	suck
kukpun	litter
kuun	breast
kupən	thread
kupi-	show
kurkə	reel of thread, thread
kusun	power
kusun-ku	strong-PROP
kutu	drag
kuwuu-	feed
Lala	gruel, porridge
ləkəə	arrow
ləkəə-či-	arrow-VBZ
ləluə	bib, apron
loo-	hang
loo-čı-	hang-FR
loča	Russian
lopto	right away
luktu	totally
Makta-	praise
maal-	die out
mama	elderly woman, old woman

mamaarı	grandmother
maŋbo	river
maŋga	difficult, expensive, strong, hard, serious
mapa	old man, bear
mapaarı	grandfather
ması	strong, hard
masılto-	fasten, strengthen
mədəə	message
mədəliku	request
mədəsi-	ask, require
məlǰi-	compete
məən	oneself
məənčiəri	oneself.DIR.PL
məənčiji	oneself.DIR
məənduji	oneself.DAT
mənə	oneself
məənǰiji	oneself.INS
məŋgumə	made with silver
məŋgun	silver
məəpəəri	oneself.ACC.PL
məəpi	oneself.ACC
mərgəən	hero
mıawan	favorite
mıočaačı-	gun.VBZ
mıočaan	gun
mıxoraan-	bow, bow down
mii	I
mimbiə	I.ACC
mimbiwə	I.ACC
mindu	I.DAT
minǰi	I.INS
miŋguči-	moan
miruə	dowry
moo	tree, bar, wood, stick
moo-kaan	rod-DIM
moo-lsı-	gather firewood-HAB
močogo-	return, turn back
modan	time (turn)
modorı-	smear

modorɪ-go-	smear-ITER
mogo	unskillful
mojɪn	intact
moktolɪ-	break
moolo-	walk
moŋgɪ-čɪ-	knead-FR, massage-FR
moŋgon	neck
mučuun	charcoal
mudən	riverbank
muə	water
muə-lsi-	fetch water-HAB
muələn-	drown
muiki	snake
muirə	shoulder
murči-	think
murun	mind
murun-ku	thought-PROP, mind-PROP
mutə-	be able to
mutə-gu-	be able to-ITER

Naa	land, earth
nadaačɪa	seventh
nadaan	seven
naɪ	person, man
naɪŋgɪ	other's property
nakan	heated floor, *ondol*
namčɪan	comfortable
namo	sea
namo-	fold
namo-go-	fold-ITER
naanaɪ	Nanai
nanta	leather
naŋgaačɪ-	throw away
naŋgala-	leave, throw
naŋgala-go-	leave-ITER
naokta	soft grass
naonǰoan	young
naonǰokaan	boy

narı-	cast a net
nəə	certainly
nəə-	put, set
nəktə	boar
nəku	child
nəəku-	put
nəmdə	thin
nəmi	thin
nəu	younger brother
nəučə-	keep, store
nəuči-	keep, store
nıkan	China
nılčalı-	crush
nıŋmaan	fairy tale
niičəəkəən	bird
niə-	exit, go out
niə-gu-	exit-REV
niə-gu-u-	go out-REV-TR
niə-wəən-	go out-CAUS
niə-wu-	go out-TR
niəčəə-kəən	bird-DIM
niru-	write
nixəli-	open
njaaloon	raw
njama	warm, warmish
njaŋgaa	a little
njəŋnjə	spring
njəpultə	fur
njoambačı	they.ACC
njoambanı	he.ACC, she.ACC
njoančı	they
njoančıačı	they.DIR
njoančıan	he.DIR, she.DIR
njoandoanı	he.DAT, she.DAT
njoanı	he, she
njoanǰı	he.INS, she.INS
njoaŋgı	his, hers
njuŋgun	six
nuuči	small, little

nuučikəənǰuən	children
nuučiku	small, little
nuktə	hair

ŋaala	hand, arm
ŋaanı-	go to take
ŋaso-	carry
ŋəələ-	be frightened
ŋəələə-či-	fear-FR
ŋəəluuči-	frighten

o-	become, pass away
oo-go-	board-REV
obo	share
očogo-	remain
ogda	boat
oı	few
ojaa	surface
okčı-	cure
okčı-čı-	cure-FR
okto	medicine
okto-ko	medicine-PROP
olbıačı-	carry
olbın-	bring
olbın-bo-	bring-TR
omı-	drink
omı-nasι-	drink-REP
omı-nasι-waan-	drink-REP-CAUS
omo-	collect
omolgıča	waist
onılaanı	length
onımı	long
onımıoo	extremely long
oŋasa-	sleep
oŋbo	buttock
oŋbo-	forget
orkı-la-	bad.VBZ, blame
orkı-laa	bad-SUFF (somewhat bad)

orkıkta	uncomfortable
orkın	bad
oroondola-	substitute
oroondolanı	instead of
osı-	become, come, die
osı-go-	become-ITER
osı-waan-	become-CAUS
oosı-čı-	clean-FR
oosı-go-	remove-REV
osıgoaan-kıča-	revitalize-DES
osını	if
osısı-	refuse
otokoo	a little
otolı-	understand, be able to, know
Paačı-la-	mallet-VBZ (ram, hit)
pagǰıala-go-	run away-REV
paıdan	grave mark
paaǰı	separately
paaǰıla-	separate
paksı	skillful, master
palan	floor
paloa	hammer
paloa-la-	hammer-VBZ
panjoo	wooden figure representing the deceased
papa	uncle (maternal, elder)
papola-	ban.VBZ (forbid, prohibit)
papon-ko	ban-PROP
pası	part, piece
patalaan	lady
paawa	window
pəgiə	bottom
pəgui	lower
pəiŋən	knee
pəisi	down
pəəjə	forehead
pəku	hot
pərgə-	try

pərgə-wəən-	try-CAUS
pıanǰıko	sofa
pıarmaa	frozen raw fish
piktə	child, kid
poo-	saw
poaı-kta-waan-	pad-DISTR-CAUS
poaktanı	some
poaldoanı	sometimes
poanı	some, rest
poawanı	some
poja	baby
pokto	light gown
pokto	way, pathway, road
polta	blankets
polta-la-waan-	blankets-VBZ-CAUS
puiku-gu-	jump-REV
puiku-nəsi-	jump-REP
pujə	injury
pujə-ku	injury-PROP
pujəli-	get hurt
puǰin	heroine
pujuu-	boil, cook
pujuu-či-	cook-FR, boil-FR
pujuu-wu-	cook-TR
pulə-	be left
puləə	residue
pulsi-	walk, go, frequent
puun	scent
puuŋgiči-	smell
puŋku	shawl, wraparound
puŋnə-gu-	expel-REV
puril	children
puril-ku	children-PROP
puxin	intestine
Saa-	know, understand
saa-ıča-	seek-DES
saa-waan-	know-CAUS

sagdan-go-	get old-REV
sagǰɪ	old
saago-	make sure
saɪ-	mark
saɪnaa	perhaps
saman	shaman
saola	water container
saolɪn	banquet
saorɪ	wood chip
saorɪ-	whittle, make *saori*
saorma	offering for the deceased, gift
sarbɪ	sharp
sarɪn	banquet
saawaasɪ	maybe
səə	age, year
səčən	nimble
səəgǰən	red
səək	easily
səkčiə-	lay, spread
səəksə	blood
səktəpun	mattress
səəl-	prick
sələ	iron
səlkə	half-moon silver ornament
səlxəən	crossbar
səəpə	sable
səpərsi-	cut
səurə	silk
səwən	figure for spirit
sɪa-	eat
sɪa-waan-	eat-CAUS
sɪalta	charcoal
sɪan	ear
sɪan-ko	ear-PROP
sɪaptaŋgɪ	food
sɪdo-	scrape
sɪlɪa	plate
sɪlko-	wash
sɪlko-go-	wash-ITER

sɪra-go-	continue-ITER
sii	you
sii-	plug, string
sii-	take time, pass
sidəri	bracelet
siksə	night
siksəŋgiələə	evening
sikuun	new
silčuksə	phosphorus
silə-ku	broth-PROP
sili-čə-	braid-PASS
sili-či-	braid-FR
sili-gu-	braid-ITER
siluun	dry
sim	quietly
simbiə	you.ACC
sinči	you.DIR
sinəǰii	poor
sinəǰii-ləə	poor-SUFF (somewhat poor)
siŋəəktə	flowering cherry
siŋgərə-	insult
sirəktə	thread
sirxə	twine
siun	sun
sogbo	fish skin
sogdata	fish
sogǰama-sɪ-	fish-DUR
soɪrakta	bead
sokta	ski
solbon	fortune-telling ceremony
solɪ	fox
soloogo-	leave
somalaan	pouch
soŋgo-	cry
soŋgomo	feel like crying
soopon	water bowl
soron-	sin
suu	talisman
suə	you.PL

suglən	present, gift
suuktu	branch
sumul	sinew
suŋgurə	at full length
susuuči-	see off
susuəči-ndə-	see off-INT

Ta-	do
tačıočı-	study
tado	then
tadu	then
taja	there, that place
tajaǰı	opposite side
taako-	be familiar with
taakoalı-	meet
takto	warehouse
taktoola-go-	step on-ITER
talaa	sliced raw fish
talo	birch bark
taoda-	respond
taon	every
taosı	to that place
tata-	pull
tata-go-	pull-REV
tawa	fire
taawo-	light up
təə-	sit, sit up
təə-gu-	sit-ITER
təə-si-	lie down-DUR, sit-DUR
təə-si-ičə-	lie-DUR-DES
təə-u-gu-	sit-TR-ITER
təə-wəən-	sit-CAUS
təčičə-	keep, wear
təi	that
təǰə	truth
təǰə-	believe
təǰuuči-	try
təlgəči-	bone

təluŋgu	legend
təəm	once, only
təən	hem
tənii	just
təŋ	very
təəŋku	saddle
təpčiu-	begin
tərək	just, exactly
tətu-	wear, dress
tətu-gu-	wear-REV, dress-ITER
tətu-wəən-	dress-CAUS, put on-CAUS
tətuə	clothes, clothing, dress
tətuə-	dress
tətuə-ku	clothes-PROP
təuči-	load
təwə	cargo
təxə	base
tɪas	full
too-	go
too-bo-	go-TR (carry)
tooɪ	riverside
toɪga-	hit
toɪkaan-	beat
toɪksa	birch bark of special treatment
toɪŋga	five
toɪŋgɪačɪa	fifth
tokon	center, middle
tookpaačɪ-	go up
toktoo-	make an agreement
tolɪ	breastplate
tompo	thread (made with fish skin)
toŋdo	right
toŋga-sɪ-	touch-DUR
toŋgala-	touch
toŋgala-waan-	touch-CAUS
topto	rope
tora	pillar
torɪ	bridewealth
totamaarɪ	therefore, so

totamı	therefore
totapaarı	then
totapı	then, after that, later
totapı-maarı	therefore
totapıa	later
totaraa	and then
tuu-	fall
tuu-gu-	fall-REV, sink-ITER
tuə	winter
tugbu-	fall
tugbugu-	put down
tugdə	rain
tugdə-	rain
tui	so, that way
tuiŋku-	quake
tujəə	so much, like that
tujəə tujəə	so much
tuju-	treat
tuju-n	treat-NMLZ
tuǰu-	lean
tukpən	nail
tukpən-	nail
tukpən-gu-	nail-ITER
tukuru	bottle
tukuru-ku	bottle-PROP
tul tul	always
tuliə	garden, yard
tunjəpu-	walk with stick
tunjəpu-n	walk with stick-NMLZ
tuŋdə	willow
tuŋgən	chest
turgən	fast
turgəsuən	quickly
turgun	reason
tutu-gu-	run-ITER
Ui	who
uikə	door

uilə	above
uiptəŋgi	upwards
ujə	top
uji-	tie, process
uji-gu-	tie-ITER
uju-	tie, bind, braid, process
ujuun	alive, living
uǰi-	raise, bring up
uǰi-wəən-	bring up-CAUS
uləən	good, sufficiently, well
uləənǰi	good
uləəsi-	love
uliksə	meat
ulpi-	sew, embroider
ulpi-čə-	sew-PASS
ulpi-gu-	sew-ITER
ulpi-lu-	sew-INCH
ulpisu	artfully embroider
uməkəəči-ndə-	fish-INT
uməkən	fishing gear
un-	say
un-gu-	say-REV
undəxən	board
unəəči-	compare
untii	boots
urə-	grow, grow up
uruuči-	bring up, raise
utuŋgi	canoe
uwui	upper

Waa-	catch, kill
waa-nda-go-	catch-INT-ITER
waaıča-	hunt
waaıčaŋko	game
waısı	to the shore
waaraŋkola	acacia

Xa	what
xaa-go-	go ashore-REV
xačın	kind
xado	how much, how many
xadowa	several
xagoarı	what for
xaı	what
xaı-	do what
xaıdo	where
xaıgoanı	for what
xaıgoarı	what for, for what
xaıgojı	why
xaımaarı	why
xaımı	why
xaıs	again, still
xaǰa	scissors
xaǰa-čı-	scissors-VBZ
xaǰa-la-	scissors-VBZ
xaǰon	thing, clothes, goods, stuff
xaal(ı)	when
xala	tribe, family
xalačı-	wait
xamačaa	what, which
xamasıı	backward, back
xamıa	back
xamoroı	last
xaŋgısı	away
xao-	wash
xao-čı-	wipe-FR
xao-čı-go-	wash-FR-ITER
xao-go-	wipe-ITER
xaosı	where to
xapol	broom
xapolı-	sweep
xas	again
xasısı-	chase
xawaŋga	quickly
xədun	wind

xədun-	blow
xəjə-	float
xəǰəni	Nanai
xəm	all
xəmdə	abdomen
xəmtu	all
xərə	frog
xərəktə	skin
xərgən	funeral repast, memorial ceremony
xəri-	treat
xərkə-	wind round
xəsə	word, language
xəəsi-	call
xətə-	withstand, obtain
xətu	torn
xətuə-	cut
xətuli-	cut
xəur	coffin
xəwəən	lake
xɪsaŋgo-	say, speak, talk
xoo-go-	be cured-REV, heal-REV
xoo-go-waan-	be cured-REV-CAUS
xoan-	be capricious
xoaŋgoan	cucumber
xoda	price
xoɪpon	earring
xoǰɪ-	finish
xoldon	side
xolgɪ-čɪ-	dry-FR
xolgɪ-čɪ-go-	dry-FR-ITER
xolgo-	dry
xolgokto	dried
xolto	fish soup
xoonɪ	how
xonjakaan	ring
xonjaan	spoon
xonjapton	thimble
xooŋko	bow of the boat
xora-	give birth, survive

xora-go-	stay alive-ITER
xorakta	bark
xorɪ-	help, protect
xorɪ-čɪ-	help-FR, protect-FR, save-FR
xoro-	remove
xoroačɪ-	hold fist
xosakta	nail
xoto	brainpan
xuəksə	sleeve
xuəl	across
xuimu	navel
xujə	horn
xujun	nine
xuktə	tooth
xuku-	wrap
xukuən	bag
xulə-	dig
xulǰii	warm
xuməgdən	ritual stick
xumu-	bury
xumu-gu-	bury-REV
xumu-lu-	bury-INCH
xumu-n	bury-NMLZ
xupi-	play
xurəən	hill
xurmə	needle
xurmi	short
xusə	male
xusənəj	man
xusəni	male, man

4.1.2. English-Nanai

A little	njaŋgaa, otokoo
abdomen	xəmdə
above	uilə
acacia	waaraŋkola
across	xuəl
adult	daaɪ
affair	ǰaka
after that	totapɪ
again	guči, xaɪs, xas
again and again	guči guči
age	səə
agree	čɪxala-
alcoholic drink	arakɪ, arkɪ
alive	ujuun
all	xəm, xəmtu
alone	əmuučən
already	ələ
always	tul tul
ancient	balapčɪ
and then	totaraa
angelica	əuxəxin
animal	bəjun
appear	agbɪn-
appear-TR	agbɪn-bo-
approach	ača-, ǰɪǰan-
apron	ləluə
arm	ŋaala
around	ǰakpa, kəəndəli
arrive	ɪsɪ-, ǰi-
arrive-ITER	ɪsɪ-go-
arrow	ləkəə
arrow-VBZ	ləkəə-či
artfully embroider	ulpisu
as if	əmutuu
ask	gələ-, mədəsi-

ask for	gələ-
ask for-REV	gələ-gu-
at full length	suŋgurə
at that time	čado
attach	kapıra-
aunt (maternal, elder)	dada
autumn	bolo
away	xaŋgısı
awning	jaotaan
Baby	poja
baby bed	duri
back	xamasɪ, xamɪa
backbone	darama
backward	xamasɪ
bad	čukin, orkɪn
bad.SUFF (somewhat bad)	orkɪ-laa
bag	xukuən
ban-PROP	papon-ko
banquet	saolɪn, sarɪn
bar	moo
bark	xorakta
base	čikəli-
base	təxə
basin	altama
be	bi-
be-CAUS	bi-wəən-
be-OBLG	bi-gilə-
be able to	mutə-, otolɪ-
be able to-ITER	mutə-gu-
be born	balǰɪ-
be born-ITER	balǰɪ-go-
be capricious	xoan-
be cured-REV	xoo-go-
be cured-REV-CAUS	xoo-go-waan-
be diligent	kičə-
be extinguished	guup-
be familiar with	taako-

be frightened	ŋəələ-
be glad	agda-
be in time	korpɪ-
be injured	koorxɪǰɪ-
be left	pulə-
be suitable	ajasɪ-
bead	soɪrakta
bear	mapa
beast	bəjun
beat	toɪkaan-
beautiful	gučkuli
become	o-, osɪ-
become-CAUS	osɪ-waan-
become-ITER	osɪ-go-
begin	təpčiu-
behind	čɪa, xamɪala
believe	təǰə-
betray	ǰələči-
bewitch	ǰuki-
bewitch-FR	ǰuki-či-
bib	ləluə
big	daaɪ
big-EXTR	daaɪ-ookaan
big-SEL	daaɪ-ǰɪma
bind	uju-
birch bark	talo
birch bark of special treatment	toɪksa
bird	niičəəkəən
bird-DIM	niəčəə-kəən
blade	ǰəjəku
blame	orkɪla-
blankets	polta
blankets-VBZ-CAUS	polta-la-waan-
blood	səəksə
blow	xədun-
boar	nəktəkəən
board	undəxən
board-REV	oo-go-
boat	ogda

body	bəjə
boil	pujuu-
boil-FR	pujuu-či-
bone	gɪrmaksa
bone	təlgəči-
boots	untii
bottle	tukuru
bottle-PROP	tukuru-ku
bottom	pəgiə
bough	gara
bow	buri
bow	mɪxoraan-
bow (of the boat)	xooŋko
box	guisə
boy	naonǰokaan
bracelet	sidəri
braid	uju-
braid-FR	sili-či-
braid-ITER	sili-gu-
braid-PASS	sili-čə-
brainpan	xoto
branch	suuktu
bread	əpən
break	bojaa-, bojalɪ-, moktolɪ-
breast	kuun
breastplate	tolɪ
breathe	ərsi-
bride	gɪamata
bridesmaid (follow-AGT)	daxala-mǰɪ
bridewealth	torɪ
bring	ɪra-, olbɪn-
bring-REV	ǰapa-go-
bring-TR	olbɪn-bo-
bring up	uǰi-, uruuči-
bring up-CAUS	uǰi-wəən-
broken.VBZ	bojačɪ-
broom	xapol
broth-PROP	silə-ku
burn	ɪwan-, ǰəgdə-, ǰəgǰi-

burn-FR	ǰəgǰi-či-
burn-ITER	ɪwan-go-, ǰəgǰi-gu-
bury	xumu-
bury-INCH	xumu-lu-
bury-NMLZ	xumu-n
bury-REV	xumu-gu-
buttock	oŋbo
Call	xəəsi-
call-DUR	gərbiə-si-
canoe	utuŋgi
cap	komtaan
cargo	təwə
carry	ɪra-, ŋaso-, olbɪačɪ-
carry (go-TR)	too-bo-
cast a net	bota-, narɪ-
catch	ǰapa-, waa-
catch-FR	ǰapa-čɪ-
catch-INT-ITER	waa-nda-go
catch a fish	bota-
celebrate	anjaara-
center	tokon
certainly	nəə
charcoal	mučuun, sɪalta
chase	xasɪsɪ-
chest	tuŋgən
child	nəku, piktə
children	nuučikəənǰuən, purig~puril
children-PROP	puril-ku
China	nɪkan
clean-FR	oosɪ-čɪ-
close	dasɪ-
cloth	boso
clothes	tətuə, xaǰon
clothes-PROP	tətuə-ku
clothing	tətuə
coffin	xəur
collect	omo-

come	ǰi-, osɪ-
come back	ǰiǰu-
come to mind	ǰooŋgo-
comfortable	namčɪan
companion	ǰɪa
compare	unəəči-
compete	məlǰi-
consider	bodo-
continue-ITER	sɪra-go-
cook	pujuu-
cook-FR	pujuu-či-
cook-TR	pujuu-wu-
cover	buniə-, dasɪ-
cover-PROP	dasɪ-ko
cover-REV	dasɪ-go-
cover up	dasɪ-
crack	kaltaaǰɪa
cradle	əmuə
crock	kagba
crossbar	səlxəən
crush	nɪlčalɪ-
cry	soŋgo-
cucumber	xoaŋgoan
cup	kotaan
cure	okčɪ-
cure-FR	okčɪ-čɪ-
custom	ərdən, kolɪ
cut	čaalɪ-, səpərsi-, xətuə-, xətuli-

Daughter	asɪa piktə
day	aon, ini
days	ərin
dead	buikin
deceive	argala-
decently	ajaǰɪɪ
demon	ambaan
descend	əu-
descend-REV	əu-gu-

destroy	bojalı-
die	bu-~bui-~bur-, osı-
die-TR	bur-bu-
die out	maal-
difficult	maŋga
dig	xulə-
direction	baaro, baaroa
directly	čuul
disease-PROP	ənuu-ku
dishes	alıo
dislike	ırbasi-
distant	goro
do	aŋgo-, ta-
do-TR	təpčiu-wu-
do what	xaı-
dog	ında
doll	akoan
doll.VBZ	akoačı-
door	uikə
down	pəisi
dowry	miruə
drag	kutu
dress	baaroolı-, tətu-, tətuə-
dress	tətuə
dress-CAUS	tətu-wəən-
dress-ITER	tətu-gu-
dried	xolgokto
drink	omı-
drink-REP	omı-nası-
drink-REP-CAUS	omı-nası-waan-
drown	muələn-
dry	siluun
dry	xolgo-
dry-FR	xolgı-čı-
dry-FR-ITER	xolgı-čı-go-
Ear	sıan
ear-PROP	sıan-ko

earring	xoɪpon
earth	naa
easily	səək
eat	sɪa-
eat-CAUS	sɪa-waan-
eight	ǰakpon
elder brother	aag
elder sister	əikə
elderly woman	mama
elk	bəjun
embroider	ulpi-
embroidery	ɪlga
embroidery-VBZ	ɪlga-la-
empty	gəun
end	duə
endeavor	busəsi-
enough	ələ
enter	ii-
enter-CAUS	ii-wəən-
enter-REV	ii-gu-
enter-TR-REV	ii-wu-gu-
esophagus	kota
ethic group	golo
evening	siksəŋgiələə
every	taon
exactly	tərək
examine	jarsɪ-
exchange	ǰuəčin
exit	niə-
exit-REV	niə-gu-
expel-REV	puŋnə-gu-
expensive	maŋga

Fabric	boso
face	dərəl
fairly	ambaan
fairy tale	nɪŋmaan
fall	tuu-, tugbu-

fall-REV	tuu-gu-
fallen away navel	čuŋguru
family	ǰooŋkan, xala
far	goro
fast	turgən
fasten	masılto-
fate	ǰuulgəən
father	amaa, amın
father-in-law	aŋpa
fathers	amınaa
favorite	mıawan
fear-FR	ŋəələə-či-
feast	anjaa
feed	kuwuu-
feel like crying	soŋgomo
felly	kərgiən
female	asıa, əktə, əktəni
fetch water-HAB	muə-lsi-
few	oı
fifth	toıŋgıačıa
figure for spirit	səwən
filbert	ačaŋkora
find	baa-, baogo-
finger	čumčuən
finish	korpı-, xoǰı-
fire	tawa
firestone	borakta
first	boŋgo, ǰuləsi, ǰului
first anniversary	baar
fish	sogdata
fish-DUR	sogǰama-sı-
fish-INT	uməkəəči-ndə-
fish skin	sogbo
fish soup	xolto
fishing gear	uməkən
fishing rod	boŋnan
five	toıŋga
flint	čiun
float	xəjə-

floor	palan
flowering cherry	siŋəəktə
fluid food	boda
fluid soup	boda
fly-REV	dəgdə-gu-
fold	namo-
fold-ITER	namo-go-
follow	daxala-
food	sɪaptaŋgɪ
fool	əədən
foot	bəgǰi
for what	xaɪgoanɪ, xaɪgoarɪ, xaɪgojɪ
forbid	kamalɪ-, papola-
forehead	pəəjə
forget	oŋbo-
fortune	ǰuulgəən
fortune-telling ceremony	solbon
forward	ǰuləsi
four	duin
fox	solɪ
freeze	gəkči-
frequent	pulsi-
friend	anda, ǰɪa
frighten	ŋəəluuči-
frog	xərə
front	ǰulə, ǰuliə
frost	gəkčiun
full	tɪas
funeral bib	əəriptun
funeral repast	xərgən
fur	njəpultə
Game	waaɪčaŋko
gap	aldan
garden	tuliə
gather firewood-HAB	moo-lsɪ-
get	baa-
get hurt	pujəli-

get husband-VBZ-INT	əǰi-lə-ndə-
get ill-INCH	ənu-lu-
get ill-INCH-CAUS	ənu-lu-wəən-
get old-REV	sagdan-go-
get rid of	ačoa-
ghost	ambaan
gift	suglən
girl	arčokaan
give	buu-
give-CAUS	buu-wəən-
give-REV	buu-gu-
give birth	xora-
glass	kočı
go	ənə-, ənu-, pulsi-, too-
go-REV-CAUS	ənə-gu-wəən-
go around	kəəndəli-, tookpaačı-
go ashore-REV	xaa-go-
go away	ənu-
go out	niə-
go out-CAUS	niə-wəən-
go out-REV-TR	niə-gu-u-
go out-TR	niə-wu-
go to take	ŋaanı-
god	boa, əndur
gold	aısın
good	aja, gəə, uləən, uləənǰi
good-VBZ-REV	aja-na-go-
goods	ǰaka, xaǰon
grab	ǰapača-
gradual	əlkə
gradually	əlkəǰiəni
grand-female	daaı-əkə
grandfather	daamın, mapaarı
grandmother	daaın, mamaarı
grave mark	paıdan
graver	jaoko
great	daaı
groom	aojan
grow	urə-

grow up	urə-
grown-up	daaɪ
gruel	lala
guard	ətuu-
gun	mɪočaan
gun.VBZ	mɪočaačɪ-

Hair	nuktə
half	dolɪn
half-moon silver ornament	səlkə
hammer	paloa
hammer-VBZ	paloa-la-
hand	ŋaala
hang	loo-
hang-FR	loo-čɪ-
happiness	kəsi
happiness-PROP	kəsi-ku
hard	maŋga, masɪ
hardworking	ǰoboso
hat	aapon
have expired	abolɪ-
he	njoanɪ
he.ACC	njoambanɪ
he.DAT	njoandoanɪ
he.DIR	njoančɪan
he.INS	njoanǰɪ
head	ǰɪlɪ
heal-REV	xoo-go-
hear	doolǰɪ-
hear-CAUS	doolǰɪ-waan-
heat-FR	ɪwa-čɪ-
heated floor	nakan, kan
heaven	boa
help	bələči-, xorɪ-
help-FR	xorɪ-čɪ-
hem	təən
here	əjə
hero	mərgəən

heroine	pujin
hers	njoaŋgɪ
hill	xurəən
hinder	kočalɪ-
his	njoaŋgɪ
hit	paačɪla-, toɪga-
hold fist	xoroačɪ-
holiday	anjaa
horn	xujə
hot	pəku
house	ǰoo~ǰoog
how	xoon, xoonɪ
how many	xado
how much	xado
hunt	boatoačɪ-, waaɪča-
hunter	boatoŋgo
husband	əǰi
hut	čooro

I	mii
I.ACC	mimbiə~mimbiwə
I.DAT	mindu
I.INS	minǰi
ice	ǰukə
if	osɪnɪ
illness	ənuu
illness-PROP	ənuu-ku
illness.VBZ	ənusi-
imitate	amda-
in the forest	duilə
in the taiga	duilə
in turn	iduǰi
inappropriate	ačaasɪ
injure-DUR	ənu-si-
injury	pujə
injury-PROP	pujə-ku
inner	dookɪa
inner corner	ǰokon

insect	kolaan
inside	doo, dookıa
inside-PROP	doo-ko
instead of	oroondolanı
insult	siŋgərə-
intact	mojın
interesting	ərdəŋgə
interesting-VBZ	ərdəŋgə-si-
intestine	puxin
invite	gələ-
iron	sələ
island	boačaan
Judge-ITER	ǰoǰa-go-
judge-NMLZ	ǰoǰa-n
Juulin	ǰuulin
jump-REP	puiku-nəsi-
jump-REV	puiku-gu-
just	baı, baıbıı, tənii, tərək
just now	əsii
Keep	nəučə-, nəuči-, təčičə-
keep-FR	ǰapa-čı-
kid	piktə
kill	waa-
kind	xačın
kindle	ıwan
kindle-FR	ıwa-čı-
knead-FR	moŋgı-čı-
knee	pəiŋən
knife	kučəən
knife for sewing	gırsoo
know	otolı-, saa-
know-CAUS	saa-waan-
Lady	patalaan
lake	xəwəən

lamp	ixərə
land	naa
language	xəsə
large	daaɪ
large-SUFF (somewhat large)	daaɪ-laa
last	xamoroɪ
last long	goɪda-
later	totapɪ, totapɪa
lay	ii-, səkčiə-
lay on a table	ǰirkəgu-
lazy	baakɪ
lean	tuǰu-
leather	nanta
leave	naŋgala-, soloogo-
leave-ITER	naŋgala-go-
left	ǰəuŋgiə
leg	bəgǰi
legend	təluŋgu
lend	ɪŋsoo-
lend-FR	ɪŋsoo-čɪ-
length	onɪlaanɪ
lie	bi-, čɪkɪ-
lie-DUR-DES	təə-si-ičə-
lie down	akpan-
lie down-DUR	təə-si-
lie down-REV	akpan-go-
lie down-REV-CAUS	akpan-go-waan-
light gown	pokto
light up	ǰəgdə-, taawo-
light up-FR	ǰəgǰi-či-
like that	tujəə
likely	biǰərə
listen	dosɪǰa-
litter	kukpun
little	nuuči, nuučiku
little branch	gara
live	balǰɪ-, bi-
living	ujuun
load	təuči-

loaded	daoko
locker	joso
lonely	əmuučən
long	goropčı, onımı
long-EXTR	onımı-ookaan
long ago	balana
long time	goro
look	ičəǰə-
lots of	gərəən
love	ajapo-, uləəsi-
lower	pəgui
luck	kəsi
Make	aŋgo-
make-INCH	aŋgo-lo-
make-REV	aŋgo-go-
make an agreement	toktoo-
make efforts	kičə-
make sure	saago-
male	xusə, xusəni
man	naı, xusənəj, xusəni
many	əgǰi
many-SUFF (somewhat many)	əgǰi-ləə
mark	saı-
massage-FR	moŋgı-čı-
master	paksı
match	jəŋsilə-
mattress	səktəpun
maybe	saawaası
meadowsweet	bolookto
meat	uliksə
medicine	okto
medicine-PROP	okto-ko
meet	ačan-, taakoalı-
memorial ceremony	xərgən
memorial service	kasaa
memorize	əǰə-
mercy	guǰiən

mercy.VBZ-ITER-CAUS	guǰiəsi-gu-wəən-
message	mədəə
method-PROP	ərdən-ku
middle	tokon
mind	murun
mind-PROP	murun-ku
misfortune	kɪsɪako
moan	miŋguči-
money	ǰɪxa
month	bɪa
most	čuu
mother	əniə, ənin
mother-in-law	əŋpə
mothers	əniənəə, əninəə
mourning	burpuun
mouth	aŋma
move gently	əmusi-
much	əgǰi
Nail	tukpən, xosakta
nail	tukpən-
nail-ITER	tukpən-gu-
name	gərbu
Nanai	naanaɪ, xəǰəni
navel	xuimu
navigate	jara-
near	əjə, ǰɪǰa
neck	moŋgon
neck-flap	apɪto
need	gələ-
needle	xurmə
net	jarako
new	sikuun
next	ǰakpa, ǰɪaja
night	dolbo, siksə
nimble	səčən
nine	xujun
no	anaa

not	aba, əčiə, əǰi, əm
not-VBZ	aba-na-
not-VBZ-ITER	aba-na-go-
now	əsi
Oar	gɪol
oarlock	gara
obtain	xətə-
odd	gaksɪdaan
offering food	dooboča
OK	aja, gəə
old	sagǰɪ
old man	mapa
old woman	mama
on the spot	čala
once	təəm
one	əm, əmun
one (of the pair)	əmǰiə
one-SEL (one of two)	əm-ǰimə
one of a pair-PROP	gaksɪa-ko
one person	əmuni
one year	baar
oneself	məən, mənə
oneself.ACC	məəpi
oneself.ACC.PL	məəpəəri
oneself.DAT	məənduji
oneself.DIR	məənčiji
oneself.DIR.PL	məənčiəri
oneself.INS	məənǰiji
only	baɪ, təəm
only one	əmukəəkəən
open	dəgbəli-, nixəli-
opposite side	bado, tajaǰɪ
ordinary	baɪbɪɪ
other	goɪ
other-SEL	goɪ-ǰɪma
other's property	naɪŋgɪ
otherworld	buni

outside	boa, boakıa
owner	əǰən
Pad-DISTR-CAUS	poaı-kta-waan-
pair	budər
part	pası
pass	sii-
pass away	o-
patch	ǰipərə-
pathway	pokto
pattern-PROP	ılga-ko
people	gərəən, gərəəni, gurun
people.PL	gursəl
perform a memorial service	kasaata-
perhaps	saınaa, biǰərə
permanently	bortı
person	naı
phosphorus	silčuksə
picture-PROP	ılga-ko
piece	pası
pierce	kučəəli-
pillar	tora
pillow	čiptun
pine	ǰaagda
pity	kaıran
place	bado, bəun, boa
plate	sılıa
play	xupi-
plug	sii-
pole	goaon
politely	gookoǰı
poor	sinəǰii, guǰiələ
poor-SUFF (somewhat poor)	sinəǰii-ləə
porridge	lala
pot	ənjuə, kalan
pouch	somalaan
pour	jəwəri-
pour.DUR	jəwərsu-

power	kusun
praise	makta-
prepare	bargɪ-
present	suglən
pretty	gučkuli
price	xoda
prick	səəl-
principle	gɪan
process	uji-, uju-
produce	ərdələ-
prohibit	papola-
protect	ətuu-, xorɪ-
protect-FR	xorɪ-čɪ-
pull	tata-
pull-REV	tata-go-
push	ana-
put	əsəli-, nəə-, nəəku-
put down	tugbugu-
put on	baaroolɪ-
put on-CAUS	tətu-wəən-
Quake	tuiŋku-
quant	goaon
quickly	turgəsuən, xawaŋga
quiet	əlkə
quietly	əlkəə, doolaa, kaokaa, sim
Rabbit	gormaxon
rain	tugdə
rain	tugdə-
raise	uǰi-, uruuči-
ram	paačɪla-
rarely	əmbə
raw	njaaloon
raw fish (frozen)	pɪarmaa
raw fish (sliced)	talaa
reach	ɪsɪ-
reason	turgun

red	səəgǰən
reel of thread	kurkə
refuse	osɪsɪ-
region	kaltaaǰɪa
rejoice-REP	agda-nasɪ-
remain	očogo-
remove	ačo-, xoro-
remove-REV	oosɪ-go-
request	mədəliku
require	gələ-, mədəsi-
residue	puləə
respect	kidu-
respond	taoda-
rest	poanɪ
return	ənu-, močogo-
revitalize-DES	osɪgoaan-kɪča-
rich	bajan
rich-SUFF (somewhat rich)	bajan-laa
right	aaŋgɪa
right	toŋdo
right away	lopto
ring	koŋgɪrɪ-
ring	xonjakaan
rise	garpa-
ritual stick	xuməgdən
river	maŋbo
riverside	tooɪ
road	pokto
roast	čɪro-
robe	amɪrɪ
rod-DIM	moo-kaan
roof	guičə
rope	topto
row-AGT (rower)	gɪolɪ-mǰɪ
rule	gɪan
run-ITER	tutu-gu-
run-REV	čoča-go-
run away-REV	pagǰɪala-go-
Russian	loča

Sable	səəpə
saddle	təəŋku
safely	ajaǰɪɪ
sail	čɪsa-
salmon	dawa
same	əm
save-FR	xorɪ-čɪ-
save a child's life	ɪlɪočɪ-
saw	poo-
say	gusərə-, un-, xɪsaŋgo-
say-REV	un-gu-
scatter	čəktəri-
scent	puun
scissors	xaǰa
scissors-VBZ	xaǰa-la-, xaǰa-čɪ-
scrape	sɪdo-
sea	namo
search	gələ-
second	ǰuəjə, ǰuəjəčiə
see	ičə-
see-CAUS	ičə-wəən-
see-INT	ičə-ndə-
see-ITER	ičə-gu-
see off	susuəči-, susuuči-
seek	gələ-
seek-DES	saa-ɪča-
seek-REV	gələ-gu-
senior	daaɪ
separate	paaǰɪla-
separately	paaǰɪ
serious	maŋga
serve	dəŋsi-
set	nəə-
seven	nadaan
seventh	nadaačɪa
several	xadowa
sew	ulpi-
sew-INCH	ulpi-lu-

sew-ITER	ulpi-gu-
sew-PASS	ulpi-čə-
shaman	saman
shamanic caps	ǰəilən
share	obo
sharp	sarbɪ
shavings	saorɪ
shawl	puŋku
she	njoanɪ
she.ACC	njoambanɪ
she.DAT	njoandoanɪ
she.DIR	njoančɪan
she.INS	njoanǰɪ
short	xurmi
shoulder	muirə
show	ičə-, ičəuči-, ičuən-, kupi-
side	xoldon
silk	səurə
silver	məŋgun
sin	soron-
sinew	sumul
sink-ITER	tuu-gu-
sister-in-law	əukən
sit	təə-
sit-CAUS	təə-wəən-
sit-DUR	təə-si-
sit-ITER	təə-gu-
sit-TR-ITER	təə-u-gu-
sit up	təə-
six	njuŋgun
ski	sokta
skillful	paksɪ
skin	xərəktə
sleep	ao-, oŋasa-
sleeve	xuəksə
slingshot	dəəŋgurə
small	nuuči, nuučiku
smear	modorɪ-
smear-ITER	modorɪ-go-

smell	puuŋgiči-
snake	muiki
snot	inoksa
so	totamaarı, tui
so much	aso, tujəə, tujəə tujəə
soak	čakpa-
sofa	pıanǰıko
soft grass	naokta
some	poaktanı, poanı, poawanı
sometimes	poaldoanı
son	xusə piktə
soon	ələə
soul	ərgən
soup	čoolon
speak	xısaŋgo-
spear-VBZ	gıda-la-
spend a night	aoŋga-
spend a night-FR	aoŋga-čı-
spend time	bıaŋsa-
spoon	xonjaan
spray	čəktəri-
spread	dəri-, ǰəəri-, səkčiə-
spread-ITER	dəri-gu-
spring	njəŋnjə
stand-DUR	ılı-sı-
stationary	kirim
stay	dərəǰi-
stay-ITER-CAUS	dərəǰi-gu-wəən-
stay alive-ITER	xora-go-
step	duərə-
step on-ITER	taktoola-go-
stern	kətən
stick	moo
still	xaıs
store	nəučə-, nəuči-
stove	golǰon
strengthen	masılto-
string	sii-
strong	maŋga, ması

strong-PROP	kusun-ku
study	tačɪočɪ-
stuff	xaǰon
substitute	oroondola-
suck	kuuči-
sufficiently	uləən
summer	ǰoa
sun	siun
surface	ojaa
surround	kəəndəli-
survive	xora-
sweep	xapolɪ-
swell	ǰool-
Table	dərə
tableware	alɪo
taiga	duəntə
taiga (here and there)	duipə
taiga side	dujə
take	baa-, ǰapa-
take-CAUS	ǰapa-waan-
take-FR	ǰapa-čɪ-
take-REV	ǰapa-go-
take away-REV	ǰapa-go-
take care	ətəxi-
take care of	kərəl-
take time	sii-
talisman	suu
talk	gusərəəndu-, xɪsaŋgo-
tasty	amta
teach	aloosɪ-
tear-FR	gudə-či-
tell	gusərə-
tell-ITER	gusərə-gu-
ten	ǰoan
thank-ITER	banjaala-go-
thanks	banɪxa
that	təi

that.ACC	čaa
that place	taja
that way	tui
then	čado, čadu, tado, tadu, totapaarɪ, totapɪ
there	taja
therefore	totamaarɪ, totamɪ, totapɪmaarɪ
they	njoančɪ
they.ACC	njoambačɪ
they.DIR	njoančɪačɪ
thief	čowoo
thimble	xonjapton
thin	nəmdə, nəmi
thing	ǰaka, xaǰon
think	murči-
third	ɪlaačɪa, ɪlɪačɪa
this	əi
this way	əusi
thought-PROP	murun-ku
thread	kupən, kurkə, sirəktə
thread (made with fish skin)	tompo
three	ɪlaan
three peoples	ɪlaanɪ
threshold	kəndərxiən, kəndərxin
throw	naŋgala-
throw away	naŋgaačɪ-
tie	uji-, uju-
tie-ITER	uji-gu-
timbered wall	korɪan
time	əər, ərin
time (turn)	modan
to end	jək
to that place	taosɪ
to the forest	duisi
to the shore	waɪsɪ
together	gəsə
tomorrow	čɪmana
tooth	xuktə
top	ujə

torn	xətu
totally	luktu
touch	toŋgala-
touch-CAUS	toŋgala-waan-
touch-DUR	toŋga-sɪ-
tread	gɪraan-
treat	doobo-, tuju-, xəri-
treat-NMLZ	tuju-n
treat for the deceased	saorma
treat the deceased	dooboča-
tree	moo
tribe	xala
truth	təǰə
try	kičə-, pərgə-, təǰuuči-
try-CAUS	pərgə-wəən-
turn	kəčəri-
turn back	močogo-
turn over-INT	susuəči-ndə-
twine	sirxə
twins	adoo
twins-PROP	adoo-ko
two	ǰuə~ǰuər
two people	ǰuəni
Uncle (maternal, elder)	papa
uncle (maternal, younger)	gučəkə, gusin
uncle (paternal, younger)	əksən
uncles	gusinəə
uncomfortable	orkɪkta
uncorking	dəgbəliku
understand	otolɪ-, saa-
underwear	əŋgərəgdə
underworld	buni
unskillful	mogo
upper	uwui
upwards	uiptəŋgi

Various	goɪ goɪ
very	čuu, təŋ
very quietly	əlkəə əlkəə
vicinity	ǰakpa
village	ɪxon
village residents	ɪxonkaan
vodka	arkɪ
voice	ǰɪlgan
Waist	omolgɪča
wait	xalačɪ-
walk	moolo-, pulsi-
walk with stick	tunjəpu-
walk with stick-NMLZ	tunjəpu-n
want	gələ-
want-REV	gələ-gu-
wardrobe	guisə
warehouse	takto
warm	njama, xulǰii
warmish	njama
wash	sɪlko-, xao-
wash-FR-ITER	xao-čɪ-go-
wash-ITER	sɪlko-go-
watch	ičəǰə-
water	muə
water bowl	soopon
water container	saola
way	pokto
we	buə
we.ABL	bunǰiəǰi
we.ACC	bumbiwə
we.DAT	bundu
we.INS	bunǰi
wear	təčičə-, tətu-
wear-REV	tətu-gu-
wedding	gɪamata
wedding boat	gɪla
well	ajaǰɪɪ, gəə, uləən

what	xa, xaɪ, xamačaa
what for	xagoarɪ, xaɪgoarɪ
when	xaal, xaalı
where	xaɪdo
where to	xaosɪ
which	xamačaa
white	čaagǰan
whittle	saorɪ-
who	ui
why	xaɪgojɪ, xaɪmaarɪ, xaɪmɪ
wide	daramɪ
wife	asɪ
willow	busuəktə, tuŋdə
wind	xədun
wind round	xərkə-
window	paawa
wineglass	kočɪ
winter	tuə
wipe	xao-
wipe-FR	xao-čɪ-
wipe-ITER	xao-go-
without	anaa
withstand	xətə-
woman	əktə, əktəni
woman.PL	əkəsəl
wood	moo
wood chip	saorɪ
wooden chamber	kərən
wooden figure	panjoo
word	xəsə
work	ǰobo-
work-INCH-ITER	ǰobo-lo-go-
world	boa
wrap	xuku-
wraparound	puŋku
write	niru-

Yard	tuliə
year	aɪŋanɪ, baar, səə
year.VBZ	aɪŋanɪ-sɪ-
you	sii
you.ACC	simbiə
you.DIR	sinči
you.PL	suə
young	naonǰoan
younger brother	nəu

4.2. Grammatical forms

4.2.1. Inflectional suffixes

-a/-ə	accusative case marker (ACC)
-a/-ə	infinitive verb ending (INF)
-a/-ə	oblique case marker (OCM)
-a(n)/-ə(n)	present indicative finite verb ending (PRS)
-ačɪ/-əči	negative past personal participle ending (NEG.PST.P)
-adaasɪ/-ədəəsi	negative present personal participle ending (NEG.PRS.P)
-arɪ/-əri	reflexive plural personal ending (REFL.PL)
-asɪ/-əsi	negative present personal participle ending (NEG.PRS.P)
-ba/-bə	accusative case marker (ACC)
-barɪ/-bəri	reflexive plural personal ending (REFL.PL)
-bɪ/-bi	first personal singular ending (1SG)
-bɪ/-bi	reflexive singular personal ending (REFL)
-borɪ/-buri	present impersonal affirmative participle ending (PRS.IMPS.P)
-bowasɪ/-buwəsi	impersonal negative present participle ending (NEG.PRS.IMPS.P)
-ča/-čə	passive participle ending (PASS)
-čɪ/-či	directive case marker (DIR)
-čɪ/-či	second personal singular ending (2SG)
-čɪ/-či	third personal plural ending (3PL)
-čɪ(n)/-či(n)	past personal affirmative participle ending (PST.P)
-da/-də	present indicative finite verb ending (PRS)
-daa/-dəə	anterior impersonal converb ending (ANT)
-dasɪ/-dəsi	negative present personal participle ending (NEG.PRS.P)
-dɪɪ/-dii	present personal affirmative participle ending (PRS.P)
-do/-du	dative case marker (DAT)
-doo/-duu	second personal singular present imperative

	ending (2SG.IMP)
-doɪ/-dui	comparative case marker (COMPR)
-dola/-dulə	locative case marker (LOC)
-go/-gu	cohortative modal ending (COHOR)
-go/-gu	designative case marker (DSG)
-go/-gu	purposive personal converb ending (PURP)
-ɪ/-i	present personal affirmative participle ending (PRS.P)
-jɪ/-ji	first personal singular ending (1SG)
-jɪ/-ji	reflexive singular personal ending (REFL)
-ǰaa/-ǰəə	future indicative finite verb ending (FUT)
-ǰɪ/-ǰi	instrumental case marker (INS)
-ǰɪaǰɪ/-ǰiəǰi	ablative case marker (ABL)
-kɪ(n)/-ki(n)	past personal affirmative participle ending (PST.P)
-l	third personal plural ending (3PL)
-la/-lə	locative case marker (LOC)
-maarɪ/-məəri	simultaneous plural impersonal converb ending (SIM.PL)
-mɪ/-mi	simultaneous singular impersonal converb ending (SIM)
-nɪ/-ni	third personal singular ending (3SG)
-o/-u	second personal singular present imperative ending (2SG.IMP)
-očɪa/-učiə	conditional personal converb ending (COND)
-orɪ/-uri	present impersonal affirmative participle ending (PRS.IMPS.P)
-oso/-usu	second personal plural imperative finite verb ending (2PL.IMP)
-oxan/-uxən	past impersonal affirmative participle ending (PST.IMPS.P)
-paarɪ/-pəəri	conditional plural impersonal converb ending (COND.PL.IMPS)
-pɪ/-pi	conditional singular impersonal converb ending (COND.IMPS)
-po/-pu	first personal plural ending (1PL)
-ra/-rə	infinitive verb ending (INF)
-ra/-rə	present indicative finite verb ending (PRS)
-raa/-rəə	anterior impersonal converb ending (ANT)
-rasɪ/-rəsi	negative present personal participle ending

	(NEG.PRS.P)
-rɪɪ/-rii	present personal affirmative participle ending (PRS.P)
-roo/-ruu	second personal singular present imperative ending (2SG.IMP)
-sɪ/-si	second personal singular ending (2SG)
-so/-su	second personal plural ending (2PL)
-wa/-wə	accusative case marker (ACC)
-wa/-wə	oblique case marker (OBL)
-wačɪ/-wəči	negative past impersonal participle ending (NEG.PST.IMPS.P)
-wadaasɪ /-wədəəsi	impersonal negative present participle ending (NEG.PRS.IMPS.P)
-warɪ/-wəri	reflexive plural personal ending (REFL.PL)
-wasɪ/-wəsi	impersonal negative present participle ending (NEG.PRS.IMPS.P)
-worɪ/-wuri	present impersonal affirmative participle ending (PRS.IMPS.P)
-xa(n)/-xə(n)	past personal affirmative participle ending (PST.P)

4.2.2. Derivational suffixes

-(a)čɪ-/-(ə)či-	frequentative affix (FR)
-(a)čɪa/-(ə)čiə	ordinal number
-bo-/-bu-	transitivizer affix (TR)
-čɪ-/-či-	verbalizer affix (VBZ)
-gɪla-/-gilə-	obligative affix (OBLG)
-go-/-gu-	iterative affix (ITER)
-go-/-gu-	reversive affix (REV)
-(ɪ)nda-/-(i)ndə-	intentional-directional affix (INT)
-ǰɪa/-ǰiə	side
-ǰɪma/-ǰimə	selective affix (SEL)
-kaan/-kəən	diminutive affix (DIM)
-(k)ɪča-/-(k)ičə-	desiderative affix (DES)
-ko/-ku	proprietative affix (PROP)
-(k)ookaan /-(k)uukəən	extreme degree affix (EXTR)

-kta-/-ktə-	distributive affix (DISTR)
-la-/-lə-	verbalizer affix (VBZ)
-laa/-ləə	nominalizer affix (NMLZ)
-laa/-ləə	sufficient degree affix (SUFF)
-lo-/-lu-	inchoative affix (INCH)
-lsɪ-/-lsi-	habitual affix (HAB)
-ma/-mə	material
-maačɪ-/-məəči-	reciprocal affix (RECI)
-mǰɪ/-mǰi	agentive affix (AGT)
-n	nominalizer affix (NMLZ)
-na-/-nə-	verbalizer affix (VBZ)
-nasɪ-/-nəsi-	repetative affix (REP)
-nkaan/-nkəən	dweller
-o-/-u-/-wo-/-wu-	transitivizer affix (TR)
-sal/-səl	plural affix (PL)
-sɪ-/-si-	verbalizer affix (VBZ)
-sɪ-/-si-/-so-/-su-	durative affix (DUR)
-waan-/-wəən-	causative affix (CAUS)

4.3. Particles

4.3.1. Suffix-Particles

=**a**/=**ə**	mirative (MIR)
=**bakı**/=**bəki**	consecutive (CON)
=**daa**/=**dəə**	additive (ADD)
=(**j**)**am**/=(**j**)**əm**	reportative (REPO)
=**kaa**/=**kəə**	contrastive (CNTR)
=**kas**/=**kəs**	emphatic (EMP)
=**maa**(**t**)/=**məə**(**t**)	consecutive (CON)
=**maa**(**t**)/=**məə**(**t**)	similative (SML)
=**noo**/=**nuu**	question (Q)
=**o**/=**u**	concessive (CONC)
=**ragda**/=**rəgdə**	limitative (LIM)
=**tanıı**/=**tənii**	topic (TOP)
=**tol**/=**tul**	exclusive (EXCL)

4.3.2. Word-Particles

bijərə	likely
gəə	well
goan(**ı**)	certainly
manjaa	only
undəə	regarding
xaı	indeed

5. Concluding Remarks

In the previous chapters we presented the transcriptions, linguistic annotations, and translations of the Nanai speech materials that depict various stages of an individual's life cycle including birth, childhood, growth, marriage, and burial. In addition, we provided an abridged Russian version of the same materials as well as an alphabetical list of Nanai words with their meanings.

As a representative member of the Southern Tungusic language group, the Nanai language belongs to the Manchu-Tungusic branch of the so-called Altaic Language family. Like all other Manchu-Tungusic languages with few native speakers there are fewer than 4,000 Nanai speakers out of 17,000 ethnic Nanais in Russia and China. More seriously, the language is not being passed down to the next generations, thus being considered seriously endangered. In this sense, the documentation of Nanai is growing as an extremely urgent undertaking for linguists. Thanks to one of the co-authors Antonina Kile, in 2005 we were able to embark on the investigation into the sound and grammatical structure of Nanai, and later in 2013 we were also able to further record spontaneous narratives analyzed in this book. Through this process, we acquired very rare Nanai-language folklore materials of great linguistic and ethnographic value.

The speech materials were divided into four topics that incorporate the traditional way of life of the Nanai people: Childhood education and child rearing rituals, Birth rituals, Wedding rituals, and Funeral rituals. Through these topics, we were able to gain a deeper understanding on the lifestyle, folklore, values and so forth of the Nanai people. In the materials, we witnessed the Nanai people leading honest and diligent lives, tending to impoverished neighbors and the elderly.

We also learned that, because there has been no widely-used writing system until recently, the Nanai people have made every effort to impart all their experiences directly to the next generation through their spoken words and actions.

These materials were dictated composedly by perhaps one of the most fluent speakers of the language, based on her own experience of having lived in the last traditional society as an ethnic Nanai. In this book, we attempted grammatical analyses, annotations, and interpretations of them and, as a result, we have become able to share the content and linguistic materials with interested readers and researchers. We hope, on the one hand, that this research will increase understanding of the cultural practices of the Nanai people and their language, and, on the other hand, that it will also play a significant role in the revitalization of the Nanai language.

References

An, Jun. 1986. *Hezhe yu jianzhi* [Introduction to Hezhe]. Beijing: Minzu Chubanshe.

Avrorin, Valentin Aleksandrovich. 1959. *Grammatika nanaiskogo jazyka* [Grammar of Nanai]. *1. Foneticheskoe vvedenie i morfologija imennyx chastej rechi* [Introductory phonetics and morphology of nominal parts of speech]. Leningrad: Izdatel'stvo akademii nauk.

Avrorin, Valentin Aleksandrovich. 1961. *Grammatika nanajskogo jazyka* [Grammar of Nanai]. *2. Morfologija glagol'nyx i narechnyx chastej rechi, mezhdometij, sluzhebnyx slov i chastic* [Morphology of verbal and adverbial parts of speech, exclamations, auxiliary words and particles]. Moskva & Leningrad: Izdatel'stvo akademii nauk.

Avrorin, Valentin Aleksandrovich. 1981. *Sintaksicheskije issledovanija po nanajskomu jazyku* [Syntactic studies of Nanai]. Leningrad: Nauka.

Avrorin, Valentin Aleksandrovich & Onenko, Sulungu Nikolaevich. 1986. *Materialy po nanajskomu jazyku i fol'kloru* [Materials of Nanai language and folklore]. Leningrad: Izdatel'stvo nauka leningradskoe otdelenie.

Bulgakova, Tatiana. 2013. *Nanai Shamanic Culture in Indigenous Discourse.* SEC Publications.

Gaer, Je. A. 1991. *Tradicionnaja bytovaja obrjadnost' nanajcev v konce XIX – nachale XX v* [Traditional household rites of the Nanai in the late 19th – early 20th centuries]. Moskva: Mysl'.

Grube, Wilhelm. 1900. *Goldische-Deutsches Wöterverzeichniss.* St. Petersburg: Commissionären der Kaiserlichen Akademie der Wissenschaften.

Jin, Hui. 2011. "A study on the phonological system of Hezhe spoken in China." Seoul: M.A. thesis, Seoul National University.

Kazama, Shinjiro. 1994. *Nānai go no itchi ni tsuite* [On agreements in Nanai]. Sapporo: Hokkaido daigaku bungakubu gengogaku kenkyūsitsu.

Kazama, Shinjiro. 1996. "Hejen go no kētōteki ichi ni tsuite [Genetical position of Hezhen]." *Gengo kenkyū* 109. 117–138. The Linguistic Society of Japan.

Kazama, Shinjiro. 2005. "Nānai go no gimonshi ni yoru hango hyōgen ni tsuite [On ironical expressions by interrogatives in Nanai]." *Kantaihēyō no gengo* 12. 129–163. Sapporo: Hokkaido daigaku daigakuin bungaku kenkyūka.

Kazama, Shinjiro. 2007. "Nānai go to udehe go no fuzoku go ni tsuite [On clitics in Nanai and Udihe]." *Asian and African Languages and Linguistics* 2. 49–83. Tokyo: Research Institute for Languages and Cultures of Asia and Africa, Tokyo University of Foreign Studies.

Kazama, Shinjiro. 2010a. "Nānai go bunpō gaisetsu [Introduction to Nanai grammar]." *Nānai go no minwa to densetsu* 12. 207–266. Tokyo: Research Institute for Languages and Cultures of Asia and Africa, Tokyo University of Foreign Studies.

Kazama, Shinjiro. 2010b. "Nānai go no asupekuto [Aspects in Nanai]." *Journal of the Institute of Language Research* 15. 181–191. Tokyo: The Institute of Language Research, Tokyo University of Foreign Studies.

Kazama, Shinjiro. 2010c. "Nānai go no hininshō keidōsi ni tsuite [On impersonal participle in Nanai]." *Asian and African Languages and Linguistics* 4. 134–148. Tokyo: Research Institute for Languages and Cultures of Asia and Africa, Tokyo University of Foreign Studies.

Kazama, Shinjiro. 2011. "Nānai go no fukubun ni tsuite [On compound sentences in Nanai]." *Hokuhō gengo kenkyū* 1. 115–138. Sapporo: Hokkaido daigaku daigakuin bunkaku kenkyūka.

Kile, Antonina Sergeevna. 1994. *Nanajsko-russkij tematicheskij slovar'* [Nanai-Russian thesaurus]. Xabarovsk: Xabarovsk gosudarstvennyj pedagogicheskij universitet.

Kile, Antonina Sergeevna. 2004. *Iskusstvo nanajcev: vyshivka, ornament. Tradicii i novacii* [Nanai art: embroidery, ornament. Traditions and innovations]. Xabarovsk: OOO Rossijskij Media Al'jans.

Kile, Antonina Sergeevna. 2011. "On the classification of ritual terminology in the Nanai language." *Altai Hakpo* 21. 35–50. Altaic Society of Korea.

Kile, Nikolaj Batunovich. 1973. *Obraznye slova nanajskogo jazyka* [Figurative words of Nanai]. Leningrad: Nauka.

Kim, Juwon. 1985. "Tungguseu jeeoeui inching eomi [Personal endings in Tungus Languages]." *Yeoksa eoneohak* [Historical Linguistics]. 277–303. Seoul: Jeonyewon.

Kim, Juwon. 1988. "Nanaieoeui moeum johwa [Vowel harmony in Nanai]." *Gugeohak* 17. 229–246. Seoul: The Society of Korean Linguistics.

Kim, Juwon, Kwon Jaeil, Ko Dongho, Kim Yoon-shin, & Jeon Soonhwan. 2008. *Sarajeo ganeun altai eoneoreul chajaseo* [Documentation of endangered Altaic languages]. Paju: Taehaksa.

Ko, Dongho & Kim Juwon. 2005. "Heoje oeoeui [+seoljeongseong] machareumgwa pachareumeui eumseong silhyeon yangsang [Aspects of phonetic realizations of [+coronal] fricatives and affricates in

Hezhe]." *Alatai Hakpo* 15. 1–14. Seoul: The Altaic Society of Korea.
Ko, Dongho & Yurn Gyudong. 2011. *A Description of Najkhin Nanai.* Seoul: Snupress.
Ling, Chunsheng. 1934. *Songhuajiang xiayou de Hezhezu* [Hezhe people in downstream areas of the Songhua river]. Nanjing: Guoli zhongyang yanjiuyuan yuyan yanjiusuo.
Onenko, Sulungu Nikolaevich. 1958. "O chasticakh v nanajskom jazyke [On particles in Nanai]." *Doklady i soobshchenija instituta jazykoznanija AN SSSR* No. 11. 95–106.
Onenko, Sulungu Nikolaevich. 1986. *Russko-nanajskij slovar'* [Russian-Nanai dictionary]. Moskva: Russkij jazyk.
Onenko, Sulungu Nikolaevich & Avrorin, Valentin Aleksandrovich. 1959. *Russko-nanajskij slovar'* [Russian-Nanai dictionary]. Leningrad: Gosudarstvennoe uchebno-pedagogicheskoe izdatel'stvo.
Onenko, Sulungu Nikolaevich & Avrorin, Valentin Aleksandrovich. 1980. *Nanajsko-russkij slovar'* [Nanai-Russian dictionary]. Moskva: Russkij jazyk.
Petrova, Tajsija Ivanovna. 1960. *Nanajsko-russkij slovar'* [Nanai-Russian dictionary]. Leningrad: Gosudarstvennoe uchebno-pedagogicheskoe izdatel'stvo.
Sem, Lidija Ivanovna. 1976. *Ocherki dialectov nanajskogo jazyka* [Outline of the dialects of Nanai]. Leningrad: Izdatel'stvo nauka leningradskoe otdelenie.

Abstract

The Life and Rituals of the Nanai People

The Nanai language, one of the Manchu-Tungusic languages of the so-called Altaic language family, is seriously endangered with only a few fluent native speakers, as well as with no intergenerational language transmission, making its documentation an extremely urgent undertaking for linguists.

In this book we present the transcriptions, linguistic annotations, and translations of a fluent Nanai speaker's spontaneous narratives on the life cycle of the Nanai people, which are divided into the following four topics: Childhood Education and Child Rearing rituals, Birth rituals, Wedding rituals, and Funeral rituals. In addition, we provide an English translation of the abridged Russian version of the materials, as well as an alphabetical list of lexical and grammatical forms with their meanings.

The goal of our research is, on the one hand, to help understand the cultural practices of the Nanai people and their language, and on the other hand, to contribute to the revitalization of the Nanai language.